The DUXBURY BOOK

1637-1987

THE
DUXBURY
BOOK
1637-1987

Compiled and edited by

Katherine H. Pillsbury

Robert D. Hale

Jack Post

The Duxbury Rural and Historical Society
Duxbury, Massachusetts

Dedicated to

Sabina Dwinnell Crosby

Printed in the United States of America

International Standard Book Number 0-941859-00-2

Library of Congress Catalog Card Number 87-70439

Preface

The 350th anniversary of the incorporation of Duxbury seemed an appropriate time to review some of the early incidents in the town's history, and at the same time tell its more recent story. Starting with a nucleus of topics provided by Dorothy Wentworth, retiring Town Historian, and encouraged by the Duxbury Rural & Historical Society, three editors: Katherine Pillsbury, present Town Historian; Robert Hale, literary pundit and bookseller; and Jack Post, publications chairman and columnist, set to work in September 1985.

Financial support would be needed (a Fund Raising Committee); illustrations found (a Graphics Committee); articles solicited, edited, and expanded or contracted; a professional designer engaged; the manuscript typed and indexed; and the whole finally printed, all the diverse elements brought together in a beautifully bound book.

No list of credits can adequately cover all those who supported the project in so many ways, but please read the lists found in the pages beyond the text for those who contributed creatively and/or financially, and share the editors' admiration and gratitude for everyone whose enthusiasm brought about *The DUXBURY BOOK, 1637–1987*.

Acknowledgments

Special thanks go to the following men and women who helped immeasurably in providing both the experience and expertise needed to assemble a completed book:

- Fran Nichols and Norman Forgit for their patience and readiness to supply photographs where needed;
- Dorothy Wentworth and Anthony Kelso for generously giving sound advice on historical facts;
- Nancy and Edwin Swanborn, curators of the King Caesar House;
- Caroline Chapin, Archivist of the Pilgrim Society and Ross Urquhart of the Massachusetts Historical Society for their help in locating materials and illustrations;
- David Bohl of the Society for the Preservation of New England Antiquities for his expert photography of antique illustrations;
- Marilyn Rowland for her careful typing and indexing;
- Francis Leach for the organization of the sources and footnotes.

The editors are grateful to the members of the Graphics and Funding Committees for their interest and support. Their efforts enabled the idea of this book to become a reality.

Funding Committee	Graphics Committee
Jack Post, Chairman	Katherine Pillsbury, Chairman
Charles E. Cousins	Joan B. Hacker
Carleton Knight, Jr.	Carleton Knight, Jr.
Robert W. Leach	Lanci Valentine
Joan E. Leitzes	Robert C. Vose, Jr.
David W. Stookey	
Robert C. Vose, Jr.	

Colophon
Design and production by Cornelia Boynton / Ciao Design
Composed in 11 on 14 Trump Medieval with italic display by Grafacon, Inc.
Printed on 70 pound Lustro Dull by Arcata Graphics / Kingsport
Binding by Arcata Graphics / Kingsport

Contents

Timeline

A Town for Summer

❦ Modern Duxbury

Introduction

When the Town of Plymouth was contemplating the fit form for the celebration of its three hundred and fiftieth anniversary in 1970, a member of the Board of Selectmen, known for his dislike of the Pilgrims and their descendants, remarked that it was an ill wind that blew the *Mayflower* into Plymouth Harbor, and voted against an appropriation at the town meeting. Sadly, his vote prevailed, and among the many things not done in connection with that anniversary was the publication of a modern history of the ancient colony and town of Pilgrim founding. Fortunately, wiser, cooler heads prevailed in the counsels of the town of Duxbury for we now have, in celebration of the three hundred and fiftieth anniversary of the foundation of this town, a well-produced volume of historical essays, rich in diversity, taste, and substance. The production of local history is an industry as old as the American town, and the quantity and frequency of these often parochial essays in piety and self-indulgence have contributed to the poor reputation of what we refer to with some caution as "local history." The effort represented in these essays presented in behalf of Duxbury and its lively history will do much to restore the reputation of this aspect of literary history, and will certainly do as much, if not more, to enhance the already distinguished reputation of the Town of Duxbury as a place that takes its history seriously.

Visible across the bay from Plymouth, Duxbury has always held a fascination for its older sister, the county town and capital of the Old Colony. It was, after all, to that small collection of inlets, coves, hillocks, and acres of marsh-lands that Plymouth's most distinguished inhabitants migrated: Myles Standish, the captain; Elder Brewster, the parson; John Alden, he who would be asked to speak for himself. In Plymouth history, these are names to be conjured with, and they are to be found not in the old mother town, but across the bay in Duxbury. Governor Bradford says it was the marsh hay that attracted them, and the inconvenience of returning to church in winter time that kept them. But in Plymouth, as we stand upon our hill and gaze across the bay at the monument to Myles Standish on Captain's Hill (the tallest statue in the world—Myles above the sea, as the South Shore schoolboy joke goes), we wonder if Standish, Brewster, Alden, and the rest of those migrants knew something we ought to know. And now we know they did, and the history of the town they settled and which has flourished in their wake is now made available to all of us in this well-produced and seemly volume.

Duxbury has long been fortunate in its sense of its own past and in sensible, public-spirited citizens who have come forth to serve it in each generation. The founders of the Duxbury Rural and Historical Association, those who care for the Ezra Weston *King Caesar House*, and those who labor annually amid the poison ivy fields of Clark's Island in behalf of Pulpit Rock, people like Gershom Bradford, the redoubtable and fruitful Dorothy Wentworth, and now, the editors and contributors to this book, all of these have carried the history of Duxbury from ancient times to our own, setting an example and providing encouragement for generations to come to do the same.

Change may lay its inevitable hands upon the places of our hearts. To pass through the still-elm-shaded streets and lanes of Duxbury, to see the tidal mysteries of the Bluefish River, the splendid houses neighbor to Ezra Weston's, the stolid dignity of the First Parish Church, the most peaceful of graveyards beside it, the elegant Nathaniel Winsor, Jr. House and its three relations, Captain's Hill, the beaches, even the "yuppification" of Hall's Corner, is to see something of the splendid continuity of an old town. It is a town not simply *preserved* as in Sturbridge Village, not *restored* as in Williamsburg, or *imagined* as in Plimoth Plantation, but lovingly lived in and wisely cared for by generations of ordinary folk who knew a good thing when they saw it, and refused to tolerate the shoddy or the tacky. What we see with our eye in the casual passage through the precincts of the town, we now have interpreted for us in deft and useful prose by people who know what they are talking about. This special book is about a special place. It gives pleasure to the eye and to the mind and gives credit to the town and the people who write about it. How fortunate for her neighbors near and far that Duxbury in its three hundred and fiftieth year should be both so well preserved and so ably served by those who would share her with the world beyond her streets and shores.

Peter J. Gomes

The Beginnings

Native Americans

Statue of Massasoit, Coles Hill, Plymouth.
(Frederick Potter)

*I*n July 1975, Professor James Mueller of Bridgewater State and his archaeology class were digging in Duxbury on the Howland Farm at the head of Morton's Hole, south of Chestnut Street. They found usual artifacts of the colonial period, a few coins, arrowheads, and clay pipe fragments typical of a long-used campsite, and finally, to their delight, a piece of stone spear point of unusual design. At only half a dozen sites in New England had such finds been made. They knew it to be a Clovis point, named after Clovis, New Mexico, where the first one was discovered embedded in the skeleton of an extinct beast which could be carbon-dated with some accuracy at 7200 B.C.! It was the oldest hard evidence of man's existence in our area at that early time. The Clovis date is a benchmark for other measurements, and the name given to the human culture of the period 7200 to 5000 B.C. is Clovis Man or Paleo-Indian.

In our mind's picture of primeval days, the third and most important dimension is *time*, infinite and incomprehensible. Even 9000 years is but a moment in geologic time. Changes in living and environment seemingly came about slowly indeed, to us who today rush from one new thing to another.

Think what our New England shoreline must have looked like in Paleo days. The ice sheet had absorbed so much of the ocean that its level was almost two hundred feet lower than now, exposing most of the Continental Shelf which runs from New Jersey to the Grand Banks—hundreds of square miles of fairly level land. We know that it was covered with vegetation, because mastodon bones are still being brought in by fishermen. Those elephantine animals were vegetarians. Undoubtedly, there were people there, too.

A change in lifestyle took thousands of years, defined usually by some related development. The era from 5000 to 3000 B.C. was named the Early Archaic culture, marked by the invention of the *atlatl*, or throwing stick. Almost every country boy has learned to throw horse chestnuts or green apples from a pointed stick, and knows how much further they will go than when thrown by his unaided hand. The primitives learned too, and adopted this extension of their arms. They would laboriously form a stone the size of a plum and drill a hole in it with a stone drill rotated between their palms and force it onto their spear shaft to its middle. It not only added some weight and stability to the spear, but provided a point where a hook on the atlatl could engage the spear and propel it. A perfect specimen of such a weight was found in her garden some time ago by Mrs. John Nash of Chapel Street in Duxbury.

From 3000 B.C. to A.D. 300, the slow motion progress continued, this being the Late Archaic period, distinguished by the increased use of permanent dwellings within stockades. The permanent houses were circular with sapling frames, thatched roofs, and hide-covered sides and doorways, compared to lean-tos, tepees, and other portable shelters. Little villages tended to promote raising of food crops, such as corn, beans, and squash, rather than complete dependence upon fish, game, and wild plants.

From A.D. 300 well into the Historic Time is called the Ceramic-Woodland culture, during which the people learned to make pottery that could be used directly over a fire. Previously, they had to depend upon bowls scraped out of quarried soapstone for heavy, clumsy utensils which too much heat would crack, or upon clay-plastered baskets in which they could heat food by dropping in hot stones. The new pottery was made by rolling long clay ropes between the palms and then

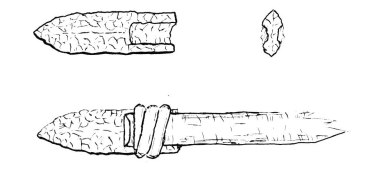

Clovis spear point (7200 B.C.). Spear formed by winding thongs around recessed stone point and shaft. *(Frederick Potter)*

winding them spirally to form a pot. This could be smoothed and decorated to the desired finish. It was dried, then fired and became a permanent, fire-safe utensil. Better food and nutrition were valuable results.

It was probably late in this period that the famous Oyster Shell Mounds at Damariscotta, Maine were started. About two miles north of the bridge over the Damariscotta River are five immense, and numerous smaller, mounds of shells, mainly oysters, left by primitive people after their feasts over several hundred years and abandoned long enough ago that large trees have matured, died, and turned to dust on the hillocks of the discarded shells. It has been estimated that to transport them elsewhere would require 108 trains of 40 freight cars each! Many of the oysters were over a foot long, so that it would not have taken many to feed even the hungriest brave. Just imagine the number of meals, cooked and raw, eaten in the area and the effect of that vast food source on the life of the adjacent population. We suggest a visit to the mounds as the only way to become a believer in the facts.

Prehistoric times ended about A.D. 1600, followed by much more rapid change due to the Indians' contact with European explorers, traders, and settlers. The native Americans were eager to trade for European tools and utensils. Bows and arrows, in use for the past thousand years, gradually gave way to powder and ball.

The Pilgrims were fortunate in settling here just when they did . . . only a couple of years earlier, the Indian population had been left weakened by a plague, probably chickenpox, to which they did not have immunity. The local Indians also raised a substantial amount of produce on cleared land which the settlers could use. There were several Indians, notably Samoset and Squanto, who could speak English, act as interpreters, and help in many other ways.

The Pilgrims were fortunate to find Massasoit as leader of the Wampanoag Federation, consisting of some 5,000 individuals from many Southeastern New England tribes. For fifty-four years, Massasoit worked closely with the Pilgrims, and was saved at least once by them when he was captured by Indian enemies and faced execution. He had two sons, Wamsutta and Metacom, who took the English names of Alexander and Philip. In turn, first Alexander and then Philip became sachems after their father died in 1662.

By the time of Massasoit's death, English law had added provocative limitations to Indian freedom and the westward push of hordes of new immigrants was forcing the native Americans into smaller and smaller areas. Faced with increased threats to their traditional way of life, Philip decided to fight. In 1675 and 1676, the Wampanoags, joined later by the Narragansetts and Nipmucs, conducted an initially successful and fierce guerrilla warfare all up and down the frontiers of the English settlements, penetrating as close to Duxbury as Plymouth and Norwell. The English forces, under the able leadership of Captain Benjamin Church, an early Duxbury settler, finally prevailed in the summer of 1676. As a result of what had become known as King Philip's War, local native Americans who survived lost their independence, most of the remainder of their lands, and were scattered and subjugated. The war marked an end to the strong political and economic influence of the Indians on the settlers.

Among the legacies of the Historic Indians, we are today very conscious of their names for lakes, rivers, cities, towns, and streets, not only here, but across the country. Locally, we are familiar with names such as Mattakeesett, Massachusetts, Nipmuc, Narragansett, Mashpee, King Philip's Path, and many others, all attesting to the many tribal groups and their prominent leaders.

FREDERICK T. POTTER

Squanto

By the time the *Mayflower* landed at Plymouth, Squanto (Tisquantum) had already been to England and back twice, the first time with explorer Captain George Weymouth in 1605. He returned with Captain John Smith in 1614, only to be captured along with other Indians by Captain Thomas Hunt, who took them to Spain to be sold as slaves. Squanto managed to get back to England and joined Captain Dermer's ship bound for Plymouth in 1619. When he arrived, he discovered that his tribal village at Patuxet had been completely eliminated.

Old Paths of Duxbury

*T*wo paths, used for centuries by native Americans, played an important role in the early history of Duxbury. The Pilgrim settlers called these ancient paths the Green's Harbor Path and the Bay Path. The Green's Harbor Path followed an easterly route through Duxbury on its way from Plymouth to Green's Harbor (Marshfield) and Scituate, a course approximated by Route 3A today. The Bay Path followed a more westerly course through Duxbury, leading north through what is now Pembroke and Hanover to the Puritan colony at Massachusetts Bay (Boston). This path took much the same course as today's Route 53.

Long before the arrival of the Separatists at Plymouth, the local Algonkians had developed a network of paths across southeastern Massachusetts. The paths followed the natural contours of the land, avoided wetlands, and forded rivers at narrow places. Many paths fanned out from the Wampanoag village at Patuxet (Plymouth); some leading north to the seat of the Massachusetts tribe near present-day Wollaston, others leading south to Nauset (Cape Cod), and west to the tribal villages of Nemasket (Middleboro), Titicut (North Middleboro), Cohannet (Taunton), and Pokanoket (Bristol, Rhode Island), the seat of the Wampanoag tribe.[1]

Edward Winslow and Stephen Hopkins, with the native Squanto as guide, traveled the Nemasket Path in July 1621, when they visited the Wampanoags at Pokanoket. Other exploratory expeditions along the already established paths helped to familiarize the settlers with the surrounding countryside.[2]

The earliest mention of the Bay Path is in Phineas Pratt's March 1623 account of a journey from Wessagusset (Weymouth) to Plymouth to warn the authorities of a threatened Wampanoag attack.

Then looking round me I ran southward toward three of the clock, but the snow being in many places I was distressed because of my footsteps . . . Then hearing a great howling of wolves, I came to a river. Then water being deep and cold and many rocks, I passed through with much ado. Then I came to a deep dell or hole, there being much wood fallen into it . . . The day following I began to travel . . . and about three of the clock I came to that part . . . Plymouth Bay where there is a town of later time . . . Duxbury. Then passing by the water on my left hand . . . to a brook and there was a path . . . fearing to go beyond the plantation, I kept running in the path; then passing through James River (Jones River) . . . running down the hill I . . . an Englishman . . . coming in the path before me . . .[3]

After land was granted in Duxbury in 1627, the settlers began to use both the Bay Path and the Green's Harbor Path. Duxbury's fertile land along the northern edge of Plymouth Bay could be easily reached by water, but foot travel along the old paths was often necessary, as Duxbury families journeyed back to Plymouth and settlers drove their livestock from Plymouth to their Duxbury farms.

By 1634, the Court at Plymouth felt it necessary to formally lay out a highway. The Governor and Assistants at Plymouth Colony "apoynted for laying out highwayes for Duxbyside, Capt. Miles Standish, Mr. Williams Collier, Jonathan Brewster, William Palmer, Steven Trace."[4] In May 1637, a jury consisting of twelve men from Plymouth and Duxbury laid out the main road, known as the Green's Harbor Path, and a side

path, the Duxburrow (Ducksburrow, Duxborrow) Path, which led specifically to the Duxbury grants.

The Green's Harbor Path followed the shoreline north of Plymouth, passed the Isaac Allerton farm on the south side of the Jones River, crossed the river at the Old Wading Place northeasterly of present Route 3A, followed the incline of Abraham Pierce's Hill in the present center of Kingston, passed through Governor William Bradford's farm at Stoney Brook, and entered Duxbury near Tussock Brook. Here the main stem of the path ran north through Island Creek, following what is now Mayflower Street and connected with Bow Street at North Hill. This main path continued to Millbrook on a course that parallels present day Route 3A. It passed west of Duck Hill and ran into Marshfield at present Careswell Street.

The Duxburrow Path left the main stem of the Green's Harbor Path at Tussock Brook and ran easterly through the Governor Thomas Prence farm to the site of the Duxbury Meeting House. A branch ran to the farms of Myles Standish and William Brewster at the Nook. The Duxburrow Path itself turned north through John Alden's farm and joined the Green's Harbor Path at Millbrook.[5]

The Green's Harbor Path, "laid out to remain a waye forever," was one of the first court-ordered roads in America.[6] Its exact location became obscured over the years, but during 1917 and 1918, Henry Fish of Duxbury and Elizabeth Paulding Eames of Marshfield uncovered its course. In his 1924 booklet, *Duxbury, Massachusetts, Ancient and Modern*, Henry Fish mapped out the trail through Duxbury. Elizabeth Eames corresponded with him and together they reconstructed the old way through the two towns.

References to the Green's Harbor Path are frequently made in early deeds and in boundary records. In

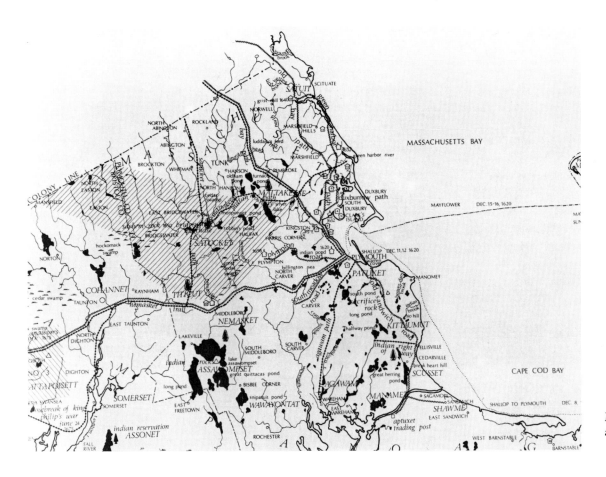

Map showing local native American tribes and trails, with early Pilgrim paths, c. 1620–1690. *(Courtesy Cynthia H. Krusell)*

setting the bounds between Duxbury and Marshfield in December 1640, the line is described as running from "a great rock that is flatt on the topp, called parting rock . . . and shall range from thence norwest to the South River, and on the contrary South East with payth between Scituate and Duxborrow and from then payth to divide them to the bridge over Green's harbour fresh."[7]

Along these two old paths the settlers drove cattle to their farms, traveled to their neighbors, and walked to their mills and to their meeting house. Their representatives to the Court at Plymouth rode along these paths to attend court sessions and in a much later period, the mail riders and stagecoaches continued to follow the old routes through Duxbury.

CYNTHIA HAGAR KRUSELL

7

Captain Myles Standish

Statue of Myles Standish, fourteen feet high.

Captain Myles Standish had already earned the respect and gratitude of the people of Plymouth long before he moved across the bay to Duxbury. Intelligent, decisive, and pragmatic, Standish reacted swiftly to any challenge posed by hostile native Americans. In the first three critical years, he established a strong defensive posture that protected Plymouth when the little plantation was feeble and its very existence seemed threatened.

The short, muscular Captain was born in 1584 in the Isle of Man where his family had lived for four generations, having migrated to the island from Ormskirk in Lancashire.[1] The Standishes of Ormskirk and Man were a junior branch of the eminent Standishes of Standish in Lancashire.

While serving with the English forces in Holland, Myles Standish made friends with the Pilgrims, who later recruited him to provide protection for their proposed settlement in the New World. In Myles Standish, the Pilgrims found not only an experienced military professional, but also an unusual soldier, one who soon demonstrated his ability to lead in the economic and civil affairs of the colony as well as to train and command its citizen-soldiers.

In 1625, Captain Standish went back to England where he laid the groundwork for the agreement between Plymouth Plantation and the London merchants, by which the people of Plymouth were able to buy out the merchants' interest and acquire ownership of the assets of the company. Furthermore, after Isaac Allerton completed the arrangements for the new contract, Myles Standish, William Bradford, and Allerton agreed to undertake the payment of the colony debt in return for a monopoly of the fur trade. The men became known as the "Undertakers" and they invited several other leaders to join them, including four men who would subsequently move to Duxbury: Thomas

Prence, William Brewster, John Alden, and John Howland. These financial arrangements made possible the early land grants that became the basis for the settlement of Duxbury.

In 1631, Captain Standish sold his two acres in Plymouth and moved his family and livestock to a new home on his 100-acre grant at the southeastern end of the peninsula, once called the *Captain's Nook*, but now known, in part, as Standish Shore. In 1637, an additional grant extended his boundaries to include the easterly side of Captain's Hill. This was probably his share as heir of his deceased wife, Rose, who had not survived the first terrible winter in Plymouth. In 1623, Myles Standish married Barbara, who had arrived that year on the *Anne*, and by 1627 they had three boys, John, Alexander, and Charles. There was probably an additional son, Myles Jr., by the time the Standishes settled into their Duxbury homestead. With them came Hobomock, Myles Standish's faithful Indian friend, who lived with the family until his death in 1642.

Unlike most of the early settlers who selected sheltered valleys for their homesites, Myles Standish built his long, narrow house on a high bluff with a commanding view of the Plymouth harbor and the channel leading to the open sea.[2] Like his Duxbury neighbors, Myles Standish had to provide the necessities for a growing family. (The records show that he was paid for his service to the Plymouth Colony only occasionally, and sparingly at that.) He planted rye, peas, wheat, and Indian corn, as well as flax and hemp, and he raised sheep, cattle, and horses. After 1640 he could take his corn to the Duxbury mill to be ground, and he could sell his surplus livestock and commodities at the Duxbury fair, held each October by order of the General Court.

During his Duxbury years, Myles Standish was frequently away from home on colony business, often for

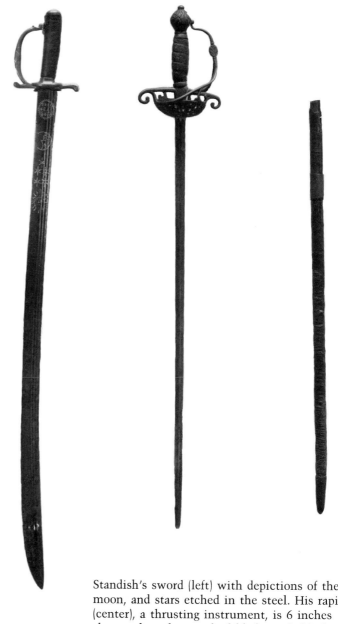

Standish's sword (left) with depictions of the sun, moon, and stars etched in the steel. His rapier (center), a thrusting instrument, is 6 inches shorter than the standard blade, probably because of his stature. The rapier scabbard (right) is made of wood, covered with leather and bound with iron. *(The Pilgrim Society, Plymouth, Massachusetts)*

several days at a time. He continued to be elected assistant governor for most of his life. There appear to be only four years between 1625 and 1656 that he did not serve. In two of those years, he was the deputy from Duxbury to the General Court. He was acting governor of Plymouth Colony during Bradford's absence in May 1653. The assistant governors were a powerful group of elected officials who performed executive and judicial functions, when they sat as the Court of Assistants, and legislative functions as well, when they met with the General Court. They also acted as the governor's council to advise on important decisions. Myles Standish was treasurer of the colony for twelve years, from 1644 through 1656.

Captain Standish continued to perform his military duties when called upon to do so. He trained the militia in Duxbury, Plymouth, and Marshfield and was appointed commanding officer of the entire colony militia in 1649, retaining his rank of Captain. He was seventy years old in 1654, the last time the summons came to command the troops. Captain Standish stood ready and willing, but the campaign was cancelled.

Along with all his military and civil duties, Myles Standish, often working with John Alden, surveyed the bounds of countless land grants and established the boundaries for entire towns. He was often the colony's agent in purchasing land from the Indians, perhaps because he was proficient in the Indian language. One of the largest such transactions was his purchase of 196 square miles from Massasoit in 1649/1650. Most of this land was granted by the Plymouth General Court to the people of Duxbury, and for six years was called Dux-burrow New Plantation before it became the Town of Bridgewater.[3]

Despite Standish's total dedication to the success of Plymouth Colony, he never joined the Pilgrim Church, although he regularly attended services. His impressive library indicates that he was a Protestant with Puritan leanings, more liberal than the Pilgrim Fathers. In fact, in 1645 Standish supported a petition for complete religious toleration in Plymouth Colony. This movement was favored by many of the deputies, but failed when Governor Bradford refused to let the matter come to a vote in the General Court.

Differing religious ideas did not prevent Myles Standish and Elder William Brewster, his Duxbury neighbor, from becoming cherished friends. Standish got along well with the Elder's sons, Jonathan and Love, but he quarreled with Francis Eaton's sons when they moved back onto their father's grant, which adjoined that of Standish. The Captain took Samuel Eaton to court over boundary disputes and, in another case, got a 30-shilling judgment against Benjamin Eaton for one of Standish's sheep, killed by young Eaton's dog. These were minor irritations for Standish, but his temper really flared when his old enemy, Thomas Morton, of Merrimount fame, moved to Duxbury in the winter of 1643. Standish had arrested and deported Morton for selling guns to the Indians. In 1637, Morton published *New English Canaan*, in which he satirized the Pilgrims and ridiculed Standish, calling him "Captain Shrimpe."[4] When Morton appeared on Standish's farm to hunt for ducks and geese, Standish was incensed. There was little Standish could do about it, since fishing and hunting rights were free to all men by order of the General Court when land grants were first issued. Happily for Standish, Morton's stay in Duxbury was brief.

Myles Standish was a passionate man, moved deeply by his loyalty to his friends and his love for his wife and children. He had lost two young sons, John and Charles, and later a daughter, Lora, probably his favorite child. He had also deeply loved his daughter-in-law,

Detail of the deed by which Massasoit (Ousamequin) transferred 196 square miles of land to townsmen of Duxbury. This purchase became the Duxburrow New Plantation until it was incorporated as the Town of Bridgewater in 1656. A literal transcription (23 March 1649):

the m̃k of ousameqin

En Consideration of the Aforesaid bargayn and sale we the said Myles Standish samuell nash and Constant southworth doe bind orselves to pay unto ye said ousameqin for and in Consideration of ye said tract of land as followeth

7 Coates a yd & halfe in a coat
9 hatchets
8 howoes
20 knives   Myles Standish
4 moose skins   Samuell Nash
10 yds & half of Cotton   Constant
                       Southworth

(The Old Bridgewater Historical Society, West Bridgewater, Massachusetts, translated by Stella J. Snow)

Mary, who lived only a short time after her marriage to Josias Standish. When drawing his will, Myles Standish had four surviving sons: Alexander, Josias, Myles Jr., and a second son named Charles. He asked that he be buried as near as possible to the two deceased young women, Lora and Mary.

After thirty-six years of loyal service to Plymouth Colony, Myles Standish died in October 1656. He was buried with honor in Duxbury, between the graves of Lora and Mary, as requested, in the Old Burying Ground next to the first Meeting House on what is now Chestnut Street.

FRANCES D. LEACH

Elder Brewster

The Brewster lilacs, brought from Holland by Elder Brewster, still bloom each spring. *(Elizabeth D. Post)*

Elder William Brewster was revered in Plymouth Colony. An elder of the congregation, his spirit, guidance, and judgment helped the struggling colony survive its early years. A part of the Brewster story not well known is the family's long connection with Duxbury, the land "on the other side of the Bay."[1] William Brewster had a substantial farm in the Nook section of South Duxbury, an area now known as Standish Shore. He and his sons, Jonathan and Love, were influential men in Duxbury during its infancy.

The story of the lives and lands of these Brewsters is not found in any one place, but comes from a meandering trail through colony court records, deeds, estate settlements, and town reports. The family emerges from these documents as human, and as afflicted "in the thorns of life"[2] as any other.

Their Duxbury story begins in 1627, with the second land division, and it begins in sadness. Mary Brewster, William's wife, died in April 1627, after a long illness. She was about fifty-eight, and left behind her husband, their two sons, Love, sixteen, and Wrestling, thirteen, and ten-year-old Richard More, a servant. Living nearby with their own families were the older married children, Jonathan Brewster, Patience Prence, and Fear Allerton.

The eighty-acre Brewster grant of land can be determined quite accurately since William Brewster very soon began to buy land from his neighbor, Francis Eaton. The Brewster lands were also in the Nook, which has the bay and Eagles Nest Creek as constant boundaries. The grant included land on both sides of the creek, on the east stretching south from Eagles Nest Point, and on the west from the upland ridge just north of the present-day Marshall Street.

The Nook farm was good land; wild, but not untamable. The Patuxet Indians had used it for years as a summer campground. It had several clean running springs, cleared upland, and light woods along the creek. Eagles Nest Creek also provided valuable salt hay marshes and a sheltered harbor. William Brewster could look south from his farm and see his near neighbors, the Standishes and Eatons, and out across the bay to Plymouth. To the north he could see the Morton's Hole farms, and the scattered farms along the Bluefish River.

Tradition and local lore have always placed the Brewster farmhouse near where a clump of lilacs bloom and Lombardy poplars grow. That is correct. This site is on the edge of the upland, overlooking the upper reaches of the creek, off what is now Marshall Street. A spring only a few feet north of the housesite supplied the Brewster household with water, and 360 years later, it still runs clear. The date William Brewster built his Duxbury house can also be pinpointed. He bought one acre from the widow of Francis Eaton, making the date after 1633, when Eaton died. In 1634, Love Brewster married, and stayed on in his father's house to care for him and the farm, so the house by the lilacs was built then, probably in anticipation of Love's marriage.

Elder Brewster retained his Plymouth house and his membership with the congregation at Plymouth. There has always been a question of where he spent most of his time. When he died in 1644 at his home in Plymouth and inventory was taken, many of his possessions were listed at that residence. But several Duxbury deeds and some court records point towards his being a resident of this town. It seems safe and logical to say that William Brewster spent the warm months on his Duxbury farm with Love's family, and the winter months in Plymouth. Perhaps as he grew older, and Love's family grew larger, he might have spent less time in Duxbury, but we have every reason to claim him as an early resident of the town.

Brewster died on the 10th or the 18th of April, 1644, without a will, a fact which could have meant endless haggling over his estate. But the settlement was a model of thoughtfulness and fairness, thanks to Brewster's four close friends: Myles Standish, William Bradford, Edward Winslow, and Thomas Prence. This extant record gives an important glimpse of what the Duxbury farm actually looked like, as well as some of the feelings amongst the family. A dispute arose between Jonathan and Love, a serious one, which was settled by the four older friends this way:

> For the debts which were alleadged against the said Jonathan the elder brother by the said Love the younger as aforesaid we conceive that if their father had not acquitted them before his death yet hee would never have charged his Eldest sonn with them in regard of his great charge of children and so beleeving it was donn actually or intentively or both we discharged Jonathan of all the said debt his brother made him debtor to the estate aforesaid. And for the Dwelling house aforesaid of the said William wherin the said Love Brewster resided, we were so well aquainted with the purpose of the said Wllam now deceased and the evidence offerred for profe seemed to us so strong as wee beleeving the said Wllm had actually or intentively or both given said house to his sonn Love and Sarah his wyfe and their and their heires etc.[3]

Elder William Brewster was noted for his compassion, so it is not surprising to find from his settlement that he was caring for his grandson, Isaac Allerton, Jr., who would later become the first colony resident to attend Harvard. The farm in Duxbury was divided as it

13

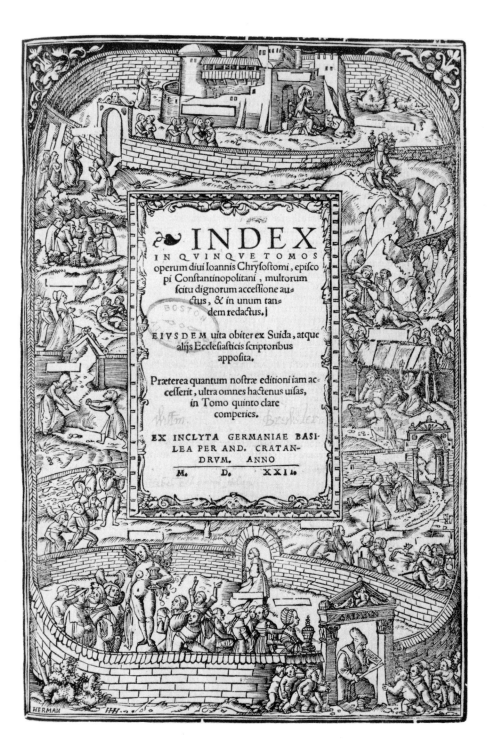

fell naturally, with Jonathan getting the land on the west side of Eagles Nest Creek, and Love receiving the land on the east side. "And the reason wherefore we gave Love the less quantitie was and is because the quallity of Loves land in goodness is equall to the quantitie of Jonathans as we judg."[4]

Jonathan Brewster

The eldest son, Jonathan Brewster, was married with two children in 1627 when he received an 80-acre grant in the land division. His first Duxbury farm was not in the Nook, but located below Tremont Street, between Icehouse Pond Creek and present day Soule Avenue.

Jonathan Brewster was one of the first men to bring his family across the bay to stay year-round; his name appears on the 1632 document in which Duxbury men promised to return to Plymouth in the winter. The isolation of his frontier farm can only be imagined, but the farm just to the north was Thomas Prence's, whose wife was Patience Brewster. A curious entry in an old Brewster Bible may give a clue to the hardships Jonathan's family suffered in the early years. Ruth Brewster, a daughter, was born in 1631 "att Jones River."[5] This is a strange entry, since none of the Brewsters owned land at Jones River, so perhaps the baby arrived unexpectedly on the arduous journey back to Plymouth.

Jonathan was an ambitious, adventurous man, frequently away from his Duxbury farm. In 1633, he took part in an expedition that explored the Connecticut River, and despite great danger from the Dutch and the Indians, established a trading post, of which Jonathan

Title page with Renaissance woodcut border, of a folio St. Chrysostom (Basle, 1522), signed Willm. Brewster. One of the several hundred books in Brewster's library. *(Boston Athenaeum)*

was made agent. This venture did not last long. In 1635, two groups of Massachusetts Bay colonists flooded into the valley, and land and trading post eventually had to be forfeited to them. Perhaps Jonathan was lucky, for only a short time later this area was engulfed in the Pequot Indian war.

He was not back on his farm long before he was involved in another ill-fated venture. Jonathan received a grant at the North River in 1638, and established a ferry. The traffic on the inland route to the Massachusetts Bay plantations made such a venture profitable, but only a year later Jonathan was fined in court for "neglecting" his ferry. He paid his fine in corn, a legal tender, and in 1641 sold the ferry business. One of the buyers later drowned in a crossing, not an uncommon fate for operators of ferry boats of the period.

One reason Jonathan Brewster may have neglected his ferry was that he was busy building a new family home on part of his father's farm in the Nook. He sold his first farm in 1638 to Comfort Starr, Duxbury's aptly named first doctor. Jonathan's new farm was on the east side of Eagles Nest Creek, on a rise of land opposite Love's home. The farm had a nearby spring, orchards sloping to the creek, plenty of tilled land, fresh and salt meadows. The path out of the Nook went from Love's house across the narrowest point of the creek and through the dooryard of Jonathan's farm.

Jonathan lived on his Nook farm for ten years. One hopes those were happy, since his later years were not. In 1648, he abruptly left Duxbury for Monhegan, Connecticut. His departure seems odd, but a letter between his two friends, Roger Williams and John Winthrop, Jr., provides the answer.

Sir (though Mr Brewster wrote me not a word of it) yet in private I am bold to tell you, that I hear it hath pleased God greatly to afflict him in the thorns of life.

He was intended for Virginia, his creditors in the Bay came to Portsmouth and unhung his rudder; carried him to the Bay, where he was forced to make over all—house, land, cattle and part all to his chest.[6]

Evidently Jonathan was a trader, perhaps even owning a ship, but lost his Duxbury farm to two Dorchester merchants when he could not give them an accounting on their goods. Myles Standish and William Collier were empowered to make the transfer of the farm, an unpleasant task to do for a neighbor. Jonathan went to Monhegan, now Norwich, Connecticut, and set up a trading post with money borrowed from his brother-in-law, Isaac Allerton. He chose Monhegan because of his long friendship with John Winthrop, Jr., who lived there. Both men were interested in alchemy, and their fascinating letters are full of traded information that reveals Jonathan had a type of laboratory, something he must have originated during his time in Duxbury.

Jonathan Brewster's life in Connecticut was not any easier. He was isolated, in constant anxiety about Indian attacks, and complained about the lack of even basic supplies. He also quarrelled with the local minister, and worried about his "manifold miscariadges."[7] In a letter to his sister-in-law, Sarah Brewster, he wrote, "I feare I shall next year go further from you, for I with my whole family resolve for old England,"[8] but this became yet another failed venture. Jonathan died in September, 1656, soon after an incident that probably confirmed his darkest fears.

Mr Brewster further complaineth that som Narragansett Indians the last spring did assault and kill a Monhegan Indian Imployed in his service and flying to Mistris Brewster for Succor; yett they violently took him from her and shott him by her side to her great affightment.[9]

Jonathan Brewster had a hard life in New England, one can only hope he found a better one.

Love Brewster

Love Brewster was the son who appears to have been the closest to his father. He, his brother, Wrestling, and Richard More all came over to Duxbury soon after the land division to work the Elder's farm. Wrestling Brewster is a mystery; Bradford states he "dyed a yonge man unmaried,"[10] but where or when is not recorded. Richard More left Duxbury in 1637, after selling his land on Eagles Nest Point, a share of the land said to have been given to him by William Brewster.

Love married Sarah Collier on May 15, 1634, the same day that her sister Rebecca married Job Cole. William Collier must have had quite a feast at his home for this double wedding. Love and Sarah settled into the Nook farm, with the understanding that it would be theirs after the Elder's death. Love Brewster kept a lower public profile than his brother, holding no public office except when he helped lay out the 1637 path from Plymouth. He volunteered for the Pequot War, but was not called; he was a yeoman, and farming occupied all of his time.

The Brewster farm was successful; there are several references to men whom Love hired as servants to help. Unfortunately, two of these proved to be embarrassments to the family. Richard Bishop left his service and got married, and his wife later murdered their small daughter, in one of the rare such crimes in Plymouth Colony.

The most notorious of the Brewster servants was Thomas Granger, who was hanged in 1642 for bestiality. Bradford mentions this case in some length because he felt it revealed the moral rot occurring within the colony. Certainly it was a great shock for Elder Brewster and his family to find it occurring on their own farm. It must also have been a financial hardship for them, since the animals involved were sacrificed before Gran-

ger's eyes, and then buried in a pit. "A very sade spectakle it was,"[11] concluded William Bradford.

Hard upon this horror was the death of William Brewster in 1644. Love, beset by the problems with his brother over the estate, and disputes over land boundaries, took sick in 1650, lingering for five months before he died at age forty. He left behind a young widow and four small children, two under five. Sarah Collier Brewster was thrust into unusual circumstances. Only thirty-five when her husband needed nursing, she also had to run the farm and care for their children. Her life is not a blank, as so many of the lives of women were in those early years.

Love's will is interesting because Sarah was made sole executor, handling all the major duties. "I give and bequeath unto my beloved wife Sarah Brewster all the Residue of my whole estate, both goods and Chattles and land at Duxburrow for the bringing up of her and my children to the time of her life and after her desease I doe give the aforesaid lands to my eldest sonn."[12] He also trusted her with his books, many of which were his father's, "and for those books I have that my wife would distribute them to herselfe and Children at her discretion."[13]

Sarah Brewster was left well off, but with a large farm to manage. Contrary to earlier histories, the Love Brewster farm was not sold out of the family, but remained a Brewster farm for another 130 years. Sarah ran this farm and raised her family with help from her father; there is a record of his petitioning on her behalf for some undivided common lands. She also settled the boundary disputes with the Eatons, so that the farm would be preserved for her sons.

In 1656, Jonathan Brewster wrote to Sarah, "In my judgement I would advise you to marry one whome you could love."[14] She appears to have taken his advice, since she waited fifteen years, until her sons were grown, before marrying Richard Parke of Cambridge Village, now Newton. But Richard Parke died the following year. By 1671, Sarah Brewster Parke had returned to Duxbury to live with her sons, Nathaniel and William, on the Brewster farm in the Nook.

In 1678, Sarah argued with the next door neighbor, William Pabodie. She pulled up boundary stakes on his land, claiming it was Brewster land, and so was charged with trespass. Sarah was not afraid to stand up in court and demand that the settlement be made according to the original division of the Elder's farm. This was yet another instance when Sarah fought for her name and the lands of the Brewsters. Her son, Deacon William Brewster, eventually settled the case when he bought the disputed part of Eagles Nest Point.

Sarah Parke went to live in Plymouth in 1682, but her troubles were not over. A church record for that year states that "A sister recommended to from another (church) yet was not accepted to our communication, till some offence was removed betwixt her and a brother, which upon hearing by some Godly wise were comfortably issued, and she was accepted by the (church)."[15] Another record on the same case is badly torn in some strategic places, but does list a fragment of her name and William Pabodie's, so the problem seems to have been some lingering feeling between the two. Sarah's last years seemed peaceful; she died in 1691 at age 76. The record for that year states that those lost were, "some of them of the best."[16]

Sarah Collier Brewster Parke is an extraordinary example of an ordinary Duxbury woman who demonstrated fortitude and perseverance through hardship. She outlived her parents and sisters, two husbands, and two children, worked her family's farm, fought several disputes that threatened it, and lived to see the day when the colony founded by her family was dissolved into the larger, more powerful, Massachusetts Bay Colony.

ANTHONY KELSO

OLD BREWSTER PLACE

John Alden

ost school children know that John Alden was one of the Pilgrims, a signer of the Mayflower Compact (the 7th), and finally, of his courtship of Priscilla. His Duxbury house stands today, maintained by the Alden Kindred of America, Inc. His life is described in several books, one of the best being *The Aldens in the Alden House* by Duxbury's own Dorothy Wentworth.

How did Alden get to the house off what was to become Alden Street? Why America? Why Duxbury? What kind of man was he? Finally, why was John Alden on the *Mayflower*? He was not a Separatist, although he ultimately embraced this philosophy in the New World. He was on board because of an English Parliamentary statute of 1543, the Barrell Law. This law insured the kingdom a plentiful supply of oak staves for making barrels to hold the beer which was so essential to the Englishmen of the day. It stated, in part, that "who so ever shall carry beer beyond the sea, shall find surities to the customers of the port to bring in clapboard to make so much vessel as he shall carry forth."[1]

John Alden was a cooper, or barrel maker, by trade. The bill of service issued by the authorities called him "an artificier in the mysteries of coopering." The word *mysteries* indicated a professional or guild-like status.[2] From the records of Governor William Bradford we know that Alden was hired at Southampton when the *Mayflower* provisioned there. His employment enabled the departing ship to fulfill the requirements of the Barrell Law. In fact, the required clapboard was a large part of the cargo of the vessel *Fortune*, which returned to England from Plymouth in 1621. Alden's contract provided that he might return on the *Fortune*, but we all know that he chose to stay in the Plymouth Colony.

The Aldens' second Duxbury house (1653). *(Norman Forgit)*

The circumstances of his crossing give us the first clues to John Alden's character. He was disciplined enough to have acquired a trade. However, with his life before him, assuredly many opportunities at hand, and without the impetus of a religious zeal, he chose a dangerous undertaking. The man was also an adventurer.

He decided to cast his lot with the Plymouth Colony, and eventually married Priscilla Mullins, who had been orphaned after her father, mother, brother Joseph, and family servant Robert Carter, had all succumbed in the first New England winter. About 1624, Alden's daughter Elizabeth was born.

It is known that the Aldens constructed a small home in Plymouth, which has been replicated by the Plimoth Plantation. However, the settlement was not to be their final home. In 1627, John Alden, Myles Standish, and others bought out their English backers, enabling them to divide up the settlement as they saw fit. Lots were drawn and Alden received a grant in Duxbury, which ran westerly from the Bluefish River.

At first, the Aldens spent three seasons of each year on the Duxbury land, returning to Plymouth in the winter. In 1632, when the Governor allowed a permanent settlement to be formed in Duxbury, the Aldens, having invested so much time and effort on their Duxbury property, sold their house in Plymouth and moved to Duxbury year-round.

By this time they were a family of six. The house John Alden constructed as a homestead for their farm was a narrow structure, 380 square feet, with a small root cellar at one end. The outline of this house, which was excavated by Roland Wells Robbins in 1960, can be seen behind the Alden School. Three-hundred-eighty square feet make tight quarters for six people; yet, while they were still living in this same house, the Aldens had six more children. One can imagine that their next

and larger house resulted from someone putting his or her foot down. So it was that in 1653 the Aldens completed their second house, not too far from the first. It has been in the Alden "family" ever since.

It is hard to imagine the adventurous John Alden as a simple farmer. In fact, existing records indicate that he was a farmer by necessity, but was also involved in other far-reaching activities. First, as a master carpenter, he probably assisted in the construction of many of his neighbors' homes, and also found time to create serrated cabinets, chests, and cupboards for prosperous colonists.

Site excavation of the Aldens' first Duxbury house (1960). The dry-laid stone work forms a six-foot square root cellar. *(Randall W. Abbott/The Pilgrim Society)*

The second Alden Kindred reunion, August 28, 1902. *(A.E. Alden/Alden Kindred of America)*

Secondly, he was heavily involved in the political life of the town and colony. He sat on each Governor's Council except for the first, serving as an acting governor in 1664–1665, and again in 1667. From 1656 to 1658, he was treasurer of Plymouth Colony. He sat on several war councils necessitated by Indian hostilities. From 1641 to 1649, he represented the Town of Duxbury at the General Court and on several important occasions was authorized to act as agent or attorney for the colony. It was probably in this capacity that he travelled to the colony's distant settlement at Kennebec, Maine.

Finally, he was active, along with Myles Standish, as a surveyor, and helped lay out many of the early grants. It is said that he laid out the course for a canal through Cape Cod, a canal which was constructed centuries later.

John Alden was approximately eighty-eight years old when he died. He had outlived all the other men who had sailed on the *Mayflower*. During his lifetime, he developed into a well-rounded individual, improving on his existing skills, adding mechanical, agricultural, and nautical capabilities. He had contributed to colonial society as magistrate, military man, and surveyor. In short, he had become the kind of man who was needed in the New World to insure the survival of his own family and of the colony itself. Duxbury can be proud to count John Alden as one of its founders.

JOHN ALDEN KEYSER, JR.

One of Duxbury's oldest houses, the gambrel-roofed Alexander Standish House built in 1666 on the west side of Captain Myles Standish's farm. Alexander, the Captain's oldest son, married Sarah Alden, daughter of John and Priscilla Alden. *(Cecil B. Atwater/Duxbury Rural and Historical Society)*

Detail from sampler (c. 1644) stitched by Lora Standish, beloved daughter of Captain Myles, when she was about twelve. Earliest known sampler in the United States, on display at Pilgrim Hall. *(Allen Harney/The Pilgrim Society, Plymouth, Massachusetts)*

King Caesar House, Duxbury, built 1808–1809, by
Ezra Weston, Jr., known as *King Caesar.* Owned
and operated as a museum by the Duxbury Rural
and Historical Society. *(Carleton Knight, Jr.)*

View south towards the Weston Wharf and Duxbury Bay from the front hall of the King Caesar
House. *(Cecil B. Atwater/DR&HS)*

Detail of French wallpaper in west parlor of King Caesar House. "Le Parc Français" by Jacquemart et Benard. *(Clive Russ/DR&HS)*

"Ship *Argus*, Joseph Drew, Master, entering Marseilles Jan. 1823" by Antoine Roux, French 1799–1872. *(Clive Russ/DR&HS)*

23

Ship Mary of Boston engaging 3 French privateers   Naples 1800

"Ship *Mary* of Boston Engaging Three French Privateers, Naples, 1800" Gamaliel Bradford, Captain. By Michel Felice Corne, active in Salem and Newport between 1799 and 1845. *(Clive Russ/ DR&HS)*

The Nathaniel Winsor, Jr. House (1807), a three-story Federal house with Duxbury's only Palladian window. *(Carleton Knight, Jr.)*

The First Parish Church, dedicated 1840. There were three meeting houses before this, the first two near the Old Burying Ground, the third also on Tremont Street. *(Cecil B. Atwater/ DR&HS)*

View of Mr. Joshua Winsor's House by Rufus Hathaway (1793–5). This landscape depicts Winsor's home with his warehouse and wharf at the right. The artist's legendary humor and attention to detail is subtly recorded in paint by means of the small figure standing aboard the ship whose shot gun has brought down two geese seen falling simultaneously. *(Private collection)*

George Soule

In the Nuclear Age it is almost impossible to visualize the living conditions in 1637, when Duxbury became a town. Electric lights, central heating, and modern plumbing have banished all memory of tiny houses boasting none of these comforts; but one thing was available to the Pilgrims—plenty of land. When new arrivals crowded Plymouth, some of the *Mayflower* passengers moved over to Duxbury.

The first grants of land in Duxbury were drawn by lot, but undoubtedly preference determined some locations, for naturally, Myles Standish wanted to look across the bay to Plymouth, and Elder Brewster wished to live near Standish. Mayflower Pilgrim Edward Winslow's grant was at Careswell (Marshfield), and that probably influenced George Soule's acquisition of land this side of the marshes at Powder Point, for the wealthy Winslow had financed Soule's passage on the *Mayflower*.[1] Perhaps Soule was a poet at heart, for he chose to live in the most beautiful section of Duxbury, with enough arable land for the necessary gardens, and immediate access to Duxbury Bay, where fishing could delight a man, as well as provide food for hungry children.

In Bradford's *History*, Soule is called a servant of Edward Winslow, but apparently his duties were not of a menial nature, for aboard the *Mayflower* on November 11, 1620, Soule signed the Compact adopted by the Pilgrims.[2]

Very little is known about George Soule. Apparently he was an able businessman, for as early as July 1627, he was one of the group of fifty-eight "Purchasers or Oldtimers" who assumed Plymouth Colony's debt to "The Adventurers," as they called the promoters and capitalists who financed the voyage of the *Mayflower*. In 1633, the Court ordered residents of the Colony to pay taxes. George Soule was assessed 9 shillings, whereas his wealthy friend, Winslow, was assessed 2 pounds, 5 shillings.[3]

An aerial view of Powder Point (c. 1965) shows George Soule's original grant. His homestead was probably located on the northwest side, overlooking the Back River.

Justin Winsor tells us that George Soule was a member of the military group that took action between 1633 and 1636 against the Pequot Indians, which resulted in their total subjugation and almost total extinction; and in 1642, Soule served on a committee for raising forces to handle possible attacks by the Narragansetts.[4]

According to Winsor, George Soule did not settle in Duxbury much before 1637. He was not especially involved in town government, but he did frequently represent Duxbury at the Court of Deputies. Apparently he prospered, for Mitchell's *History of Bridgewater* tells us that Soule was one of the original proprietors who purchased land in what is now Bridgewater. Soule also acquired considerable land in Middleboro and in Dartmouth.[5]

His friend, Edward Winslow, was assistant governor of Plymouth Colony for many years, and also governor for a few terms, but about 1646 he returned to England. Soule's life was less spectacular. He never returned to England, even for a brief visit, and he lived at Plymouth for only a few years before he settled at Powder Point, where he spent the remainder of his long life. A gravestone in Standish Cemetery marks the approximate location of his burial which took place sometime before January 1679.

Little is known about George Soule's wife. Her name was Mary Becket (or Bucket) and she came to Plymouth in the summer of 1623 as a passenger on the 140-ton ship *Anne* from London. The *Anne*, along with its companion vessel, the 44-ton pinnace, *Little James*, brought ninety-five passengers, about a third of them women. Among the new arrivals were Elder Brewster's two daughters, Patience and Fear; Myles Standish's future wife, Barbara; and the widow, Alice Southworth, who would marry William Bradford.

George Soule's Soliloquy, 1637

Across the Bay I see the Eagle's nest,
that hides the fields this side of Brewster's house,
so close to Standish dwelling on the crest
of ridge below the hill the Redmen roam
in retrospect. We came across the foam,
through crashing waves, almost two decades past,
and now I fish, or spade the fertile loam
that skirts the marsh and flooding tides held fast
by Nature's law. No love can ever last
a longer time than mine for England's shores,
but now my heart is bound to lands so vast
we only dream what endless mileage stores.
Perchance my sons will venture far afield
to seek horizons from my eyes concealed.

—Isabelle V. Freeman

Mary Becket and George Soule had nine children. Their first son Zachariah died childless before 1663. Their son Benjamin was "killed in action by Indians before Pawtucket" during Pierce's Massacre in King Philip's War in 1676. Other Soule children, Nathaniel, George, Susannah, Patience, and Elizabeth, all married and settled at some distance from Duxbury; but son John and daughter Mary married and remained in Duxbury. John's first wife was Rebecca Simmons, who mothered six children. His second wife was Esther (Nash) Sampson. They had six more children.

George's daughter Mary, was "placed to Jonathan Winslow in 1652 for 7 years."[6] Not much is known now of the early practice of putting a girl in another family

29

in order to acquire as much experience and education as possible, while performing her duties in the home, but it was fairly common in the colonial days. It does not imply poverty on the part of the parents. Mary Soule married John Peterson before 1672. They had nine children, four of whom died young.

We cannot say that all descendants of John Soule and Mary Soule Peterson stayed in Duxbury, for such is not the case, but a great many of them did, and many of their descendants still live in Duxbury. Unfortunately, George Soule has never been given the attention enjoyed by his fellow settlers, Myles Standish and John Alden, but he and his descendants have contributed enormously to the establishment and growth of the town. Perhaps the world has forgotten George Soule, but his descendants remember him with admiration and deep respect.

ISABELLE V. FREEMAN

Other First Families

Alden, Brewster, and Standish are names that come to mind when one thinks of the earliest settlers of Duxbury. Yet these were only the better known. The town had other first settlers who played important roles, but their names are less familiar. William Collier, Francis Eaton, Francis Sprague, and later, William Pabodie, were among the influential men who struggled to establish themselves and their town. These other early settlers should be remembered for their part in the history of the town, and for their colorful personalities that glimmer through the records, even after all these years.

Collier, Sprague, and Eaton all came to Duxbury by chance, drawing by lot their grants of land. They, along with Pabodie, lived in and around the Nook and Morton's Hole, the area west of present-day Hall's Corner. Here stood the town's meetinghouse, burying ground, stocks, and militia training ground. Today, only the burying ground remains, but in the early years Morton's Hole was the center of town.

Francis Sprague

Francis Sprague, his wife Anna, and their children, Mercy and John, came to Duxbury in 1632 and were among the first to stay year-round on their grant. Francis Sprague had a sixty-acre farm in the vicinity of the present-day Hornbeam Road. The small creek that runs just south of this point of land is still known as Sprague's Creek. The exact location of the Sprague house is not known, but it might have been close to present day Washington Street. Proof that the Spragues were here as early as 1632 is found in a court document

31

The Gundalow

From the very first, saltmarsh hay was valuable, easily harvested, and needed for fodder. Ownership of marshland was granted and transferred just like more solid real estate. Through most of the nineteenth century, farmers went out to gather the hay in wide-bottomed, shallow boats known as *gundalows*. These boats drew little water and could be rowed or poled, so were especially adapted to the marshes. They could carry up to eight tons of hay, brought aboard over long gangplanks.

Katherine Pillsbury

of July 1633, wherein Francis is ordered to "mow at the Eagle and about his own ground where he mowed last year."[1] This order referred to the valued salt hay marshes that line Eagles Nest Bay, so prized that in the early years they were kept in common and given out each year.

Sprague was a farmer, like all early Duxbury settlers, but he served over the years as a constable and surveyor of highways. It is not these duties he is remembered for, however. Sprague was the first ordinary keeper in Duxbury, receiving a license in October 1638 "to keep a victualling on Duxburrow side." He must have enjoyed his own spirits, because that same year he was brought before the court for "drinking o'ermuch." Only a year later, his license was taken away, but this formality did not stop him. He continued to pour until 1641, when he was ordered not "to dray any wyne or strong water untill the next generall (Court) without speciall lycence." He must have received this license, but continued to get into trouble over the years. Francis Sprague could have been an impetus for a 1645 Plymouth Colony law that stated "if any victualler or ordinary keeper do either drink, drunke himself or suffer any person to be druncken in his house, they shall pay five shillings." At various times over the following years Sprague was also brought before the Court for killing a mare, beating his neighbor's servant, and selling firearms to the Indians. He lost his ordinary license for the last time in 1666.[2]

The Sprague children were chips off the parental block. Mercy Sprague was warned in 1652 for "mixed dauncing," a practice believed to stir up bodily lust. A few years later, she created a major scandal by leaving her husband, William Tubbs, for another man, and then running off to Rhode Island. Tubbs tried to disown her, and got an illegal writ of divorce in 1664, for which he was fined. Finally, in 1668, he received a legal divorce since Mercy, "being a woman of ill fame and light behavior apparently manifest, hath for the space of four years and upwards absented and withdrawne herselfe from her husband into another colonie, pretending she is att libertie, and that, notwithstanding, all the meanes and waies her husband can use with safety, shee will not be reclaimed nor pswaded to returne and abide with him as shee ought to doe." Mercy Sprague Tubbs must have been a woman of some independence, not afraid to speak her mind. She informed the court at Plymouth, "she will never returne againe unto him while her eyes are open."[3]

John Sprague, Mercy's brother, was fined for drinking, gaming, and uncivil reveling, but he was granted an ordinary license in 1669, after his father lost his. John married the girl next door, Ruth Bassett, and soon after was killed in King Philip's War. He met a particularly gruesome death, being part of Captain Michael Pierce's company of Plymouth Colony men who were ambushed by the Narragansetts at Pawtucket in the spring of 1676. Francis Sprague died in the same year as his son. The Sprague farm passed to John's children, who continued to live on it for another twenty-seven years, but not with the reputation their forebears had. The Spragues could not have been the easiest neighbors—particularly for the town's minister on the adjoining farm—but they certainly added a colorful episode to the story of Duxbury's early settlement.

William Collier

One of the Sprague's neighbors, William Collier, was a man of sterling character and reputation. Among the earliest to settle in Duxbury, arriving in 1633, he was one of the wealthiest men in Plymouth Colony. Referred to as a "gentleman," he and Edward Winslow had the highest tax assessments in the colony. Collier had been a London brewer, one of the merchant adventurers who financed the colony. He was one of the few such men to remain loyal to the struggling colony. An older man when he came to settle in Duxbury, Collier brought with him his wife, Jane, and their four daughters.

The location of the Collier farm has never been pinpointed. Court records indicate his first land grant was at Morton's Hole, since he was ordered to mow the salt meadow there. In July 1635, Collier was granted another parcel of land, "lying up in ye woods called by the name North Hill." Tradition has the Colliers moving to North Hill, but this cannot be proven. As late as 1662, Collier was still attempting to establish boundaries for his North Hill land, but there is no suggestion that he was living there. He had earlier given some North Hill land to a son-in-law, so it seems logical that he used this later grant for his children. Wild animals were evidently a bother to Collier, because his "woolf-trap" is mentioned in 1638.[4]

Before he died in 1671, William Collier made an agreement with Benjamin Bartlett, who had married Collier's granddaughter, Sarah Brewster. Bartlett was to buy "house and land which the said William Collyare Now liveth on," as well as a parcel of North Hill land.[5] Bartlett could not take possession of the farm and lands until Collier's death. This deed indicates that Collier was still living in the vicinity of Morton's Hole, perhaps on the high ground near the meeting house.

William Collier was an asset to Plymouth Colony. He was for many years an assistant governor and a member of the Council of Commissioners for the United Colonies of New England, a body that attempted to regulate disputes between the New England colonies. In 1658, the colony provided him with a servant, "because he can not easily come to public business, being aged and having much private business." Evidently, this servant did not work out, because a year later Joseph Prior was brought before the court for, "pilfering and pryloring practices, and other unworthy carriages relating therto, viz in alluring a younge maide, kinswoman to William Collier to healp him, the said Prior, to sundry things pertaining to the said William Collyare without his knowing." Prior was released after "shewing and expressing great humiliation," but only two years later was put in the stocks for stealing from another employer.[6]

The Collier house was also the place where Wamsutta, first son of Massasoit, was brought for questioning in July 1662, for "entertaining hostile designs against the English." Wamsutta, or Alexander, continued on to Marshfield where he caught a deathly fever. His death precipitated the colony's drift towards King Philip's War.

Collier was also influential in other local Duxbury events. He received a license in 1660 to sell "strong waters" to his neighbors as he saw fit.[7] Perhaps this was to counteract the wild behavior at the Sprague ordinary. And he was part of a group that shaped, or tried to, the character of the town.

In 1637, soon after the arrival of Ralph Partridge, Duxbury's first minister, the congregation petitioned to insure that the town would have men who could support a church and minister. This action appears to be a result of the lingering bad feeling caused by the splintering of the Duxbury congregation from Plymouth. "That seeing the church of plymouth now called home their members who held much lands on that side, and they being few, and the lands there were desposed in great part to servants and other yeong men, from whom they could expect little help," the Duxbury congregation asked that lands on this side of the bay be granted only when "such as these foure viz, Mr William Collyer, Mr Ralph Partrich, Jonathan Brewster and William Basset should approve as fitt for their societe."[8]

Francis Eaton

Francis Eaton was another early settler, coming to his eighty-acre Duxbury grant in 1631. His farm lay in the Nook, between the farms of Standish and Brewster. Francis Eaton had the distinction of having the earliest recorded land sales in Plymouth Colony. In June 1631, he sold his four acres in Plymouth to Edward Winslow, in consideration of "the second cow calfe," which Winslow was to deliver "the same at the age of six moneths." Francis Eaton must have been preparing to live on his Duxbury farm. Six months later, we find him selling one share of land in the Nook, "commonly called Nothingelse," to William Brewster.[9]

Because of his trade as a carpenter, Eaton was valuable to the colony, advising and assisting with many of the first houses. Eaton is likely the man Bradford describes as "an ingenious man that was a house carpenter," who converted one of the colony's shallops to a more sturdy boat with decking, so it could be used for trading along the coast.[10]

Unfortunately, Francis Eaton's family life was marred by sadness. His wife died the first winter and left him with a son, Samuel, "a suckling child." His second wife died only a few years later, and by 1627 he married Christian Penn. In 1627, the Eatons had a daughter, Rachel. By 1633 when Francis died, they had two more children, Benjamin and an "ideote child." This last child was still living in 1650 when Bradford made his list of first comers, but no sex or name is given, and this child remains a sad, unsolved mystery.[11]

Francis Eaton was likely one of the victims of the smallpox epidemic that raged through Plymouth during the summer of 1633. He died insolvent, owing work to various families, but his widow was absolved of her husband's debts. The inventory of Eaton's estate is

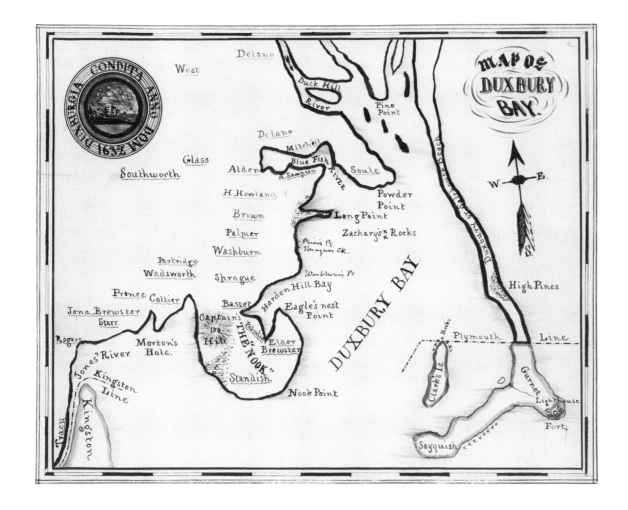

Map by Justin Winsor locates the areas where the first settlers lived. *(The Massachusetts Historical Society)*

telling in its sparseness: he owned not much more than his carpenter tools and the clothes on his back.

After Francis Eaton's death, the Eaton family split apart. Christian Eaton married Francis Billington and moved to Plymouth. This family had hard times, many children, and no means to provide for them. Samuel Eaton and his half brother, Benjamin, were both apprenticed out. The Eaton farm in the Nook remained in the

family, held for Samuel, but the tenants are unknown.

By 1647, Samuel Eaton, then in his mid-twenties, returned to the Duxbury farm, setting off boundary disputes. From 1648 through October of 1652, Samuel Eaton had running fights with his Nook neighbors on either side, the Standishes and the Brewsters. The boundary dispute with the Brewsters was particularly acute because of earlier purchases of Eaton land by the

Brewster family. No one appeared to know who owned what land, and the original plan had been lost. The problem was compounded when Jonathan Brewster left town, followed by the untimely death of Love Brewster in 1650. The settlement of the boundaries with Samuel was left to Sarah Brewster, Love's widow. It must not have been easy. The Eaton house was quite close to the Brewster house, since a deed gives the right to use a water spring on Brewster land to both parties.

The Eaton children, like many of the second generation of colonists, had a hard time living up to the ideals of their fathers' generation. Samuel Eaton was brought before the court in 1651 for mixed dancing with Goodwife Halle, when both were married to others. In March 1651/2, he was sentenced to sit in the stocks for pilfering and stealing. Only a few months later, he, his wife, and his sister were involved in a case involving a man who had branded a colt so that its true owner would not recognize it. Samuel Eaton was in Duxbury until 1663, when he received a land grant in Middleboro and moved there.

Constant Southworth's will, dated 1678, and proved March 16, 1678/9:

"To my daughter Elizabeth Southworth my next best bed and furniture, provided she doe not marry William Fobbes, but if she doe then to have 5 shillings."*

Later that year Elizabeth Southworth did marry William Fobbes.

* Plymouth Colony Records, Wills IV, 1:18

Benjamin Eaton lived for a time with his brother, Samuel, at the Nook farm. He got into trouble with his formidable neighbor, Captain Standish, to such an extent that the court ordered him "to provide himselfe a service, if not the Court would provid him one." But apprenticeship did not seem to help, because two years later Benjamin, with others, was charged with "vain, light and lacivious carriage at an unreasonable time of the night." He was released with an admonition. Later he moved to Kingston, and apparently settled into respectability.[12]

Rachel Eaton was a sad case, married young to Joseph Ramsden, a drunk. They lived in Plymouth, and at one point Rachel was accused of going in the company of young men. But in a May 1652, court record the truth appeared, "wheras Joseph Ramsden hath for som time liued with is family remotely in the woods from naighbors, wherby his wife hath been exposed to great hardship and perill of loosing her life, and other inconveniences haue followed therupon, the Court haue ordered, that said Joseph Ramsden bee warned by the cunstable of Plymouth to bring his wife and family, with all convenient speed near unto so naighborhood, that soe shee may bee in a way of healp, as nessesitie shall require, as he will answare the neglect thereof at his perill."[13] Four years later, the court again ordered Ramsden to move his family into town, but a short time later Rachel Eaton Ramsden died. There was no inquest or suspicion in the court records, but one can not help wondering if her circumstances contributed to her death. The Eaton family tragedies embody many of the contradictions of the early, harsh life in Duxbury. Ownership of land was a way to better yourself, even if it brought you into conflict with your neighbors, and the godly life often clashed with human nature and desires.

William Pabodie

William Pabodie was one of the second generation of Duxbury settlers. His father, John Pabodie, had a homestead farm on the Bluefish River. William grew up there, married the neighbor's daughter, Elizabeth Alden, oldest daughter of John and Priscilla. William was a surveyor, an essential man in the growing colony. He laid out and surveyed much of the land of the colony, particularly new inland tracts such as Bridgewater. This job must have meant many days and nights away from home, but he found time to be a farmer, boatman, and served Duxbury as town clerk and deputy to the Colony court.

Since Pabodie was successful early in life, he was able to purchase the substantial Jonathan Brewster Nook farm in 1650. He paid seventy pounds to the Dorchester merchants who had foreclosed on the farm two years earlier. The Pabodie-Brewster farm had ninety acres of good land that ran along the west side of Eagles Nest Creek. Included in the sale was a good-sized dwelling house and "outhouses, Barnes, stables, orchyards, gardens, meddowland and pastures." The Pabodies had five children by 1650 (the family would grow to a dozen), so this farm was essential for their support. All but two were girls, who married prominent Duxbury boys and settled nearby. John Pabodie, the oldest son, died tragically in 1669 when he was twenty-four. An inquest found "that he ryding on the road, his horse carryed him underneath the bow of a young tree, and violently forceing his head into the body therof brake his skull."[14]

In 1657, William Pabodie purchased half of Eagles Nest Point, across the creek from his farm. Twenty years later, he got into a dispute over this land with his neighbors, the Love Brewster family. Neighborliness in the Nook must have been at an all-time low in 1679 when Pabodie brought suit against Sarah Brewster, charging her with trespassing. It was a forty-pound charge that claimed she "did pull up and deface the bound markes of the said Paybodyes land, and make claim to said land."[15] Sarah apparently thought she had a strong case, if she pulled up boundary markers on a surveyor's own land. The case was settled out of court and later that year Pabodie sold his share of Eagles Nest Point to Sarah's son, Deacon William Brewster.

William Pabodie took no chances with another neighbor in 1683. Alexander Standish, son of Myles Standish, had a salt meadow he could not reach except by crossing some of Pabodie's land. Pabodie gave him a right-of-way to this land in an elaborate deed, "provided still, that the said Alexander, his heirs and assigns, shall carefully at all such times shut such gates, and put up such bars as they shall have occasion to open, or make use of in carting or passing to or from such meddow so the said Paybody nor any that succeed him be not damnified there-by."[16] A case for good fences making for good neighbors.

William Pabodie left Duxbury in 1684 for Little Compton, Rhode Island, then on the far western frontier of Plymouth Colony. Pabodie was sixty-four. One wonders what provoked him to move that far; perhaps he had surveyed that area and realized that the farmland was superior. He died in Little Compton in 1707. Many of his daughters stayed in Duxbury on land given to them by their father. Samuel Bartlett, who married Hannah Pabodie, took over the Pabodie-Brewster farm and began a new era in town by building boats on the banks of Eagles Nest Creek.

ANTHONY KELSO

Seventeenth Century Houses

*D*uxbury houses of the seventeenth century were simply built by carpenters to provide the necessary shelter with a minimum of sawed lumber. Sawn boards were hard to come by, saw mills were few and far between, and not one was in Duxbury, so every piece of worked timber was valued. No seventeenth-century house survives today in Duxbury exactly as it was built, but some exist still as sections of later houses.

These remaining parts, as well as a few excavations, show that the first houses were long and narrow, very narrow, with a chimney between two ground level rooms, with a loft overhead. The size of the first Alden house in Duxbury, as determined by excavation, as well as by its preservation as part of a later house, was 38 by 10½ feet. The dimensions of other seventeenth-century houses in Duxbury vary, but the differences are slight.

The central fireplace in these early houses provided heat and a place for cooking. Sometimes a second, smaller fireplace was built behind the main fireplace in order to provide heat for the second room. The ladder to the loft stood beside the chimney, or flat against a wall. Traces of such a ladder are evident in the Thomas Delano house (1667), on High Street.

The Hunt house (1641), is the earliest dated house in Duxbury, but it has had at least two additions since then. The additions have not spoiled the aged look of this Cape cottage with its long, pitched roof. It has survived through the years with little modernizing, simply because it was long used for grain storage. When Alpheus H. Walker bought the farm in 1906, there was a new, more modern house nearer the curve along Tremont Street, and there was no one living in the old house. It had become a storage place, stripped to the bare interior, but so well built that it withstood years of neglect, waiting to be restored to a dwelling house. In 1962, the house and an acre of land about it was set off from the old farm and sold to Robert H. Hose who restored it, preserving its seventeenth-century architecture while making it a home once more.

The Hunt house originally stood back from one of Duxbury's first *highways*, the Green's Harbor Path, which followed a route west of Tremont Street, connecting Plymouth with Marshfield. In September 1641, Edmond Hawes exchanged ten acres of land for "two thousand feet of sawne boards" and built a house. He had hardly finished it when he sold it to Edmond Hunt in 1642. It was passed down in the Hunt family, father to son, for the next 228 years until Barker Hunt's widow sold it out of the family in 1870. So, since the Hunts owned the house for so long, and Edmond Hawes for such a short time, it has been called the Hunt House.

The second John Alden house in Duxbury was built in 1653 along another early highway, the Duxburrow Path. Familiar the country over, it was one of the first Pilgrim houses in Duxbury to have a full second story, reflecting architectural planning, and was carefully placed on an attractive knoll facing south to make the most of the sunlight.

The exterior walls of this braced frame house were formed by horizontal planks, covered originally with shakes, now by shingles. The gunstock corner posts rise the full two stories, and there are visible corner braces. It is plain but sturdy construction, similar to English frame houses of the period.

To the right of the front door is the Great Room. Across the ceiling there is a half-exposed 12 by 12-foot summer beam which supports the second-story floor joists. The clamshell plaster in this room is original. Lacking lime for making plaster, the colonists ground up clam and oyster shells. Because there were so few horses

The Great Room of the Alden House, to the right of the front entrance, with its summer beam across the ceiling. (*Norman Forgit*)

in the colony, the carpenters would use animal hair, rather than horsehair, to bind the plaster.

The central, T-shaped chimney in the Alden house has two sections. One serves the kitchen, the other, three other fireplaces. The oven is at the back of the fireplace, as it is in the Delano house. Later, ovens would be located beside the fireplaces.

John Alden was too thrifty to abandon a well-built house, so brought his first house, the long, narrow one, west across the fields to form the rear part of his new house. He seems to have set an example thereby that was followed even into the nineteenth century. The ell on the north of the house is another old, narrow house, perhaps also seventeenth-century, which was moved from an unknown location when the Aldens needed a summer kitchen.

The John Alden House has never been out of the Alden family. It is presently owned by the Alden Kindred of America, assuring its preservation.

North of the Alden house, along the Green's Harbor Path in the area still known as Millbrook, there are probably several seventeenth-century houses near the first mill site, but only one, *Cranberry Cottage*, has been documented. It was owned by Constant Southworth, for many years the treasurer of Plymouth Colony, and commissary general at the beginning of King Philip's War. He had bought a grist mill at Millbrook from William Hiller (Hillier) in 1646 and settled nearby. It is thought that the original Cranberry Cottage burned in 1665 and was rebuilt, so the present house bears that date. The back ell is the oldest section of the small house. Other houses in the area, the *Crab Island* house,

Duxbury's oldest dateboarded house, the Hunt house (1641) was built with sawn lumber exchanged for ten acres of land, by Edmond Hawes who sold it to Edmond Hunt. *(Norman Forgit)*

also owned by Constant Southworth, and the Ford Store Boardinghouse, will probably prove to be seventeenth century as well.

Two more seventeenth-century houses in Duxbury are the Alexander Standish house on the Standish Shore and the Dr. Thomas Delano cottage on High Street. Alexander Standish, oldest son of Captain Myles Standish, built a gambrel-roofed cottage in 1666, on the western end of the Standish farm. It is a snug house, close to the ground, built around a central chimney to counter the winter cold. Dr. Thomas Delano, son of settler Philip Delano, went far from his father's farm near the Aldens when he built along the old Bay Path in 1667. His house is very much like the Standish cottage in appearance, except that it has a pitched roof and white paint, added by later generations. Since Sarah Alden Standish and Rebecca Alden Delano were sisters, one suspects there was common planning in the two houses.

In 1696, Isaac Simmons built his house in the Crooked Lane section of North Duxbury, far inland, a long way from the shore. He built in the Cape cottage style, small and sturdy, along what is now Temple Street. The house, together with its original thirty-five acres, remained in the Simmons family until 1934. The last Simmons to live there, Levi Simmons, was a blacksmith, whose shop was across the street. The house has been restored to its original condition, one of the very few seventeenth-century houses in such good state.

Top: The Delano Cottage, built by Dr. Thomas Delano for his bride, Rebecca Alden, in 1666, restored in 1933. *Bottom:* Isaac Simmons and his descendants lived and farmed on their land in the Crooked Lane section from 1696 to 1934. *(Norman Forgit)*

There are early houses, many seventeenth-century, so built into or added onto later that they have lost their identity. Some can be guessed at, if not actually proven.

When Captain Gamaliel Bradford built his impressive house on Tremont Street in 1807, he used his father's old house for the kitchen ell. It was the usual long, narrow house, chimney between two rooms, and with a second story, perhaps added by Colonel Bradford. When the Colonel bought the farm in 1762, there was a house on it, one that is mentioned in two earlier deeds, putting it back perhaps to the seventeenth century. It is likely that this house now forms the ell on the Captain Gamaliel Bradford house.

John Weston, Jr. built a Cape cottage in 1821 on part of his father's farm and he moved a seventeenth-century house, long unused, to become the kitchen ell. He pushed that old house so far into the new one, nearly to the ridge pole center, that one room of the old house is lost in the new. This John Weston, Jr. house is at the end of a lane, off Surplus Street.

In 1829, Rebecca Frazar built a house near the Bluefish River mill pond, where she proposed to keep a school for girls. The main house was all new, but onto it, at the back, she moved an old house for the kitchen ell. It is a seventeenth century house that may date from the time of Abraham Samson, who inherited the Lieutenant Nash land. It has been altered to provide rooms for boarding students, but the size, shape, and construction point to its age.

Most of the seventeenth-century houses in Duxbury bear the dateboard of the Duxbury Rural and Historical Society. They are fully documented and described under that project. Others remain which still need to be identified. This 350th Anniversary Year is a good time to give some thought to the earliest houses in Duxbury.

DOROTHY WENTWORTH

The *Crab Island* house in Millbrook was once a Southworth house, connected to the mill operations.

Clark's Island

Clark's Island actually does not belong to Duxbury, but spiritually those eighty acres in the middle of the bay have become part and parcel of the lives of all of us who look out on it every day, especially if we remember that there, on those still wild shores, the Pilgrims landed, even before they found and settled Plimoth Plantation.

Leaving the *Mayflower* lying at anchor in Provincetown, the shallop sailed early in December of 1620 to explore the north shore of Cape Cod in search of a suitable site for the colonists to settle in this bleak and forbidding New World. Approaching Plymouth Bay on December 8, the little vessel, loaded with ten Pilgrims and eight crew members, encountered an easterly gale which dismasted their boat and smashed the rudder. Rowing in past Gurnet Point, they managed to round up under the lee of Clark's Island in the gathering dusk and increasing cold. Fearful of Indians who might be lurking under the tall trees, they hesitated until John Clark, mate of the *Mayflower* and in charge of the expedition, leaped into the shallow water, preferring to brave the savages rather than freeze to death.

On the Sabbath, although they had not finished repairs to the shallop, they did no work, but instead marched to the top of the island, and at Election Rock, held a service of thanksgiving, their first ashore in the New World. In the shallop on Monday, they found a safe harbor across the bay, fresh water (the present Town Brook), a defensible hill nearby, and fields cleared for planting; and there were no Indians. They headed back to bring the *Mayflower* to this suitable site.

In the 1630s, Clark's Island had a stand of virgin timber which in the early years of the colony was cut and sold to the Puritans arriving in Boston, with the proceeds allotted to the support of the minister at Plymouth. In 1642, a salt works was established near the beach, a venture for which they imported a salt master from England, who proved not worth his salt, and had to be sent home. When King Philip's War broke out in 1675, the English rounded up the Indians who had converted to Christianity, several hundred of them, and settled them on the island for safekeeping, since no one knew for sure whether Christian Indians would be massacred by their savage brothers, or whether Christian Indians might revert to a savage state and massacre the whites. Clark's Island has never been so crowded, before or since.

For a decade after 1680, the island harbored a Pest House, a quarantine station against smallpox and other diseases brought in by ships. Those incarcerated there were served by "Mother White," who sailed her lugger single-handed for supplies, thrown downwind from the supply boat to hers in the Plymouth Channel at a location from that time known as *Mother White's Guzzle.*

The General Court had deeded Clark's Island to Plymouth in 1638, but Governor Andros, the King's representative, refused to recognize the local authority and in 1687 gave the island to a henchman. Plymouth sued for its return, sent representatives first to Boston, then to London to plead their case, and won only when King James (and Andros with him) was banished. But the litigation had proved so expensive that Plymouth in 1690 sold the island to Elkanah Watson and some friends for £120.

From that day almost to the present, the Watsons have owned Clark's Island, a remarkable family indeed, farmers perforce, but many with Harvard educations, important men on the mainland as well as on their island, where they raised vegetables, especially Clark's Island turnips, reputedly featured at the leading hotels in Boston.

The Watsons knew well the Transcendentalist Group of the mid-nineteenth century, including Emerson. Thoreau walked down to Duxbury on one occasion, planning to visit "Uncle Ed" Watson. The tide was out; so Thoreau started walking across the mud flats toward the island. The incoming tide caught him part way across, almost mired and far from shore, in danger of his life had not a local lobsterman named Sam Burgess pulled him aboard his boat and sailed him the rest of the way to Clark's. There Uncle Ed, the "Lord of the Isle," after berating him soundly for a damned fool, welcomed him with a famous Clark's Island feast of lobsters, clams, fresh asparagus, and, of course, turnips! After a full night of storytelling, the two visited Uncle Bill Watson, the recluse of the family, aboard his grounded schooner across the cove near High Pines.

Around the turn of the century, the island was famous for its gunning stands which set out up to 200 goose decoys in the water, plus 75 or more tethered live honkers on the beach to lure the huge migrating flocks within range. The 1911 record was 328 geese in one day.

With crops no longer practical in the island's sandy soil, much of the north end has been abandoned to second growth scrub. This provides protection for one of the great heronries of the East Coast, which includes snowy and greater egrets, black-crowned night herons, and glossy ibis, adjoining a colony of thousands upon

Election Rock on Clark's Island where the Pilgrims celebrated the first sabbath in New England, an event commemorated each summer by the Clark's Island Picnic.

thousands of gulls. Both are studied systematically by the Manomet Bird Observatory.

Twenty acres of the island, including *Cedarfield*, second oldest house, and Election Rock itself, is now owned in trust by the Duxbury Rural and Historical Society, an inheritance from Sarah Wingate Taylor of the Watson family, a dedicated teacher and historian who each summer until her death in 1965 conducted the Pilgrim Rock School of American Studies at the island. Her traditions are being maintained by the Society with an annual series of lectures in Duxbury on historical subjects, and with a picnic and a commemorative service each summer at Clark's Island.

JACK POST

Notes on the Name Duxbury

Despite the vagaries of seventeenth and eighteenth century spelling, Duxburrough or Duxborough appeared with remarkable consistency as the name of the town in the official Town Records until 1779.[1] Then, Duxbury became the spelling of choice for thirty-four years until 1813, when Duxboro was adopted by the town clerks. Finally, eleven years later, in 1824, Duxbury was introduced again, and so it has remained ever since.

There appears to be no clue in any surviving early town records or in those of Plymouth Colony to indicate who named the town or why the name was chosen.

When the town was incorporated in 1637, its name was given as "Ducksborrow," leading some to suppose that the wildlife that come to the bay each fall may have been celebrated in the naming of the town. Duxborrow, however, became the spelling used most frequently in the Plymouth Colony Records.

In 1793, an article in the *Massachusetts Historical Society Collections* proposed that the town was named Duxborrow in honor of Captain Myles Standish, arguing that *dux* meant leader and *borrow,* town. It was, therefore, the leader's town.[2] James Thacher, in his *History of Plymouth*, 1835, took issue with this theory. "The compliment would have been merited," he wrote, "but it is doubtful whether, among such a people, it would have been proposed or admitted."[3] Dr. Thacher, however, did not hazard a guess about the name.

Justin Winsor, in his *History of Duxbury* (1849), was convinced that "the town was named Duxbury out of respect to Captain Standish, from Duxbury Hall, the seat of the Standish family in England."[4] Winsor's theory was accepted by many townspeople and nineteenth-century writers as well, but it must be challenged in light of evidence available today.

When Myles Standish was born in 1584, there were several Standish families in Lancashire. The most illustrious of these were descended from a common ancestor but had been identified as distinct families since the late thirteenth century. Myles Standish himself claimed descent from the Standishes who held the manor house, *Standish Hall*, in the Township of Standish in Lancashire. He did not claim descent from the second famous family who held the manor called *The Peel* in Myles Standish's day, and later called *Duxbury Hall*, located in the township of Duxbury in Lancashire.

In 1846, the American descendents of Myles Standish tried unsuccessfully to establish a claim to the estates of the latter family. They were hoping that the Duxbury Standishes of Lancashire held the clue to the lands which Myles Standish had left to his son Alexander. They were looking in the wrong place. In 1914, Reverend Thomas C. Porteus found the documents that proved that the long-lost lands actually belonged to the Standishes of Ormskirk and Man (of which Myles was a member), a junior branch of the Standishes of Standish.[5]

In view of the conflicting theories and contradictory evidence, it is possible to draw only one conclusion—after 350 years, no one knows for certain just why this town is called Duxbury.

Frances D. Leach

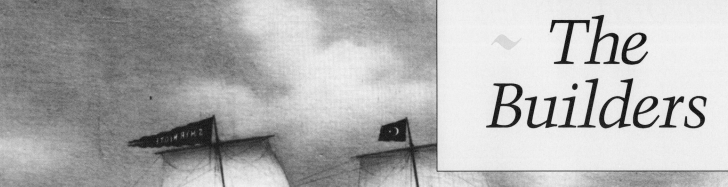

The Builders

Sea and Shore

From the very first, Duxbury's location by the sea gave focus and shape to the lives of her settlers. The original land grants here were for farmland, but each farm was laid out with either direct or indirect access to the shore. As farmers, the first settlers valued property along the coast chiefly for the salt hay which grew so freely and abundantly on the marshlands between sea and shore. Since natural meadowland was relatively scarce, they depended on the salt hay for feeding livestock.

From the first, the settlers also valued their coastal location because they depended on fishing for their own sustenance and for a commodity to trade. They also soon discovered that it was often easier to travel by water than by land.

Recognizing the need for locally-built boats, Plymouth Colony brought a boat builder over from England in 1624. He had two "catches" under construction and had completed one shallop when he took sick and died,[1] but others started to build small boats for their own use. The earliest craft were usually shallops, open-decked, double-ended boats which could either be rowed or sailed; or ketches, larger, two-masted boats with round sterns and flat decks. Both were slow and unwieldy by our standards, but sturdy and practical for fishing and sailing along the coast.

The first significant impetus to local shipbuilding came with the implementation of the English Navigation Act of 1651, which stipulated that trade between the colonies had to be conducted in either colonial or English vessels. With the protection offered by this act, colonial shipbuilding became profitable.

New England shipbuilders were able to build vessels for two-thirds the cost of those built back in England. There lumber was scarce, but here were

48

woodlands close to the shore. All along the southern coast of New England shipyards were established along tidal rivers, where there were protected spots close enough to open water to make launchings convenient.

The first shipyard on the North River dates back to the middle seventeenth century. We have no proof as yet of a Duxbury yard that early, but evidence points toward the existence of a yard here before the eighteenth century.

Samuel Bartlett had an early yard by Eagles Nest Creek, which he subsequently sold to Thomas Prence. Another indication of early shipbuilding in Duxbury comes from the diary Boston lawyer Thomas Lechford kept between 1638 and 1641. The entry refers to "John Moses of Duxbury shipwright ply (plaintiff)."

> The said John Moses Complayneth against the said defendants for yt wheras in or about the third moneth Anno Dni 1640 they did reteyne the said Complaynant to make for them a pinnace in forme as followeth that is to say thirty two foote by the keele and five foote and halfe in the hould deepe to be made proportionable according to the same with a decke and to be seeled throughout . . . [2]

Brig *Herald*, 162 tons, built in Duxbury in 1822. Owned by Ezra Weston and Martin Waterman, Master.

Ship registers held by Massachusetts State Archives list early Duxbury vessels as well. The earliest listing is for a 1703 sloop, the *Content*, "A Square-Stern'd vessel of the burthen of about Thirty Five Tuns was built at Duxbury in the Province aforsd in the present year 1703." Two more Duxbury-built vessels appear in the register for 1704, the sloop *Elizabeth*, "being a Square Stern'd vessel of Thirty Five Tuns and the brig *William*, being a Square Stern'd vessel of Fifty Tuns built at Duxbury."[3] Certainly Duxbury shipbuilders would have had several years' prior experience to have been capable of constructing these vessels by the beginning of the eighteenth century.

By the early eighteenth century, fishing, and even whaling, had become major enterprises in Duxbury. Ship's carpenters began to build schooners, a new design originating in Gloucester. Sleek, good-looking, and practical, the schooners, averaging fifty tons, carried more sail, were faster, and could venture out further and stay longer than the older ketches and smaller sloops. The schooners and sloops would become the workhorses of the Duxbury fleet for the next 150 years, carrying, as the years progressed, not only fish, but lumber and coal, passengers and mail, textiles and dry goods, all along the eastern seaboard.

A Frigate Off Duxbury

In 1782, His Majesty's Frigate *Albermarle* fired a shot across the bow of a lugger out of Duxbury running for Boston off Gurnet Head. Even though the war with Britain was over, the Treaty of Paris was not signed until 1783, so the *Albermarle* could not be faulted or indeed controlled.

The local seamen, hailed aboard the frigate, thought they were about to be impressed into the British Navy, a common practice which might mean they would never see home again. Strangely, they were brought before the commanding officer and offered a choice. If some would return to shore and bring back a supply of fresh vegetables and fruits, they would all be set free with their sloop; otherwise, the men left aboard the frigate would indeed be impressed.

What the captain did not reveal was that scurvy had broken out on the *Albermarle*, for which the known cure was vegetables and fruits. These the captain was determined to obtain, for even at the young age of twenty-three, he ran a tight ship which included good care of his men.

In due time, the New Englanders brought back the supplies, and true to his word, the captain not only freed the men and their vessel, but, as they were leaving, the leftenant at the gangway said to them: "Captain Horatio Nelson of His Majesty's frigate *Albermarle* presents his compliments and offers this purse in payment for the supplies provided for his ship."

As the men watched the *Albermarle* fill her sails and gather way, one stated, and all agreed: "That Captain Nelson is a good man! He will go far in the Royal Navy."

Jack Post

As maritime commerce grew, the character of the town changed. The earliest shipyards, owned by Israel Sylvester, Benjamin Freeman, Isiah Bradford, Samuel Winsor, and Isaac Drew, were located along the bay from Captain's Hill to the Bluefish River. New houses were being built on smaller lots near these yards, so the town stretched out in a long, narrow ribbon close to the shore, in contrast to the arrangement of inland villages where houses were clustered around a village green. Duxbury's early streets also followed the paths and cart-ways which led inland from the shore.

Some owners of fishing vessels, like Elijah Sampson and Nathaniel Winsor, suffered losses during the Revolution when the British captured their vessels, but other Duxbury men participated in privateering, a dangerous, but potentially profitable venture. Both captains and crews shared in the division of prizes. Among the young men from Duxbury who served on board privateers were sixteen-year-old Amasa Delano, Ira Bradford, and Timothy and Warren Weston, brothers of Ezra Weston.

For everyone connected with the sea, the greatest advantage from privateering would come from the substantial improvements which local ship's carpenters were making in their designs. American ships were becoming faster and more responsive; American sea captains and seamen were developing experience and expertise. Duxbury was building a reservoir of talent which would serve the town well in the future.

In the years immediately following the Revolution, most of the country suffered a severe depression, but Duxbury's fleet was growing. Tax records for 1781 list the total tonnage of vessels here at 119, but just three years later, it was 533.[4] By that time fishing vessels were already benefiting from the fishing grounds at the Grand Banks, which had been awarded to the Americans by the terms of the Treaty of Paris. Fishing was a profitable enterprise. New markets were opening up abroad, and the first Congress had granted a bounty on dried fish for export.

As the British had done before, the new American government encouraged the shipbuilding industry. In 1790, Congress passed a law allowing American vessels to pay duties only once a year; foreign vessels had to pay each time they entered an American port. Duxbury merchants began to send their ships towards the major trading ports in North and South America, the West Indies, Europe, and the Far East. Duxbury sea captains expected to be away a year or two, as they unloaded and reloaded cargoes in several foreign ports before returning.

Foreign trade offered the merchants and sea captains possibilities for substantial gain. Long gone were the Pilgrim days when men were fined for making too much profit. The merchants were making small fortunes; the sea captains, and even the villagers of Duxbury, shared in the good times as they took out *ventures*, or shares, in the voyages.

With the new prosperity, the town changed. There was a greater division between the wealthy and the poor, and classes became stratified. Merchants and master mariners were a class above the captains of smaller vessels, while sailors and their families were relegated to the bottom of the social ladder. The First Parish Church became the fashionable place to worship, with most of the master mariners and merchants owning pews there.

On December 22, 1807, the good times ended abruptly. That day, President Jefferson signed the Embargo Act, prohibiting American vessels from leaving American ports. Duxbury citizens were enraged. Trade was curtailed, shipyards closed and there was no work. When the embargo continued into late summer, town meeting sent a petition to the President:

The inhabitants of the town of Duxbury in the Commonwealth of Massachusetts in legal Town-meeting Assembled, beg leave respectfully to represent That your Petitioners have hitherto depended on Commerce, Navigation and the Fisheries and the numerous arts subservient thereto for a subsistence; that the soil of this Township is sterile, and insufficient for the production of necessaries competent for the support of the people who inhabit it—and that if they be much longer prohibited from following their customary avocations on the Ocean, a large proportion of them must migrate or starve . . .
. . . their fish yet remains unsold, and for eighteen months past they have had no visible means to pay their debts or procure sustenance for themselves and their household.

There is in this place a large quantity of fish, which owners diligently labour among, anxiously watch over and by unwearied exertion endeavour to preserve . . .[5]

A page of the freight lists for the *Hope* from the *Record of 24 Ships of Ezra Weston.*

From 1764–1773, Joseph F. W. DesBarres worked with the British Royal Navy survey of the North American coast. The charts were published in the marine atlas, *Atlantic Neptune*, starting in 1774. They were so precise that they were copied in American atlases for the next 50 years. *(Boston Athenaeum Library)*

President Jefferson replied to the town on September 20, 1808. He was unable to grant their petition because, "To have submitted our rightfull commerce to prohibitions and tributary exactions from others, would have been to surrender our independence."[6]

Not entirely hindered by the embargo, many Duxbury merchants and sea captains decided to have new houses built. They used profits from the good years to build in the latest Federal style, and local carpenters were glad for the work. Many of Duxbury's finest houses, including two Bradford houses, the King Caesar house, and the Nathaniel Winsor, Jr. house, were built between 1807 and 1809, the embargo years.

After the embargo was finally lifted in 1809, Duxbury's shipbuilding industry revived for a short time, but had to shut down again during the War of 1812. That war probably affected Duxbury more closely than any other. From the beach, the townspeople could see the British ships which were blockading the coast. They feared a British raid on their town, so organized a local volunteer militia, the *Sea Fencibles*, placed guns along the shore, and built a small fort at the foot of Fort Hill Lane. Luckily, the threatened raids never materialized.

Once the War of 1812 was over, Duxbury merchants were eager to resume trading. The business climate was very favorable. New shipyards were established and men came into town to work. In the ten years between 1810 and 1820, the population increased by almost fifty percent and Duxbury village took on some aspects of a boom town. Certain neighborhoods, like "Sodom" at the corner of Washington Street and what is now Surplus Street, were off limits to carefully brought-up young ladies.

The merchants pressured the shipbuilders to construct vessels which would combine optimum speed with optimum cargo space, because a fast ship with ample cargo space was a profitable one. Duxbury's experienced master carpenters, like Samuel Hall and Samuel Cushman, continually improved their designs, but no one knew for sure how fast a ship would sail until she took her trial run. How a ship performed in her trials was a topic of immense local interest.

Weston family records show that citrus fruits, fresh and dried, were valuable cargoes. Fast ships brought fruit back from Mediterranean ports. It sold well in Boston, for New Englanders relished the scarce commodity. Dried fruits also were a staple provision on board seagoing vessels.

Cotton provided another profitable cargo. For the cotton trade, Duxbury ship owners especially commissioned large, heavily built ships. In 1830, Samuel Hall built the 480-ton *Mattakeeset* for Ezra Weston, Jr. It was the largest ship in New England at the time. Then in 1841, another Weston ship, the *Hope*, was launched. At 880 tons, it surpassed the *Mattakeeset*, replacing it as the largest ship in New England. Built by master carpenter Samuel Cushing at the Weston yard along the Bluefish River, the *Hope* was a three-masted ship, 159 feet long, with two decks.

But, as the ships grew larger and larger, the waters of the bay were less and less accommodating. Like dinosaurs, the *Hope* and the *Mattakeeset* were too large for their environment. They had to be towed out to the deeper waters of the "Cow Yard" off Bug Light to be rigged. Once ready, they would sail off for Boston, never returning to Duxbury. After the War of 1812 the larger, deeper-water ports like Boston grew while smaller ports like Duxbury diminished in importance.

Duxbury's master mariners and sea captains shared in the town's prosperity. Like the ships they commanded, they earned reputations for being experienced and dependable masters. With familiar names like Delano and Drew, Bradford and Loring, Soule, Winsor, Freeman and Waterman, Duxbury sea captains carried the American flag to ports all over the globe.

The good times in Duxbury lasted for about twenty years after the War of 1812. By the 1840s, the decline was noticeable. There had been a financial panic in 1837, there were no longer bounties for fish, and timber supplies were badly depleted. Newly completed railroads and new clipper ships and steamboats all competed with the older merchant fleet for business. Some workers left Duxbury for employment in inland factories; others left for the Boston shipyards. Master carpenter Samuel Hall moved to East Boston where he became a well-known builder of clipper ships. Most of the early shipyards had closed by 1840. Other yards went bankrupt, were bought and sold, and resold.

Duxbury citizens bemoaned the loss of the good old days, but clung fast to their maritime traditions. Duxbury sea captains continued to command sailing ships, but now for out-of-town owners. Duxbury shipyards continued to turn out sloops and schooners as they always had, and fishing vessels continued to head for the Grand Banks as usual, but everyone had to work harder for lower returns. Harboring their resources, "making do" as best they could, no longer buoyed by the spirit and optimism of the earlier, more prosperous time, the townspeople settled down to quiet, simple lives, remembering the past.

KATHERINE H. PILLSBURY

Seaborn Wadsworth

In 1853, the ship *Seth Sprague* bound for India lay becalmed for six weeks in the Bay of Bengal. Captain Alexander Wadsworth had his wife, companion of many voyages, aboard. She was in the last stages of pregnancy and was hoping for a swift passage to medical care at Calcutta. The fates were against her, and she died ten days after giving birth to a second son.

The captain, determined to bring his wife home for burial, ordered a special casket built, caulked, and filled with French brandy taken from his cargo. Perhaps despite the heat he could thus return her body to Duxbury.

The infant, named Seaborn, was a different problem, for without a mother, the child lacked all natural nutrients. Fortunately an able seaman named Fuller was ingenious enough to pulverize and soak hardtack, the rock-like ship's biscuit, and feed it to the infant, a diet that kept the child alive until the ship reached port and a wet nurse could be obtained. For the trip home, milk goats were tethered on the foredeck.

In the Indian Ocean a gale washed the goats overboard and prostrated the wet nurse, so again, Fuller fed soaked hardtack to the infant as the ship fought her way homeward in weather so bad that the superstitious crew wished to jettison the casket containing the mother's body, an idea the captain sternly overrode. The ship struggled on, through yet another gale which persisted into Duxbury Bay. Even then, the captain's distress persisted, for the casket was too large for the door of his house, and had to remain outside in the rain. Not until the weather cleared the next day could he lay his wife to rest in Mayflower Cemetery.

At first, baby Seaborn did not take to his new-found female relatives, for he had grown accustomed to the care of his seaman nurse, but soon he grew reconciled to his aunt's loving kindness, growing up to become a captain in the U.S. Revenue Service, and living to the ripe old age of eighty.

Jack Post

Seaborn Wadsworth, left, with (left to right) George Freeman, Wallace Wadsworth, and Tom Herrick on the porch of the Winsor and Peterson Store, 318 Washington Street.

The Bradfords

After 1783, when the voyage of the *Empress of China*, the first ship to carry the American flag to China, showed the potential of the Oriental trade, Duxbury sea captains traded along the coasts of both the Atlantic and Pacific Oceans, gaining great experience in seamanship, but more important, broadening their outlook. Their exploits were invaluable in proving that the new United States of America was able to hold her own in the world and should be treated with respect.

In 1799, the *Mary*, under the command of Gamaliel Bradford with his younger brother Gershom as mate, sailed out of Boston. The U.S. Minister to Madrid later reported:

> Captain Gamaliel Bradford commanding the ship *Mary* of Boston . . . has acquired much reputation by repulsing two (actually, there were three) privateers of superior force and entered Malaga a few days ago with a valuable cargo of fresh fish and sugar. He had not a single man killed or wounded. The French privateers soon followed him into the same port, having had two killed and thirteen wounded, some of them mortally.[1]

After returning to Boston, Gamaliel and Gershom shifted to another Letter of Marque, the *Industry*, and sailed again for the Mediterranean. Encountering privateers off Corsica, they tried to run for Lisbon rather than Gibraltar to avoid Spanish gunboats and more privateers. Unfortunately, they ran into trouble with a French privateer with eighteen-pound guns in the bow. Hoping to cripple and then board the *Industry*, rather than sink her, the French shot quantities of grapeshot through the sails and rigging. Three more privateers came to the

Urn by Paul Revere commemorating Captain Gamaliel Bradford's gallant defense when attacked by French privateers in 1800. *(Museum of Fine Arts, Boston)*

aid of the French and then moved into range of the *Industry*'s guns. During the course of the ensuing fight, Gamaliel was shot through the knee and had to be carried below, leaving his younger brother in command, with instructions to the crew to "Remain calm, keep up a steady fire and do not allow them to board."[2] The battle had been in progress for three hours and Gershom continued to fight for another two and a half. The French abandoned the attack and the *Industry* limped into port. Fortunately for Gamaliel, they met a British ship-of-the-line which had a surgeon on board, who cared for him until they reached a shore hospital where his leg was amputated. Young Gershom brought the *Industry* safely home by way of Dublin. In memory of these two encounters a powerful World War II destroyer, DD545, was christened *Bradford*. She earned twelve battle stars and a Naval Unit Commendation for service in the Asiatic–Pacific area.

On their long sea voyages, five or six months or longer away from home, captains dreamed of the families they left behind and planned for their future. Among the many letters in the Bradford's Old Homestead is a tender one from Cadiz in 1804 from Captain Gershom to his expectant wife, Sarah:

> When I left you at Dorchester that stormy morning, I had a rather rough time in the boat before I reached the brig, but just at the time when I got on board, the wind came fair and I got underway directly. Six days later I supplied a New York ship with provisions and as she was bound in, I expect you saw by the papers that the *Lydia Head* was safe so far. Seventeen days after, I supplied a Portuguese ship with some bread and fish and he very politely in return sent me some fowls which were very acceptable. What do you think I did with the wishbones, all alone by myself (don't laugh) for I must tell you. The first one, I wished for your safety in your expected trouble. I had the satisfaction to get my wish, which put me in a very good humor . . . the second bone, my right hand, for a son and left hand for a daughter, I will not tell you any more, for I know you will laugh at me but I may as well write as think and dream.[3]

The child arrived safely . . . the first of four daughters.

In 1805, the Bradfords' father, Colonel Gamaliel, died, leaving ninety acres on both sides of Tremont Street to his three sea captain sons, Gamaliel, Daniel, and Gershom. Forty acres on the west side went to Gamaliel, who built the splendid yellow house there; ten acres went to Gershom on the east side; and forty to Daniel, who built off what is now Harrison Street. No doubt the houses were planned at sea during long voyages. Gamaliel wrote to his wife, Elizabeth Hickling Bradford:

> I consider you my agent to oversee the finishing of our home and shall promise myself great improvement in it from your taste and discretion. We men, you know, always usurp the province of deep knowledge and judgement . . . I therefore take all the credit for planning, forming the outline and solid parts; but 'tis the peculiar talent of women to polish. You will therefore give the finishing hand to our future dwelling in order that it may please as well as be useful and convenient.[4]

Gershom wrote in the log book of the *Mercury*, "Last night was at work about our intended house at Duxbury."[5] After the house had been given to the Duxbury Rural and Historical Society, Mrs. George Fogg discovered his specifications for the house on a paper backing for a picture. It was to be 40 by 60 feet, with the front and rear doors opposite each other, the front door to be in the center of the house facade. There was to be a wide hallway and stairway. It took some figuring to plan the two outside doors opposite each other, with a

Captain Gershom Bradford bought the French clock in the parlor in Bayonne, France in 1805. *(Norman Forgit)*

wide hallway between. The plan worked out beautifully by having the parlor wall a little closer to the front door than that of the library. As you enter the house, you can, if the rear door is open, look right out to the expansive back yard.

Four generations of Bradfords were devoted to this house and to the items various members brought back to it. There is a French clock, bought in 1805, and carefully kept with its bill of sale: "I, the below-signed, declares to have sold to Mr. Bradford, an American captain, a swinging pendulum clock in gilded copper, with a globe of glass in a single piece. I guarantee the accuracy to the above purchaser for one year. For this clock he paid me the sum of two hundred thirty-seven francs. Bayonne, May 19, 1805 T.H. de Troyat."[6] The clock was still running accurately when the historical society accepted the house, 163 years later.

Some items, such as the wing chair in the north bedroom, reflect the practical ingenuity of the family. Four ungainly wheels were added to its traditional legs so one of Captain Gershom's daughters could get about after she became somewhat crippled. The first wheel chair, perhaps! There is a set of china from Canton, blocks of lava cut from Mt. Etna to serve as flagstones, and two South Sea shells which stood by the front door. In the house are pieces of coral and more shells brought home by Gershom II after a voyage with Agassiz. There is a commission appointing Gamaliel Bradford a major in His Majesty's service in 1757; a dress sword which belonged to William Hickling, the engineer for the fort at Cherry Valley; and a lead bullet which Captain Gershom picked up on the field of Waterloo. There is also a small likeness of young Gamaliel painted by his camp-mate in the Revolution, the Polish hero Kosciewsko.

Doorway of the Bradford House, owned by the Duxbury Rural and Historical Society and open to the public in the summer. Flagstones are made of lava blocks from Mt. Etna. *(Norman Forgit)*

That the family's interests were broad is shown in the variety of subjects covered by books in the house library and by the objects brought home and saved. Combined with this was an interest in the common weal which prompted them in each generation to involve themselves in community and national events. Colonel Gamaliel became commander of the 14th Massachusetts Regiment and served with Washington throughout the Revolution. He and his wife Sarah Alden had five sons and three daughters. All five sons also served in the Revolution, son Gamaliel enlisting at thirteen, rising to lieutenant, and being present when Washington bade farewell to his troops. One daughter, Jerusha, married Ezra Weston; two sons and a daughter married members of the Hickling family, well-known merchants in Boston. Of Captain Gershom's four daughters, Lucia and Elizabeth remained at home to be lovingly referred to as "The Aunts" and Maria and Charlotte made outside contacts. Charlotte served with the Sanitary Commission, the precursor of the Red Cross, in the front lines during the Civil War and then became head of the Soldier's Home in Washington, D.C. The letters she wrote back, all carefully preserved, give a vivid picture of those stirring times. Maria, the eldest, married the Reverend Claudius Bradford. Through him the family became friends of Daniel Webster, whose clock hangs in the library.

Maria and Claudius' daughter Lucia taught Greek and Latin at the private school in Plymouth which she and her husband, the Reverend Frederick N. Knapp, started. Their sons Gershom and Laurence both went to sea, joined the Navy during the Civil War, and later worked with the U.S. Coast and Geodetic Survey. Laurence completed a comprehensive mapping of Boston Harbor and designed the Duxbury town seal. Laurence's son Edward became a lawyer after graduating from Princeton and Harvard Law School; his son Gershom, as old family tradition dictated, went to sea.

Following his father's advice that "the only way to go," properly trained and starting right, Gershom entered the school ship *Enterprise*, an old sloop-of-war maintained in part by the U.S. Navy. "And, Mates, there aboard her was a rugged institution of learning in which one acquired a wide knowledge of life not included in its somewhat narrow curriculum."[7] After graduating, he also entered the U.S. Coast and Geodetic Survey and then later, the Naval Hydrographic Office, where he spent most of his later working years. At the suggestion of his good friend, Charles Bittinger, who had bought the Gamaliel Bradford House, he became a navigation instructor in the Shipping Board's Navigation School. During the Second World War, Gershom held classes in navigation in his own house in Washington, D.C. "There were then a large number of lieutenants in the Navy Department with scientific degrees, who had little or no knowledge of ships and navigation. Seeing this need, I offered classes in nautical astronomy and methods of finding position at sea."[8]

The diversified lives of these four generations all contributed to the history of Captain Gershom's house, which has looked serenely out on Tremont Street for more than 150 years, unchanged by man or time. Appreciating the store of interesting memorabilia in the Old Homestead and realizing that all this was American history as seen through the eyes of the ordinary citizen of Duxbury, the brothers Edward and Gershom Bradford offered their stately but modest home to the Duxbury

Elizabeth Bradford, Captain Gershom's daughter, painted the flower medallions which decorate the parlor mantelpiece. *(Norman Forgit)*

Rural and Historical Society in 1968 in an "as is" condition. They were delighted when the society accepted it as a museum of family and national history for the period 1808 to 1968. Many letters and papers are still unstudied, but there is no doubt of the value of the house and its contents for future generations.

ELIZABETH BRADFORD

The Westons
Duxbury's Caesars

On March 18, 1762, fifty-two-year-old Eliphas Weston and his teenage son, Joshua, set off in a canoe from the shore of Powder Point. The two were headed across the bay to Duxbury Beach, "to cut cedar where considerable grew,"[1] because Eliphas, a ship's carpenter, needed the timber for his small boat-building enterprise. He and Joshua felled the cedars, loaded the logs onto the small boat, and started back across the bay. But, as it so often does in March, the weather suddenly turned. They ran into a snow squall, the waves were rough, and the boat capsized. Father and son drowned in the bay.

Eliphas Weston's legacy provided the foundation for his heirs' prosperity. Born about 1710, the seventh of shipwright John Weston's eleven children, Eliphas started with few material resources, but made an astute move in marrying Priscilla Peterson of Powder Point, for she was heir to farmland which had originally belonged to her great-grandfather, George Soule. After adding some purchased land to his wife's inheritance, Eliphas had enough shore frontage to enable him to participate in coastal trading.

Eliphas left his widow and seven sons, ages nine to twenty-four, but it was his fourth son, nineteen-year-old Ezra, who would take over his father's business. In 1764, Ezra Weston founded the firm of *E. Weston*. For the next ninety-three years, this firm and its successors would expand from shipbuilding and coastal trading, to fishing and foreign trade, to manufacturing and worldwide commerce, until the name Weston was a familiar one in seaports around the globe.

A stocky man with a fair complexion and firm jaw, Ezra Weston stood about 5 feet-8 inches tall. He had a limited education, but was ambitious, shrewd, and energetic. A later writer would comment, "A resolute, industrious,

Rufus Hathaway's portraits of Ezra Weston (left), with symbols of his shipping interests: ledger, ruler, dividers, a ship under construction and one under sail, *(Clive Russ / Bertram K. & Nina Fletcher Little Collection)*; and Salumith Wadsworth Weston (right), holding a rose. *(The Abby Aldrich Rockefeller Folk Art Center, Williamsburg, Virginia)*

persevering man, he had the resolution and will and energy to carry out that which he undertook."[2] He was fortunate to come to maturity at a time when the new nation was poised for a major expansion. By using his native wits, he would capitalize on every opportunity that came his way and would create new opportunities where none had previously existed.

Ezra Weston's life would have its low points as well as high. Within a few years after his father and younger brother had drowned, another brother, Daniel, lost his life in a shipwreck off Duxbury beach. During the Revolution, his younger brother Timothy drowned when the privateer he commanded sank in the Bay of Fundy. Then he lost his twenty-year-old wife of just one year, when she died eighteen days after the birth of their first baby, Sylvia Church Weston.

At first the economy did not favor Ezra Weston's enterprises, because all commerce suffered before and during the Revolution; but once the war was over, there were new and profitable opportunities, especially in fishing. Like the Winsors, Ezra Weston sent his fishing schooners off to the prolific waters of the Grand Banks. The vessels returned to Duxbury with catches of fish which were dried on the fish flakes he had built, salted with the salt from his salt works, and stored in a long fish store he had constructed, all on the Powder Point property. Once preserved, the fish was sent in Ezra Weston's vessels to foreign ports, often in the West Indies, where the plantation owners paid well for the cargoes.

With the profits accumulating from the fishing trade, and by joining with other Duxbury entrepreneurs, Ezra Weston soon had enough capital to have more ships built. Many were constructed at the "Navy Yard" (so-called because of its size) at Harden Hill, where Benjamin Prior was the shipwright. Some of the vessels would be sold to merchants in Boston, Salem, and New Bedford soon after they were launched; others would be loaded with lumber, dried fish, and other goods to be sold and traded abroad. Often the trade was triangular, with Weston's captains turning a profit for him at each port of call.

Ezra Weston also invested in local factories. Faced by the shortage of sailcloth during the War of 1812, he started his own factory, the Duxbury Woolen and Cotton

The original Weston cottage stood east of the King Caesar house. Here both Ezra Weston, Sr. and Ezra Weston, Jr. lived before the King Caesar House was built. It burned in 1886 and a similar one was constructed at the same location.

Manufacturing Company at Millbrook. With this factory, he expanded his interests from shipbuilding and shipping to wholesale and retail enterprises, and manufacturing.

Along with success in business came political influence. Ezra Weston and his fellow merchants in Duxbury usually managed to get their way. They persuaded a reluctant town to lay out Washington Street, and later, to build a bridge over the Bluefish River. Partly in admiration, partly in envy, the townspeople called him, "King Caesar."

From 1798 on, Ezra Weston had the help of his son, Ezra Weston, Jr., in running the family business, which became *E. Weston and Son.* Ezra, Jr. was the only son of Ezra Weston, Sr. and his second wife, Salumith Wadsworth.

Ezra Weston, Jr. outdistanced his father as a merchant. "Labor and fatigue were his food and sleep; the night was to him as the day, so continual and unremitting were his exertions."[3] It was said that he would sit up all night in his chaise going to Boston so that he could do business there during the day, and then would sit up all night again on the return trip to Duxbury. He lost most of two nights' sleep, but no business time.

As indifferently educated as his father, he acquired a little polish by marrying into one of Duxbury's most cultured families, the Bradfords. In taking Jerusha Bradford, the daughter of Colonel Gamaliel Bradford, as his bride in 1793, Weston allied his family with a Mayflower family which included Harvard graduates, clergymen, and ship's captains; incidentally, a family which believed in educating their daughters as well as their sons.

Ebullient and attractive, the red-haired Jerusha's sociable nature balanced that of her blunt and taciturn husband. She was prepared to take her place as the mistress of their elegant new house, now called the *King Caesar House.* Built in 1808 in the latest style, it was a

The factory at Millbrook. Ezra Weston bought a fulling mill, originally used for processing wool, and used it for manufacturing sailcloth. Later, the Fords of Fords Store bought the building where they manufactured cloth. Drawing from the Weston Plan Book.

lighter, more sophisticated, open and elegant house which reflected the prosperity of its owners and the optimism of the day.

The King Caesar House stood at the center of the family business. From the back room which is now the library, Ezra Weston Jr. supervised his work force of about 100 men. On the 100 acres at Powder Point was a small shipyard, used mainly for repairs and small boat building, a wharf with five auxiliary buildings, a spar soak, carpenter's shop, blacksmith shop, sail loft, and ropewalk.

The ropewalk was the largest and most valuable building on the property. Built in three sections, it consisted of two, two-story buildings connected by one of a single story. It stretched 1100 feet back from what is now King Caesar Road to Powder Point Avenue, about midway between Moulton and Russell roads. Here native, and later Manila, hemp was spun and twisted into strands which were re-twisted to form the long lengths of cordage needed on board each ship.

In addition to all the commercial activities on the Powder Point property, the Westons still ran a family farm. There were orchards and vegetable gardens, several barns, and a stable.

Beyond the Powder Point property, the Westons maintained other interests. They had other farms which raised the provisions for their ships; they owned woodlots which supplied timber; and their packets and ox teams brought supplies to the shipyard. There was even a Weston store where goods brought in on Weston ships were sold. And the Westons bought and sold real estate all over Duxbury.

Ezra Weston Sr. died in 1822, but like his father before him, left no will. He had never separated the business property from the family holdings so his son-in-law, Sylvanus Sampson, Sylvia Church Weston's husband, had the difficult task of dividing the property fairly

---

The Ropewalk

In that building long and low,
With its windows all a-row,
Like the port-holes of a hulk
Human spiders spin and spin
Backward down their threads so thin
Dropping, each a hempen bulk

It was tedious work at the ropewalk, where the working day lasted eleven hours. Spinners attached one end of some hemp fibers to the whorl of a spinning wheel and wound the rest around their waists, then walked slowly backwards the length of the building, as they fed out the hemp. At the same time, boys, some as young as ten, turned the spinning wheels. For some boys employment at the ropewalk served as a first step towards being a cabin

boy aboard ship and a career at sea.

At Ezra Weston's ropewalk one horse, *Honest Dick*, turned the wheel to run the machinery for forty years. The Westons, who were always fond of animals, paid tribute to him by erecting a brick marker and tablet in his memory. The marker has been moved from its original location, but still stands close to the Weston spar soak off Powder Point Avenue.

between his wife and her half-brother, Ezra Weston, Jr. When the estate was finally settled, Weston retained control of the business, renaming it, simply, *Ezra Weston.*

Ezra, Jr. also inherited his father's nickname, *King Caesar,* sometimes even being called *Old King Caesar,* to the confusion of later historians trying to distinguish between father and son. By the 1830s, the Weston business was reputed to be a million-dollar enterprise with an annual payroll of $120,000. Tired of extending credit from his store, and finding it impractical to do his banking out of town, Ezra Weston, Jr. joined with Levi Sampson and George Loring to start their own bank, The Duxbury Bank, incorporated in 1833. Weston served as its first president, but following "embarrassments caused by the injudicious conduct of its cashier,"[4] his eldest son, Gershom Bradford Weston, took over. However, The Duxbury Bank did not last long; it closed in 1842.

It wasn't until 1834, after Jerusha's death, that Ezra Weston, Jr. opened his own ten-acre shipyard on the south bank of the Bluefish River. There the ship *Hope* was launched in 1841. Just two years later, the Westons were building their last Duxbury ship, the *Manteo.*

Ezra, Jr., who had started his career in an optimistic age, died in 1842 as his maritime enterprises were beginning to feel the pinch of hard times and depression. The firm continued for the next fifteen years under the direction of his three sons, but none of them had inherited their father's drive and ability. His eldest and youngest sons were more interested in living the lives of cultured gentlemen, while the middle son, Alden Bradford Weston, ran the day-to-day business from the Weston counting house on Commercial Wharf in Boston. E. Weston and Sons was unwilling or unable to adapt to the changing times; finally, in the midst of the depression caused by the Panic of 1857, the firm closed its doors for the last time.

From its beginnings in pre-Revolutionary Duxbury to its close just before the Civil War, the Weston enterprises had grown and flourished as Duxbury had grown and flourished. The thriving businesses led by Ezra Weston, senior and junior, had spurred Duxbury's development; in turn, the Westons had benefited from the accumulated experience of Duxbury's shipbuilders, master mariners, merchants, sea captains, and sailors. Over the ninety-three years that the Westons were in business, they built almost 100 vessels of every variety, from sloops to schooners to barks. The two Ezra Westons were self-confident, practical, ambitious men, whose hard work and determination, and for that matter, imperiousness, led their family, and Duxbury as well, from obscurity to worldwide notice. Each earned the title, "King Caesar."

KATHERINE H. PILLSBURY

Joshua Winsor

*J*oshua Winsor was born in 1749, the second of eight sons and two daughters born to Samuel and Rhoda Delano Winsor. In 1773, he married Olive Thomas of Marshfield, who bore him eight children. Following her death, Joshua married her sister, who lived less than a year, after which he married for the third time.

Like Samuel Winsor, his father, Joshua was a prosperous, prolific patriarch whose custom it was to help each child, as he or she married, to establish a home either by allowing them to build on Winsor land, or by lending financial aid in some way. Winsor land appears to have extended from what is now Winsor Street to north of Fort Hill Lane, perhaps to the Bluefish River, and from the bay to the brook which is west of what is now Washington Street.

Joshua's house stood near the present Yacht Club. It has been immortalized in a painting by Rufus Hathaway, Duxbury artist and doctor, who married Joshua's daughter, Judith. This painting was done with a sense of humor and enough skill for it to bring $100,000 at a sale in the early 1980s.

With his older brother Nathaniel, Ezra Weston, Sr., and Samuel Delano, Joshua Winsor joined in an effort to lift the local economy out of the virtual poverty which prevailed following the Revolutionary War. The Winsors, whose father Samuel had been a shipbuilder, began by building schooners for the Grand Banks fishery. The enterprise flourished, and the industry and skill of the Westons, Delanos, and Winsors burst forth dramatically so that by 1787, sixty-four Banks fishing vessels were in commission. Joshua became one of the

Joshua Winsor by Rufus Hathaway (1793), portrayed as a self-assured man with one hand on a walking stick and the other in his pocket. *(Herbert P. Vose/Vose Galleries of Boston, Inc.)*

66

town's most prominent merchants, and with his brother Nathaniel was extensively engaged in mackerel and cod fishery on the Grand Banks.[1] The Winsor wharves were the first built expressly for business. On these were warehouses for drying and storing the salted fish which had been cured on low scaffolds called *flakes*. Today, just north of the present Yacht Club, the timbers and stonework remains of Joshua Winsor's wharf occasionally prove hazardous to passing yachts.

Shipping merchants sometimes sent individual consignments along with their regular cargoes for the benefit of someone at home. On one occasion, Joshua Winsor sent to England a special box of fish on behalf of each of his three daughters. The ventures were successful and from the proceeds one of the girls bought a ring; one a pair of long white gloves in which she wished to be painted (this was presumably Judith, who later married Rufus Hathaway); and one, the silk for her wedding gown.[2]

It was said of Solomon Washburn, a blockmaker in one of the shipyards along the bay, that he must be a promising young man, for he married Hannah, daughter of Joshua Winsor, a man known for being particular about the men his several daughters married. Winsor wanted each daughter well provided for, and was patriarchal, insisting that his many children live under his eye, making it possible for at least five to build on parts of his many acres that ran along the shore. Hannah was one such child. When she married Solomon Washburn in 1805, he built on the west side of the newly laid out street that ran through the Winsor lands (now Washington Street). This house is just north of the home of her sister Judith and Dr. Rufus Hathaway and is where Solomon and Hannah's eight children were born. There were probably Winsors in three out of four houses from the Winsor Wharves to Fort Hill, all on original Winsor land.

Although his children had built on his land, none had title to the lot upon which their house was built. One day in February 1815, in his 67th year, Joshua sat down to rectify the situation and wrote several deeds, all similar in wording and all with approximate valuations. One deed was given to his daughter Hannah, "for natural

Joshua Winsor's second wife, Ruth Thomas Winsor (1793). The portrait, by Hathaway, was probably done during the eight months between her marriage and death. *(Herbert P. Vose/Vose Galleries of Boston, Inc.)*

love and affection and other good reasons, the dwelling house now occupied by Solomon Washburn"[3] and about a half acre on which it stood. The house and land he valued at $2,000, which suggests he may have originally financed the house.

In preparation for defense in the war with Great Britain in 1812, Nathaniel and Joshua Winsor procured field pieces. The record shows that "at an expense of $140 they purchased two nine pounders and also two casks of powder containing each 100 weight."[4] A fishing schooner and a sloop belonging to Joshua, and manned by two of his sons, were subsequently taken by the British during this war.

In 1798, Washington Street was *projected* by Ezra Weston, Sr., Seth Sprague, Samuel Delano, and Joshua Winsor, with bitter opposition from other factions in the town. Eventually the projectors petitioned the Court of Sessions. Their case was upheld and the road was completed. They also persuaded a reluctant town meeting to build a bridge over the Bluefish River. Joshua Winsor began work in April of 1803 and it was completed by the third of July. "On July 4, the bridge was formally opened with a parade and sumptuous collation, which went a long way toward restoring good feeling among all concerned!"[5]

Joshua Winsor, a prosperous, prolific patriarch, was instrumental in the development of Duxbury in the period between the Revolution and the Civil War. He died in 1827.

ANN LEARNARD BOWMAN

Justin Winsor's 1848 sketch of the Winsor store and wharf. *(Massachusetts Historical Society)*

Rufus Hathaway

rt in Duxbury in the period from the late 1700s to the middle of the 1800s, as in other small towns throughout the nation, focused on the decorative and was mainly practiced by itinerant painters. These artists traveled from town to town creating portraits, signs, and wall decorations in response to a need of the citizens to beautify their surroundings. Self-taught, they were unrestrained by academic theory, and they painted with a directness and honesty that reflected the spirit of the people.

Continuing scholarship in American folk art has identified more and more itinerant artists, but many remain unknown. An example of anonymous art in Duxbury from the early 1800s is a wall painting in the stairway of the Charles Drew House, built in 1835. It portrays an eagle, symbol of the nation, with wings spread, head facing to the left, with a banner inscribed *E Pluribus Unum* in its beak. The left claw grasps an olive branch; the right, four thunderbolt arrows. Primarily in shades of warm brown, the eagle has a wingspan of four feet ten inches and floats on a muted blue background. Family tradition maintains that this is the work of an itinerant painter.

Another example may be found in the main house at St. Margaret's Convent on Washington Street. Located on the walls of the entry stairway, it portrays almost life-size cattails with egret-like birds among them. The house is thought to have been built in the early 1800s and the painting could date to that period. It has been repainted since 1950, but still retains great decorative charm.

Engraving of Colonel Briggs Alden from a lost portrait by Hathaway.

Although both of these wall paintings are interesting examples of the art of the period, it is Rufus Hathaway who is the most prominent artist in the Duxbury shipbuilding era. Born in Freetown, Massachusetts on May 2, 1770, he was the oldest of the seven children of Asa and Mary (Phillips) Hathaway. According to two deeds, the Hathaways were living in Swansea by 1785 and in 1789 were disowned by the Swansea Friends Meetinghouse for lack of attendance and other matters. In the 1790 census in Bristol, R. I., Asa is listed as living with three females and two sons over sixteen. It seems probable that Rufus had left home at this time to begin his career as an itinerant painter. His father and maternal grandfather were ship's carpenters, and Rufus may have apprenticed with ship painters and carvers in the area. His earliest signed and dated painting of 1790 depicts Molly/Polly Wales Fobes, future mother of the Reverend George Leonard of Marshfield. He also painted several portraits of citizens of the Taunton/Middleboro area in the early 1790s. It is possible that he obtained these commissions during visits to his many collateral relatives who lived there.

Rufus Hathaway could have been drawn to Duxbury because distant relatives resided here; or he may have been looking for painting commissions, knowing it was a prosperous shipbuilding area. In 1793, he painted portraits of leading Duxbury citizens, including Mr. and Mrs. Ezra Weston, Sr. (shown on page 61), Mr. and Mrs. Ezra Weston, Jr. (page 71), Captain and Mrs. Sylvanus Sampson (formerly Sylvia Church Weston, the daughter of Ezra Weston and his first wife Sylvia), George Partridge, and Church Sampson. It is also thought he may have painted his undated portraits of Mr. and Mrs. Joshua Winsor (pages 66 and 67) at this time.

He may then have traveled to pursue his craft. The portrait of the Reverend Nehemiah Thomas, minister of the First Parish Church in Scituate and brother of Mrs. Joshua Winsor, is dated June 10, 1794. In 1795, he painted Joseph Robertson Tolman, also of Scituate, and in the same year he returned to Duxbury to paint portraits of Joshua Winsor's two daughters, Judith and Lucy. Perhaps at this time he painted his only known landscape, the *View of Joshua Winsor's House* (page 26). According to family tradition, the artist fell in love with Judith and they were married in December, 1795.

There is a Duxbury tradition that Joshua Winsor prevailed upon Rufus Hathaway to abandon painting and pursue medicine as a steadier and more profitable livelihood. He studied with the eminent Dr. Isaac Winslow of Marshfeld and set up practice in Duxbury, becoming the town's only doctor. However, he also continued to paint, at least occasionally.

Rufus Hathaway may have completed the portrait of Major Israel Forster of Andover, Massachusetts in 1797 and that of Seth Winsor, Joshua and Olive Winsor's third son, about 1798. Thereafter there are no portraits until 1804, when he painted the portrait of Maria (born 1794) and Jerusha (born 1802) Weston, daughters of Ezra and Jerusha Weston, both of whom died that year. An undated portrait of Ezra Weston III, who died in 1808, may have been done after his death.

In addition to twenty-nine known paintings, Rufus Hathaway painted four miniatures and a wall painting of two peacocks, removed from the now-destroyed Peterson House on Powder Point. When the Bluefish River Bridge was dedicated in 1803, a temporary archway held a carved wooden eagle by Dr. Hathaway.

Rufus Hathaway, remembered locally for his sense of humor as well as his paintings, lived on Washington Street with his wife and growing family (twelve children were born between 1796 and 1821) in a house, since destroyed, on land deeded by Joshua Winsor to his

Ezra Weston, Jr. (1793) shown with a document in his hands and inkwell and ledger behind, suggesting that at the time of the portrait, at age 20, he may have been mostly involved with the administrative tasks of the business. *(The Abby Aldrich Rockefeller Folk Art Center, Williamsburg, Virginia)*

Jerusha Bradford married Ezra Weston, Jr. on June 9, 1793 and the portrait is thought to have been done at that time. She is well-dressed in a fichu and a fashionable hat with ostrich feathers, holding a small bouquet in her hand. *(The Abby Aldrich Rockefeller Folk Art Center)*

Lady with her Pets, Molly Wales Fobes (1790). The pets—a cat, two birds, and two moths—recall the use of animals in Flemish paintings which Hathaway may have been aware of through prints. Ostrich feathers, although generally worn more vertically, were popular, and indicate she is wearing evening dress. *(The Metropolitan Museum of Art)*

daughter in 1815. In a period when men frequently held several occupations, it is not surprising that he continued to paint into the early 1800s, while also practicing medicine. It is probable his practice took more and more of his time, as there are no known paintings after 1808. Deeds recording his purchase of a mill in 1808 and 1809 define him as a physician. When he died in 1822 at the age of 52, he must have considered medicine his full-time occupation, for it is thought that he wrote his own epitaph, inscribed on his headstone in Mayflower Cemetery:

> *Thousands of journeys night and day*
> *I've traveled weary on my way*
> *To heal the sick, but now I'm gone*
> *A journey never to return.*

LANCI VALENTINE

Sylvanus Sampson

When Duxbury was about half as old as it is now, Captain Sylvanus Sampson,[1] born there in 1761, was well established as one of its leading citizens. On the tenth day of March 1800, a committee consisting of Sylvanus Sampson, Samuel Walker, and Benj. Bosworth entered into a Memorandum of Agreement with Col. Jotham Loring and Mr. Samuel Chandler to build a School House for the South East district of Duxbury. It was to be thirty feet long and twenty-six feet wide and nine feet high and have seven windows. The two builders were to supply all the materials, including an iron stove, and finish said school house in a "neet and workmanlike manner" for which they were to be paid the sum of $326.66.

Captain Sylvanus Sampson was duly chosen a selectman for the Town of Duxbury at a legal meeting on Monday, the 13th of March, 1815. He was also a sea captain, shipping merchant, farmer, storekeeper, and the son-in-law of Captain Ezra Weston—Duxbury's original King Caesar.

Young Sampson's schooling pointed him firmly in the direction of these varied roles, developing his interests in the problem-solving of commerce. His school workbook for this period was bound in a page from the Boston *Gazette & Country Journal* dated January 3, 1774 (when he would have been 12) and was filled with such posers as: "How much corn may you buy for 125 pounds when corn is half a dollar per bushel." "A man bought 20 hogsheads of fish at 4 pounds 5 shillings per quintal. Each hogshead contained 8½ quintals. How much did the whole cost him?" He then went on to learn the mariner's art, wrestling with geometry, trigonometry, plain sailing, parallel sailing—all the necessary elements of navigation. But there must have been a *little* time for mindwandering. On one page of his Book of Navigation he penned, in very

Voted that the Selectmen insert a clause in the warrant for the next meeting . . . to see if the town will vote to let sheep and cattle run at large in said town.
July 19, 1790   S. Sampson, Clerk

Rec'd of Sylvanus Sampson, Agent in South East School District, Sixty Dollars being in full of all demands for my services as Grammar Master for three months.
May 3rd 1810   Thos Power

small print: "God made Satan and Satan made Sin. God made a hole and put Satan therein. Time and Tide waits for No one. Miss Sarah Hall."

In his teens, Sylvanus probably signed on ships as an ordinary crew member just to get his sea legs, but it wasn't long before he was serving as a recordkeeper or quartermaster on fishing voyages, and before he was twenty-two, he had established a stake in the business. On June 5, 1783, he put down fifteen pounds "towards a New Schooner that Consider Drew, Ship write, Is a Building at his Yard which the Said Silvanus Sampson Is to own one Quarter of."

Captain Ezra Weston must have been impressed with the abilities of this young man because he drew him further and further into his sizeable shipping empire on Powder Point. At first Captain Sampson served as Master and/or business agent on those Weston ships that engaged in the coastal and West Indies trade. He may or may not have had a fractional financial interest in any of these ships, but he did indulge in an occasional *adventure*; i.e., he would buy goods with his own money at the home port, add them to the cargo, and sell them to his advantage in the West Indies, sometimes repeating the process on the return voyage. At the same time, he was becoming more and more involved in managing Captain Weston's various business enterprises, and then, in 1787, he married the boss's daughter, Sylvia Church Weston. She was nineteen and he was twenty-six.

Sylvanus Sampson was descended not only from Pilgrim Henry Sampson but from Elder William Brewster as well, and it was on former Brewster land in the Nook, a thirty-six acre parcel surrounding Eagles Nest Cove, then owned by his father, John Sampson, that the young couple, after living in Weston houses on the Point for a few years, decided to build their own house and set up shop, literally.

The house was built by the ship's carpenters in 1792[2] alongside the road leading south from the main part of town to the old Standish farm. It was a Federal-style, two-story-and-garret box built around a massive chimney that served five fireplaces in addition to the enormous one in the cellar where food was prepared for the household. It was not unlike other comfortable residences of the day in Duxbury—with one exception. At its west end, the part that ran along the road, Captain Sampson installed a small store where he sold goods brought back on his ships. Possibly in 1806, an addition was put on the north side of the house that centered around a huge chimney. At that time, the kitchen was elevated to the main floor.

Captain Sampson established at Eagles Nest a smaller version of his father-in-law's business at the other end of town. Soon his wharf bustled with the coming and going of his ships—sloops and schooners at first—some returning with hake and cod from the Grand Banks and others with goods from the coastal and West Indies trade. Later he added at least two brigs to his fleet and entered the trans-Atlantic trade, sending his ships to Portugal, France, Egypt, Turkey, Germany, and Russia. Incoming cargoes were mostly sold in Boston, but a percentage of these imported goods stayed on board and, with additional items purchased in Boston specifically for the purpose, made the final leg of the voyage to Eagles Nest Cove to be sold on the premises.

The range of merchandise in the Sampson's store was extraordinary. Rum, both the West Indies and New England varieties, sold at a merry clip. One innovative customer had this use for it:

Capt Sampson Sir I want you to send me one quart of your WI rum as the fish will not bite well without some rum thay all say that has folured that business
Sir your hbl srvt   *Marshall Soul*

The store was about the size of a small parlor, with an alcove added. Customers entered directly from the road, through a Dutch door secured by means of an iron bar, into a small area defined by the L-shaped counter. The alcove, back from the smaller reach of counter, was lined on two walls with shelves and on the third was a window and a bank of twenty small drawers. On the back wall, opposite the door, was a small fireplace with shelves to the right of it and to the left was a one-legged bookkeeper's desk where Captain Sampson must have spent a great deal of time keeping his accounts in order. (*Fran Nichols*)

Detail of a store ledger (1800), showing purchases of pork, candles, lumber, and shoes by Joseph Wadsworth. *(Fran Nichols)*

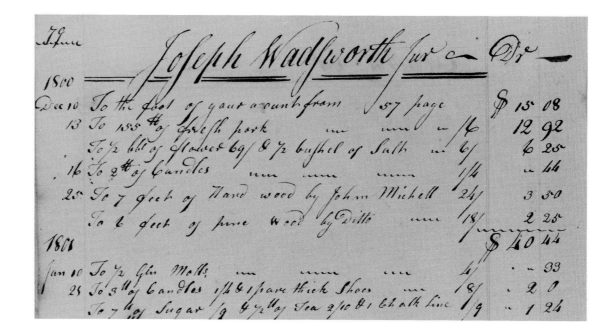

Other spirits were popular as well: brandy, Malaga and port wine, and sometimes gin. Molasses, sugar, flour, tea, corn, and fresh fish were big sellers. Windsor soap was available, but it crossed those wide pine plank counters in very small proportion to the amount of butter, cheese, candles, snuff, shot, and gun powder; also fabrics of every description—for dresses, suits, and household use—and buttons, papers of pins, hat trimmings, and shoes; chamber pots, tea pots, kettles and spiders, scythes, and nails. Books—primers, spellers, testaments, almanacs—and medicines such as turkey rhubarb, chamomile flowers, castor oil, and gum opium, were frequently asked for.

People were frequently sick, including the Sampsons (five of the eight children born to them survived) and there were several doctors around who made house calls, dispensed medicines, and prescribed cures.

Take one teaspoonful of hartshorn two teaspoons full of sweet oil. Mix together. Spread on flannel round your neck. To be repeated night and morning.

Let one of the pills be taken at night and another in the morning and continued until dizziness is produced.

Itch Ointment Take of pepper reduced to powder, of allspice reduced in like manner, of sulphur, of ginger, of spirits of turpentine, of lard; of each in an equal quantity.

Tell Polly Thomas she must wear a Wine Plaster and it will cure her Stomach. Don't forget it.

This was not an age of specialization, and all physicians had at least one other occupation. Dr. Isaac Winslow, for instance, grew and sold salt hay and pastured oxen belonging to others for a fee. Dr. Rufus Hathaway was an artist. He painted large oil portraits of little Church Sampson just before he died, Captain Sampson, Mrs. Sampson, and her father, Captain Ezra Weston. One portrait, painted in 1793, cost a total of 1 pound 17 shillings and 4 pence, including canvas, frame, and gilding the frame. Dr. Hathaway also built a corn windmill for Captain Sampson that was completed in 1802.

Wearing more than one hat was not unusual. Mrs. Sampson and the children often had to help out in the store when the captain was in Boston on shipping business or attending to the farm or the shipyard. One winter day their daughter Elizabeth, who was a student and avid reader, was sent to the dark dank cellar of the store to draw a gallon of molasses for a customer. It was slow work when the molasses was cold, so she took a candle and a book with her. So absorbed did she become in her reading that when she finally remembered her job, the barrel had emptied all over the earthen floor.

There wasn't much cash around, and Captain Sampson had to be banker as well as storekeeper.

Please to send me gal molasses 2 quarts run 7 pounds sugar and 8 or 10 dollars for I shall call next friday and we will settle it

August 1803   *Calvin Partridge*

People often satisfied bills they ran up with contra-credit such as their labor, or with goods they produced. They paid when they were able and interest was not charged on this kind of a debt.

Sir I am pretty much out of money at this time and if you will be so kind as to let Lydia Simmons have the value of four dollars two shillings and three pence out of your shop on my account and wait a few months till I can pay you you will much oblige your friend and humble servant

April 29 1800   *Abigail Thomas*

Then again, some people settled debts with a flourish.

Rec'd of Capt Sylvanus Sampson Nine shillings and Nine pence in full of all Dues Debts and demands from the beginning of the World to this Day by me

July 22, 1793   *Barzlai Goodwin*

This store in the corner of the house on what is now Standish Street is there today, almost exactly as the Sampsons left it, except that the shelves and drawers are empty now, the counter and floor are hollowed with age, and there is no Day Book open on the one-legged desk. The view from the opposite side of the house still sweeps down over fields and across marshes to the cove, where now only a small weathered boathouse marks the scene of a once-thriving shipping business. Some stonework and pilings remain of the old wharf, pointing eastward toward the open sea.

MARJORIE WINSLOW

Shipping Era Houses

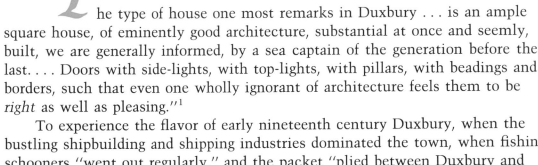

The type of house one most remarks in Duxbury . . . is an ample square house, of eminently good architecture, substantial at once and seemly, built, we are generally informed, by a sea captain of the generation before the last. . . . Doors with side-lights, with top-lights, with pillars, with beadings and borders, such that even one wholly ignorant of architecture feels them to be *right* as well as pleasing."[1]

To experience the flavor of early nineteenth century Duxbury, when the bustling shipbuilding and shipping industries dominated the town, when fishing schooners "went out regularly," and the packet "plied between Duxbury and Boston, bringing lumber and supplies for the stores," one should visit the Captain Gershom Bradford house on Tremont Street, owned by the Duxbury Rural and Historical Society.[2] Captain Bradford planned the details of his home while out at sea. Built by his friend, Benjamin Bird of Dorchester, in 1808, this is a rare early Duxbury house with a known builder. The original contract, with Bradford's specifications, may still be seen. The house is a modest, two-story, one-room-deep, I-house, with a kitchen ell. It is a simple home with fine, delicate Federal embellishments. The tall doorway has a high entablature with bow tracery and fluted decoration within its arched window. The door opens to a wide, central front-to-back hallway, that leads to the garden beyond. There are end chimneys, with the brick ends of the house covered by gray-painted clapboards to match the front. Inside, graceful carved and rope-turned moldings and original paint survive. Gershom's botanist daughter, Elizabeth, decorated the mantels with charming painted flowers. Original wallpapers and fabrics have been reproduced.

Gershom Bradford, his brother Captain Gamaliel, and sister Jerusha (wife of Ezra Weston, Jr.), built their homes at about the same time. Records indicate

Front entrance to the King Caesar House (1808–9).

The Captain Gamaliel Bradford house (1807), showing the brick end.

that the home of their brother, Captain Daniel, was built some years earlier, probably in 1796, the year of Daniel's marriage. The brothers all built on their father's land, near the corner of Tremont and Harrison streets. The four houses have details in common, such as the same parlor paint color, but they reflect quite different personalities.

Captain Gamaliel, Gershom's eldest brother, built a fine Federal home opposite his on Tremont Street. The most elegant of the three, it is a spacious, square, four-chimney home with curved windows and brick ends. The monitor roof, for added light and space in the third story, was a feature of Federal houses in the Plymouth area.[3] The ell was probably part of the 1738 home of Bradford's father, Colonel Gamaliel Bradford.

The home of Daniel Bradford stands on a knoll above Harrison Street. Originally it was a typical square, center-chimney, hipped-roofed captain's house, said to have been slightly nicknamed *Bandbox*. In the 1870s, Laurence Bradford added a five-room ell as an apartment for his mother-in-law. Tradition relates that the ell also housed the lady's cow, thus the *Cowshed* joined the *Bandbox*, forming a substantial home on the hill. At one time, the house had a widow's walk and a front entry porch. Interesting English tiles depicting Aesop's Fables surround the fireplaces in the double parlor.

On Tremont Street, just north of Harrison Street, stands the 1831 Parish House, built when the church was supported by taxes and ministers were hired for life. If an older minister became infirm, another had to be hired and the town supported both of them, paying meager salaries to each. When the Reverend Benjamin Kent arrived in Duxbury as Assistant Minister, a group of parishioners bought a lot from Captain Gershom Bradford and built a home for the young minister to rent. As handsomely built as private homes in the vicinity, this house is the only one in Duxbury to have been financed by a group of citizens. Those who paid five dollars a share in the project were master mariners, shipbuilders, merchants, carpenters, and storekeepers.

Duxbury's early farms, like the Bradford land, spread over inland acreage, with pathways leading to the shore for fishing and the gathering of salt hay. As the fishing and shipbuilding industries grew and brought prosperity to the town after the Revolution, families began to look to the shorefront area for their new homes and businesses. Washington Street, first called Commercial Street, then Main Street, was laid out in 1798, but it was not until the bridge over Bluefish River was built in 1803, linking the new road to Powder Point, that the building boom began.

With the division of old farmland into houselots, houses for Duxbury's shipowners, captains, mariners, craftsmen, and tradesmen sprang up on the main street, along the lanes to the shore, and on the old cartways. Sturdily built by shipwrights, homes reflected the new Federal style, introduced to New England builders by Charles Bulfinch and Asher Benjamin. Based on the designs of ancient Rome and the Renaissance and popularized in England by Robert Adam, the new style reached Duxbury housewrights through Benjamin's design books, and the classical examples were translated into wood for the increasingly affluent community.

King Caesar House

Many of the design elements of the house built on Powder Point for Ezra Weston, Jr. and his wife, Jerusha Bradford, in 1808, can be traced to Asher Benjamin's drawings. The doorway's elliptical fanlight, delicately traced sidelights, and the three-part window above are hallmarks of the Federal period. Slender fluted columns

The west side elevation of the King Caesar House from the Weston Plan Book shows the summer kitchen and appended utility buildings.

80

and reeded pilasters enhance the door surround. The house has generous, graceful proportions with a shallow-pitched hipped roof, brick ends (a local feature), and four tall end chimneys. The wide cornerboards have wooden facing, grooved to suggest quoins. Perhaps reflecting the owner's association with the sea, a line of rope-carved molding tops the cornice at the roofline. An elegant country Federal home, the King Caesar House was an appropriate residence for Duxbury's leading shipping magnate. It was built to face the wharf. The wharf has been restored as a park and the lawns and gardens give King Caesar's grand house a serene setting it never knew in Ezra Weston's day.

The most outstanding furnishing is the rare, hand-blocked wallpaper imported from Paris. The paper in the east parlor was printed in 1826 by the firm of Dufour and Leroy, one of France's most famous wallpaper designers. Called *The Incas*, it depicts Pizarro's conquest of Peru. The paper was restored and reinstalled in its original location in 1967. The paper in the west parlor is *Le Parc Français*, by Jacquemart et Benard.[4]

Ezra and Jerusha Weston collected fine furnishings on the worldwide voyages of Weston ships and filled their home with Oriental rugs, silver, porcelains, lacquerware, rich textiles, and other luxuries. Today, the Duxbury Rural and Historical Society, which owns the house and maintains it as a museum, has restored its early nineteenth-century appearance and furnished it with a fascinating array of artifacts from Duxbury's maritime past. A museum wing in the rear features changing historical exhibits. The house welcomes visitors in the summer months.

The area around the Surplus Street corner was also filled with activity in the shipbuilding era. There were shipwrights, carpenters, and housewrights; sparmakers, blockmakers, and blacksmiths; mariners, captains, ship-

Surplus Street

Surplus Street was once called Poverty Lane when it led to the Poor Farm; and about the same time it was Folly Street, over which one's folly led to the Alms House. When, in the Jackson administration, there were surplus funds distributed to the states to be divided among the towns, the residents of Poverty/Folly Street were loud in their opinion of how Duxbury should spend its share. They are said to have got a part of the money to improve their street, whereby it became Surplus Street.

Dorothy Wentworth

yard owners, storekeepers, and cordwainers. Today's quiet neighborhood had wharves, storage buildings, shops, and a firehouse. There were boarding houses, taverns, and a dancehall for sailors. This boisterous waterfront community, which extended to Harrison Street, was thought to be somewhat unsavory, earning the name of Sodom from the upright citizenry of Duxbury.

The children of Samuel Winsor, Sr., who operated the Winsor and Drew shipyard at Standish Shore, were among the first to follow the fast-growing shipbuilding industry to the new part of town. Their homes, grouped between the present Water and Winsor streets, were built before Washington Street was established and they, like the other late eighteenth-century houses in that neighborhood, face south, toward the old cartways to the shore. They were built as gambrel-roofed, three-quarter houses or plain, small Cape Cod houses. James Winsor, at the corner of today's Water Street, and his sisters, who married Job Sampson and Amos Brown, built nearly identical homes next to each other. The nearby houses of Samuel Winsor, Jr., on Winsor Street, Lot Stetson, Jesse Howard, and Peleg Churchill, all dating before 1800, share similarities of form and simple detail. Some have doorway sidelights; others have a row of lights over the door, a feature derived from Georgian architecture. The painting of the Joshua Winsor house on Long Point by Rufus Hathaway shows the same gambrel structure.

In the early 1800s, the next generation of Winsors and others adopted the new Federal style. The homes of Spencer Winsor and Otis Winsor, built on land owned

Half houses were built so that they could be added to without destroying the proportions. This example, the John Pierce house on Surplus Street, shows the half-cape as it was originally constructed. (Norman Forgit)

by their father, Samuel, Jr., are typical of Duxbury's many hipped-roof captains' houses, called square-riggers, "foursquare to the wind." Owners of the smaller houses expanded and refined their houses to the new taste. The Job Sampson three-quarter house on Water Street became a square rigger. The Peleg Churchill house, built by a cooper, was enlarged by more affluent owners, who installed a Federal-style, three-part Wyatt window in a central dormer, and moved chimneys to allow for a more elaborate staircase. Next door, the unadorned Cape Cod house built by shipwright James Woodward in 1801 soon had a formal portico with a heavily molded pediment and quadruple columns at each side of the entry.

Houses built as half-capes, called *sad houses* for they indicated a lack of either children or money, are now rare in Duxbury, as most were eventually extended to become full-sized Cape Cod houses. The John Pierce house on Surplus Street is one that retained its original form.

Mattakeesett Court

At the corner of Harrison and Washington streets, there is an important grouping of four fine captains' houses, all built before 1813. Each is quite different from the others; together they symbolize the height of Duxbury's shipbuilding prosperity.

The town's most elegant Federal home is the tall, yellow house of Nathaniel Winsor, Jr., built in 1807. The Winsors had become leaders in Duxbury's maritime industries: fishing fleets, shipbuilding, and coastwise trade. They were affluent and well-traveled. It is thought that Nathaniel was influenced by the mansions of Boston and Salem, for his home has a grandeur unknown in Duxbury. Certainly he was familiar with the designs of Bulfinch and Benjamin; his handsome three-story house

Mattakeesett Court. The four stately houses, with the Nathaniel Winsor, Jr. house providing the central focus, make this corner one of the best known in Duxbury. *(Fran Nichols)*

reflects the finest architecture of the day. The Palladian window is the only one in Duxbury. A semi-circular porch, following the line of the present steps, once completed the facade. Behind the elaborate tracery and carving of the doorway, a circular stair rises to the upper floors. It is thought that the large open stairwell allowed ships' carpenters to make masts inside the house. Daniel Webster, a frequent visitor in Duxbury, is said to have delivered an oration from the front steps. The house where Nathaniel Winsor once carved figureheads served in the early twentieth century as a hotel for summer vacationers.

The house on the northeast corner may date as early as 1780. The original building faces the way to the shore, not the new street, and its simple architecture relates more to Duxbury's late eighteenth-century houses than to the Federal refinement of its neighbors. A thriving tinsmith shop occupied this house for many years, and the building housed apartments before it became a single-family dwelling in this century. The white Federal house on the northwest corner has an impressive two-story porch, a Greek Revival addition.

Seth Sprague, Jr. built his home on his father's farm at the southwest corner in 1813. His substantial, square house has a monitor roof, and decorative bands of rope- and triglyph-carved molding form the cornice. The house's graceful doorway, with its distinctive wooden fan, originally faced Harrison Street. There was a smaller door on the Washington Street side, where now the larger one can not quite fit comfortably between the shuttered windows. The Sprague shipyard was south of the house, nearly opposite the store that is Sweetser's today. After the new highway was put in, the Sprague ships had to be launched across Washington Street. The Honorable Seth Sprague, Jr. was a community leader, active in politics and the church. Like many of his neighbors, he engaged in lumbering and farming as well as shipbuilding. He also ran a general store "in the end facing the street."[5] The house became a hotel in 1872, and later it was a lodging house, a livery stable, an inn, and an express company.

The Duxbury Bank building, later the Cable House, by the Bluefish River. With its tall corner pilasters it is a fine example of Greek Revival architecture. *(Norman Forgit)*

Greek Revival

In the 1830s and 1840s, homebuilders adopted the new style based on the design of the temples of ancient Greece. The fashion turned gable ends to the street and turned the gables into pediments through the use of heavy overhung cornices or plain trim bands, imitating the classical entablature. Wide corner boards or pilasters, sometimes with capitals derived from the Greek orders, are characteristic. Doorways were often placed at one side of the gable end, with a stair-hall inside, leaving room for a parlor at the front and a dining room or small bedrooms behind. With the advent of the cast iron stove, a large central chimney was unnecessary. Rooms could be added as ells, each with its own small chimney.

In Duxbury, the shift in taste from Roman-Federal symmetry and delicate ornament to the Grecian temple form with broad, plain surfaces and spare decoration, can be seen on homes of all sizes, often in combination with the earlier structures, as well as on public buildings. A concentration of interesting examples extends up the hill toward Bluefish River on Washington Street and along the surrounding streets: St. George, Cove, Cedar, and Chapel.

The Duxbury Bank at Bluefish River, founded by Ezra Weston, Jr. in 1833 for the convenience of Duxbury's maritime businesses, has Greek Revival features in its pedimented ends, massive proportions, square-headed porches, and tall corner pilasters. Simplified Ionic capitals top the pilasters and columns, a Greek Revival detail rarely found in Duxbury. The present windows in the pediments replace the original semicircular ones. This building became the office for the French Atlantic Cable in 1869, and was the office of the Western Union Telegraph and Cable Company in the late nineteenth century.

Typical of Duxbury's many small Greek Revival homes is the William Bradford house of 1841, the little red house on Washington Street. Bradford was a sparmaker and his simple home near the shipyards can be compared to the earlier Cape Cod houses of shipping era craftsmen. This house has a raised, more shallow-pitched roof, allowing for higher first floor ceilings. The gable end faces the street, with the front door at one side beneath a plain lintel. The gable has wide cornice moldings that terminate in accented corners, the suggestion of a full pediment.

The Thomas Low House (1833/4) on Chapel Street is a classic example of country Greek Revival building. Large in scale, the house has little decoration, except for the accents of white trim bands, a deep plain doorway frieze with flared cornice, and an interesting triangular window in the pediment. Far more elaborate is a house at the crest of Washington Street, bought by Zenas Faunce, Jr. in 1852, and noted for its unusual iron grillework balustrade at the second floor. Faunce's father was the anchor-smith, with an iron forge at the southwest side of Bluefish River. Zenas, Jr. is said to have had the decorative grilles made at the Faunce foundry after he had seen similar ones in New Orleans. The house has corner pilasters and full-length six-over-twelve windows at the second floor, with decorative shutters concealing the lower third, behind the grillework.

The houses built in Duxbury over a period of about sixty years mirrored the comfortable prosperity of the town's shipbuilding era. Today one can explore the village, noting the simplicity and the variety of the architectural detail. Doorways are set into small projecting porches or placed under columned porticoes, classical pediments, or high entablatures. Some are rich with carving, molding, and applied ornament; others are starkly plain. Columns, in most instances, are based on the

The house bought in 1852 by Zenas Faunce, Jr., is graced by an iron balcony, which gives the Greek Revival facade a French accent. *(Norman Forgit)*

Tuscan form, tapered with turned capitals and bases set between simple squares of wood. In the Greek Revival period, fluted Greek Doric columns without bases appeared, as well as square columns, often with cutout boards applied as decoration. Wooden quoins, in provincial imitation of Georgian masonry, embellish some captains' houses. Far more common is the use of corner-boards to define and decorate the dimensions of a house. There have been many changes through the years, but today's visitors and residents share with the author of 1906 the feeling that the "ample, square" houses of Duxbury's past are "*right* as well as pleasing."[6]

ALEXANDRA B. EARLE

Cordwainers

Shoemaking and shipbuilding, along with fishing and farming, were the four occupations that filled the lives and the pockets of Duxbury people from the late eighteenth century to 1870. Shoemaking, the least documented of the four, proved to be the salvation of the town's economy when the major employment, shipbuilding, declined.

In the seventeenth and eighteenth centuries, shoes were made either in homes by a family member to meet the needs of the household or by itinerant shoemakers moving from village to village. By the beginning of the nineteenth century, in towns such as Abington and Rockland, groups of shoemakers were brought together to form eight- and ten-man *factories*. These small shops, through a process of combination and expansion, eventually became the footwear manufacturing giants that made Plymouth County the world's leader in the making of shoes.

Duxbury's role in this manufacturing adventure did not reach the magnitude of its neighboring towns for several reasons. The sea provided a living for a large segment of the population. Fishing and harvesting of shellfish had been a source of employment from the earliest days, as had farming. Shipbuilding and its allied crafts was the major employer. Shoemaking, although not a major force in the town's economy at this time, prospered.

The year 1837 seems to be significant. One chronicler of the period noted that 42,000 pairs of shoes and 1,000 pairs of boots were produced in Duxbury that year. Whether this was the high water mark it is difficult to determine, for no other production figures are available. A large portion of the footwear produced from the 1830s through the 1850s went into a burgeoning export trade.

A shoemaker's shop.

The southern states and the Caribbean area became Plymouth County's principal customers. The number of men engaged in shoemaking seemed to fluctuate with the seasons. However, as many as seventy-five men list their occupation in town records between 1830 and 1850 as shoemaker, bootmaker, or cordwainer.

The period from 1850 to 1870 was one of the darkest in Duxbury's economic history. Shipbuilding, the largest contributor to the town's economy during the previous seventy-five years, declined drastically. A domino effect took over. The hard cash which shipbuilding and its supporting services had provided evaporated. With the exodus of shipyard workers from Duxbury to the flourishing yards around Boston and along the North Shore, there was no need for the boarding houses or the farm produce to house and feed the workers, or for the merchants who fulfilled other needs. Those who did not leave had only fishing and small farms to support them; there were few ways to generate cash. Working on shoes was credited with, as one writer of the period said, "keeping the wolf on the other side of the potato patch."[1]

During this time, many of the town's men, women, and children were involved in shoe manufacture. It was all piecework. Leather and partially-completed shoes were delivered to Duxbury from the large shoemaking centers of Abington, Rockland, and North Bridgewater (Brockton). Individual families, or workers in the factories, performed one or two of the steps of cutting, sewing or tacking in the shoe-making process. Two or three weeks after delivering the partially fabricated shoes and leather at selected points in the town, the wagons would return. The drivers would drop off new material to be processed, pick up the completed pieces, and pay the workers.

Buildings connected with shoemaking. (top) This one stands off Summer Street. *(Norman Forgit)* (bottom) The "shoe factory," once a post office and telephone exchange, stands at the corner of Washington Street and Fort Hill Lane.

A letter describing conditions in Duxbury at this time states that within a radius of one-half mile of the Millbrook section there were sixteen individual shops,

Shoemaking

Letter from William A. Jones to Sally C. Curtis and Sarah Ann Simmons. November 3, 1850.

". . . I have often though of you, Sally and John, a peging away these long evenings: I should like, much to run in and see you once in awhile, I don't think there is a little girl in all China that can drive pegs half as fast, I have not seen one, Sally, tell thy father not to give you too hard stints. . . . Sarah Ann, where is she? . . . I see her at home busy as a bee making overhauls for 6cts a pair; cheap enough; I wish I had two or three pairs, to show some of our girls what a little Duxbury girl does for 6 cts . . ."

each employing as many as four workers. Tinkertown and vicinity had several shops, one of which is said to have employed eight men. However, the work was not necessarily centered in any one section of the town. Many families scattered throughout the town picked up leather from the wagons at the drop-off points and performed the work in their homes.

By way of a social note, shoe shops became gathering places for the less arduously employed gentry. They had the reputation, later associated with barber shops, of being male gossip mills where news was circulated and tall stories woven. It was reported the Duxbury matrons were none too happy with the men who spent their free time in such idle pursuits.

The invention of machines for producing less labor-intensive shoes, and the emergence of the large factories that mushroomed in other parts of the country during and after the Civil War, brought an end to Duxbury's cottage industry. There were cobbler shops after this, as there are today, but the mass production of footwear and its economic significance bypassed Duxbury.

JAMES C. PYE

Schooling in Duxbury
1683–1945

*D*uxbury's first schoolteachers were local clergymen. As early as 1683, the sum of eight pounds was granted to the school kept by the Reverend Ichabod Wiswall. The first schoolhouse, erected in 1715, stood at the corner where Harrison and Tremont streets now meet. The spot is indicated by a granite tercentenary marker. Justin Winsor wrote,

> The Town soon after voted to set the building in the corner of the lot; but through some accident the (school)house was placed in the center of the lot, whereupon the rhyme was made, "It is to me a mystery, it is to me a riddle, that there should stand, upon any land, a corner in the middle."

The town voted that the structure should be ". . . 18 feet long, 15 feet wide and 6 feet between joints, and also the Town made choice of Mr. Seabury to get said house built . . ."[1]

By 1735, the town had voted to create four school districts: the neighborhood of Powder Point; the neighborhood of Philip Chandler's and Ensign Bradford's (Tremont and Harrison streets), the neighborhood of Nathaniel Sampson's (North Duxbury), and the neighborhood of Captain's Hill. There were two school masters for the four districts. Each served for half of the year, one at the north end, and the other at the south end of town.

Most of the early schoolmasters who were not clergy taught for only two or three years, but Benjamin Alden kept school in Duxbury for thirty-three years beginning in 1776, earning $7.00 a month when he began and $14.00 a month at the end. Another school master, Isaac Boles, "was a man of learning, but was so continuously intoxicated that he accomplished little good."[2]

Honorable George Partridge (1740–1828), teacher, soldier, and statesman.

Millbrook School, corner of routes 14 and 3A (c. 1887). The tall man by the door is Charles F. Thomas, the teacher. Directly in front of him is Sylvia Alden. Pupils in the back row, left to right: third from left, Etta Fairbanks, Nellie Delano, 9th from left, Fred Walker, Percy L. Walker, Sidney Soule. Lower right, right to left: Winthrop Delano, 4th from right, Alpheus Walker, Sr., 9th from right, Ben Ryder and 12th, Grace Delano Walker. *(Mr. and Mrs. Donald Walker)*

By the nineteenth century, the town was divided into twelve neighborhood school districts, most of which were to exist for over a century: District #1 was the Village School; District #2, the Nook; District #3, Island Creek; District #4, Tree of Knowledge; District #5, Ashdod; District #6, Alden; District #7, Millbrook (now the American Legion building); District #8, Powder Point (the Point); District #9, Tremont School; District #10, Crooked Lane; District #11, the Union School (Surplus Street); District #12, High Street School.

From 1800 to 1879, "The Point School" stood at the northwest junction of what is now Powder Point Avenue and King Caesar Road. This structure, 24 by 26 feet, was built in 1800 for $200. It stood on poles over the depressed salt marsh. Former pupil John Bradford later wrote that at high tide students fished through knot holes in the floor. In 1840, the first-known student government in America was founded at the Point School. Students "made all the rules, appropriated money, arranged classes, and even declared an occasional holiday, while the teacher merely taught."[3]

In the 1830s, Rebecca Frazar ran a private school at her house on St. George Street. After her death, her niece continued the school and it was there that Mary Ashton Rice taught for several years before her marriage in 1845. She had agreed to teach on three conditions: that she would have no more than twenty-five pupils, that none be younger than twelve, and that they include both sexes. Later she would describe her students as successful shipmasters' children who were aware of the world, many of them foreign-born. She remarked on the "brainy qualities of the people of Duxbury."[4]

Miss Rice departed from the tradition of the day by using contemporary publications rather than "school readers." She organized classes in botany and astronomy, encouraged her pupils to call upon her socially during evenings and Saturdays, and organized a post office system for the exchange of letters students wrote to one another in this "little self-centered community."[5] She insisted that her classes be self-governed by the pupils. She also formed an orchestra.

Miss Rice and her students went on fishing excursions, sometimes catching "enough mackerel for breakfasts for the whole town." On one holiday excursion to Clark's Island where they enjoyed lunch and games and playing the violin, teacher and pupils were stranded until high tide at 2 A.M. The students returned to Duxbury singing, "Home Again! Home Again! from a foreign shore," and declaring that "rowing was the tallest sort of fun."[6]

"The launching of a ship was as sure to break up my school in Duxbury . . . as the arrival of the mail in *Ole Virginny*," wrote Miss Rice. Lucky students were invited to stand on board the vessel being launched, and always a half-holiday was declared.[7]

In 1844, construction of a private, three-year high school, Partridge Academy, was completed on the site now occupied by the Town Offices. The academy was supported by a bequest of $10,000 of the Honorable George Partridge. The will stipulated, "In case of applications for admission into said school or academy being at any time beyond the regulated number, the applicants from the town of Duxbury shall have priority . . . free of assessment or expense . . ."[8]

In 1866, the town of Duxbury attempted to organize its own public high school. Classes were held in the Masonic Hall in the village and at Bosworth Hall in West Duxbury. However, the price of male teachers for

First School House

The Town records for 1736–37 report that "The said town, Duxborough, also at the said meeting (March 14, 1736) did by their vote give their School House to Ebenezer Wormal." This was the same building for which the Town Meeting of 1709 had voted "a school house shall be built at the charge of the lower end of the town, and set on the Town Commons on the westward of Joseph Chandler's lot near Plymouth road, and the dimensions of said house as followeth, 18 feet long, 15 feet wide, by 6 ft. 8 in. between joints."

In 1972, William B. Nash, present owner of the Wormall House, climbed through a trap door in the ceiling of his house, which had been considerably enlarged from the dimensions given above, presumably in 1736 when Wormall had received it as a gift from the town. He found that the measurements of his present dining room corresponded exactly with the schoolhouse, and deducted from the finish of the planking and siding up under the roof that the schoolhouse must have been moved and joined to the 1736 house. In this section, the rafters are few and over six feet apart. Two rafters are simply tree trunks with the bark removed.

The connecting ell in the center of the house (below) is now thought to be Duxbury's first school house.

the high school, double the rate paid to the female teachers, proved to be too high for the town. In 1868, an agreement was reached for all Duxbury students of high school age to attend Partridge Academy. Thus, the academy became Duxbury's high school.

In the earliest days there was no separate school committee. Occasionally, the town meeting would choose *agents* to build a school or interview a teacher, but often the full meeting would make decisions on school matters. Eventually a three-member superintending school committee evolved. Sometimes it was referred to as the *prudential committee*. The school committee

School Committee Minutes

Excerpts from the minutes of the 1870s and 1880s give a flavor of the informal but changing nature of the times:

Voted that the town instruct the Committee to choose one of their number to act as superintendent over the schools.

The town voted to authorize the School Committee to employ female teachers to teach two (high schools) of nine months each, providing such schools can be sustained for nearly the same amount of money that is necessary to support one school of nine months taught by a male teacher.

Voted to repair the bell at #2, to put in a new pump, and to have the well cleaned out.

The schools will close on July 3 and begin on August 31.

All teachers are requested not to strike any scholar on the head or pull their ears.

assigned its members to make formal visitations to the schools, publishing the resulting teacher evaluations in the town report. In 1874, for example, the annual report carried the comment that Miss Ida Sears of District #7 ". . . had not the full power to subdue some vicious scholars . . . and did not succeed according to her desserts." Although Massachusetts law did not permit women to vote until 1881 (and then only for school committee), in 1876 Mrs. Mary R. Crocker, a Duxbury teacher since 1863, was elected to the school committee.

Pranks abounded. In 1879, the Duxbury School Committee voted "to write to Mr. Marsh in regard to his son, requesting him to pay the expenses attending to finding of the bell stolen from schoolhouse #2 (The Nook) in the possession of his son, and if paid would prevent it coming before the town." The committee minutes for January 1866, read: "Complaint was made to the General School Committee by Gershom Bradford and Daniel A. Glass that there was a good deal of disorder in their school in District #3 (Island Creek), such as getting out of the windows, breaking the glass and the benches and tearing off the corner boards of the schoolhouse, etc., and that the teachers seemed to have no control of the scholars, and that their school money was thrown away." These vignettes from the good old days are but samples of the rich material available as we examine the history of schooling in Duxbury.[9]

There were 447 students in Duxbury between the ages of five and fifteen in 1872, a number which decreased to 339 by 1883. During this period the school committee closed schools, voted a ten-percent wage decrease for teachers, and shortened the three school terms from eleven weeks to ten weeks each. The vicissitudes of an individual neighborhood school could be seen in the experience of the Tarkiln School #4, which had thirty-eight scholars in 1874, but only twenty students in 1878. In 1880, the school was closed because of a diphtheria epidemic and again in 1894 for scarlet fever. By the early 1900s, Tarkiln sixth- and seventh-graders were being transported to grammar school in the village.

Children who lived nearer to a Kingston school than one in Duxbury were allowed to attend school in Kingston. One year Duxbury paid to Kingston a total of $14.43 for the education of three Duxbury students for the entire year. In 1883, Marshfield was charged $.25 per week for each Marshfield child sent to the Millbrook school. In the 1890s, Duxbury's first superintendent of schools, Dr. E. H. Watson, also served Scituate and Marshfield simultaneously. Duxbury paid $260 of his annual salary.

As the twentieth century opened, 229 Duxbury students were being educated much as they had been fifty or seventy-five years before. Fifty-four of the students were in Partridge Academy, which had three teachers, twenty-three were in the Grammar Class (8th grade), twenty-six in the Village School, twenty-six in South Duxbury, twenty-three at Island Creek, twenty-nine at Tarkiln, thirteen at Ashdod, thirty-five in North Duxbury, twenty-eight at Millbrook, thirty-five at the Point School (now on Cedar Street), and eight at the High Street School. In its annual report, the school committee indicated both its desire for a four-year high school and a concern for tardiness. In 1904, fifty corporal punishments were reported. It was not until 1907 that the state passed a compulsory school attendance law for children seven to fourteen.

After the resignation of Herbert E. Walker as principal of Partridge Academy in 1911, succeeding principals served as heads of both the academy and the high school. The next-to-final year of the academy, 1925–1926, saw the creation of Duxbury High School's first football

team. Norman Hardy was captain and quarterback, Ralph Blakeman the left halfback. With the exception of an 18–13 win over Hanover, Duxbury lost games to Cohasset, 13–6, Hingham, 14–0, Hanover, 47–0, and Kingston, 63–0 and 44–0. This was also the initial year of girls soccer, a sport which was practiced "at recess and after school," as was girls basketball and volleyball. The Camp Fire Girls Club organized school dances.

When the new high school (Upper Alden) opened in September 1927, the school had 203 students in grades five through twelve. The new school enabled the town to

Partridge Academy served as the high school until the 1920s. It burned in 1933; the site is now occupied by the new town hall.

Powder Point School for Boys, an independent boarding school, was founded in 1886 by Frederick B. Knapp on property bought from the Weston estate. The 15-acre campus included: (right to left) Powder Point Hall, which contained classrooms, dining hall, dormitories and gym; Grove House and *the Cottage*, each housing 15 boys and a master. Recreational facilities included the beach, playing fields, tennis courts, baseball diamond, a track, and 9-hole golf course.

close five neighborhood schools: Ashdod, Millbrook, the Point, South Duxbury, and High Street, leaving sixty-four students in grades one through four at Tarkiln and eighty-two students in grades one through four in the Village.

The school curriculum always reflected the times. In 1937, the town was concerned with the entry of children into *pre-primary* (kindergarten) classes; and, in 1940, driver education classes were initiated at the high school. In 1941, air raid protection training was added, as well as an Americanization class for Duxbury's adult aliens of Portuguese descent. In 1943, the school department gave its excess typewriters to the Army and Navy. The effect of World War II upon the Duxbury schools was evident at the graduation of the 15 members of the Class of 1945. Only two graduates were boys.

At the close of World War II in 1945, three school buildings were being used—the Alden High School, Tarkiln, and the Village School on Washington Street. That same year the Island Creek school building was moved to its present location southeast of the Upper Alden School, becoming the "Home Ec Cottage." In its annual report, the Duxbury School Committee was concerned about the "abnormal size" of the eighth grade. There were 38 children in that grade, but most of the rooms would accommodate only 25 pupils. Thus, 1945 marked the end of a chapter in Duxbury educational history. Growth of the schools and the town was on the horizon.

DONALD GERRY KENNEDY

Early Churches

The early settlers in Duxbury abhorred the word *church* because it conjured up such fearful fantasies of papalism, idolatry, and oppression. They had made the perilous journey to this new land in order to separate themselves from that combination of church and state known as the "Church of England." The preferred term that often crops up even today in back country New England is Meeting House. The word *meeting* had a mystical significance that included a sense of sacredness of place and of a community of believers. It is still used by the Society of Friends. By using this term, the colonists indicated that they had divested themselves of the taint of institutionalism, and placed their faith squarely on the perceived revelation of God in the life of Jesus Christ, and in the "body of believers."

The word *gathering* also had a mystical significance. The first Duxbury gathering in meeting occurred, as far as we can ascertain by incomplete records, in 1632. The original meeting house was built close by the Old Burying Ground, a location marked by a granite monument erected as part of Duxbury's 300th anniversary celebration in 1937. This small building was soon outgrown; so a second, larger meeting house was built in 1706, close to the first. This site, too, has a granite marker.

In 1785, the third meeting house was erected off Tremont Street, close to what was regarded as the center of the town. When the fourth was built in 1840, near the site of the third, ship's carpenters produced the lofty and distinctive architectural gem, known today as the First Parish Church.

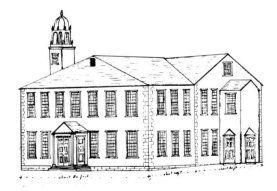

The Third Meeting House, torn down in 1840 to make room for the present First Parish Church.

The worshipping fellowship sheltered here has been in continuous existence since 1632, and in that time had to weather many a storm, including the First Great Awakening that swept the country in the 1750s, stressing evangelical and spiritual revivalism. Half a century later, the church was influenced by the growing Unitarian movement led by Dr. James Freeman, a lay reader and later a minister at King's Chapel in Boston. Unitarianism, developing from the liberalism of the time in reaction against the rigors of Puritanism, was eloquently fostered by William Ellery Channing of the Old South Church in Boston.

A few years later, the Unitarian church in Duxbury was receptive to the Second Great Awakening, humanitarian in direction, emphasizing education, philanthropy, human welfare, and missions. This spirit provided the motivation for free public education, and the public library system throughout New England.

As Duxbury mushroomed with its prosperous shipbuilding industry, Unitarianism became the expression of a new level of human achievement. Duxbury's one great worship center, flowering in its magnificent edifice, became a fitting reminder that here was a cultured and cosmopolitan congregation. As we sit in these pews today and look up at the lofty ceiling, the damask-curtained reredos, and the carved mahogany platform and podium, we know we are in touch with a great day and time.

In 1800, the First Parish Church was Duxbury's only place of worship, but by 1815, Methodists, led by a circuit rider from Scituate, began to worship in people's houses in and around Ashdod and West Duxbury. At one of those services, Seth Sprague, who had wavered in his faith, found it again in the simple honesty and sincerity of these devout people. Touched by the fresh Gospel approach in 1821, he invited them to use one of the many buildings on his 200-acre property in the Snug Harbor area for their services. Two years later, he helped them build a church of their own, donating the land and a large share of the construction costs.

Seth Sprague early became involved in the great issue of the day, slavery, and was elected chairman of the Abolitionist Committee of Plymouth County, and of a local committee as well. When the Regional Conference of the Methodist Church declined to take a stand on the slavary issue, he felt he could no longer remain a member, "in effect providing support for slavery." He read his letter of resignation before the congregation in church one Sunday morning, walked to his pew, slammed and nailed the door shut with six horseshoe nails, and stomped out of the building. Fifty-nine of the seventy-three parishioners followed. The remaining congregation continued to worship there for a short time, but before long transferred to the Ashdod Methodist Church, which had been built c.1831. The congregation later moved to West Duxbury, which had developed as a shopping and business center, where in 1868, it erected the High Street Methodist Church which is still flourishing.

Meanwhile, Seth Sprague helped to build another church when in 1844 he donated land for the present Pilgrim Church. It was known as the Wesleyan Methodist Church until the 1870s, when it was received into the Conference of Congregational Churches. Then it became the Pilgrim Congregational Church, commemorating thereby the 250th anniversary of the landing of the Pilgrims.

This church became the center of political and cultural life for Duxbury's middle and working classes, as the Unitarian had for the wealthier people. A convenient gathering place, with the only available assembly hall of any size, it welcomed all sorts of visitors, circuit lec-

West Duxbury United Methodist Church, High Street, built in 1868. The congregation moved from the Ashdod Methodist Church. *(Philip Swanson)*

turers, returning explorers, theatre troupes, and graduation classes among them. The Congregational Sunday School Picnic in the late summer, and the whole holiday it inspired for the town, became an important social event. Members of the congregation were leaders in all the humanitarian causes of the day, especially the temperance movement, which drew widespread support.

We must bear in mind that Sunday worship at this and other churches was the important event of the week. Some families made an all day trip of it, bringing their own lunches, and feedbags for the horses. Friends met at the churches to get caught up on the news, to plan for trips or weddings, even to initiate business. In the earliest days, the worship service would often last three hours, with a two-hour sermon. Ushers would move up and down the aisles with a football-shaped bulb at the end of a pole which they used to tap the head of a dozing parishioner. Church income derived mostly from pew rents, which were levied on a descending scale, depending on the distance from the pulpit. The treasurer re-arranged the charges as people changed pews and kept track of those in arrears.

For a short time there was a Universalist Church in Duxbury. The First Universalist Society voted in 1826 to buy land for a meeting house from Samuel Winsor. One of the early ministers was the Reverend Mr. Livermore, who married the schoolteacher Mary Rice. The church closed in 1846 and the meeting house was moved.

Pilgrim Congregational Church (left) and St. John the Evangelist Church (right) once housed Methodist congregations. In the 1870s, the former joined the Conference of Congregational Churches, and in 1894, Lucy Sprague Sampson bought the latter for Episcopal services.

Episcopalians, at first members of the Church of England in America, diminished in numbers during the Revolution when many accepted the King's invitation to migrate to Canada, but membership had recovered by the mid-nineteenth century. In Duxbury, the first Episcopal services were conducted in 1873 by employees of the French-American Cable Company soon after they opened the Cable House. Later, services were held at an extensively renovated schoolhouse on Chapel Street. The first recorded service conducted by a clergyman, Gustavus Tuckerman, was held on April 14, 1886, and the following year the Church of St. John the Evangelist was established as a mission of the Diocese of Massachusetts.

Seth Sprague's daughter, Lucy Sprague Sampson, became the moving spirit for the fledgling congregation of Episcopalians. In 1894, she bought for $25 the church building that her father had helped the Methodists build, and in June 1900, Bishop William Lawrence came to Duxbury for its consecration. St. John's continued as a mission for many years, flourishing in summer and closing down in winter, until as more Episcopalians came, they began to hold winter services in the church office, heated by a parlor stove. Many clergymen came for short stays, and one, the Reverend Mr. E. J. V. Huiginn, was instrumental in verifying the location of the grave of Myles Standish. After World War II, under the leadership of the late John Philbrick, the mission received parish status, and has flourished to the present.

ROBERT E. MERRY

Road and Rail

The nineteenth century saw many changes in land transportation. Traveling by boat was still possible, but with roadways widened, travel by stagecoach became practical and dependable. Arrivals and departures from village centers were occasions of great interest, for with the stage came not only passengers, but mail, news, and gossip. Duxbury, typical of many small villages where people wanted to travel beyond their narrow environs, had local drivers and its share of stage lines going in different directions. Colonel Charles Hatch and Benjamin Keene were the first to drive north to other coastal towns. Hiram Walker ran one of Duxbury's earliest lines, which ran from High Street to Hanover Four Corners. In 1810, Leonard and Woodward of Plymouth ran a line of coaches from Sandwich through Plymouth, Kingston, Duxbury, Pembroke, Hanover, Scituate, Hingham, Weymouth, and Quincy to Boston. This route followed the Braintree-Weymouth Turnpike, built in 1803. Fare from Boston to Plymouth was $2.50.

Between the 1820s and 1850s, travel by stagecoach had become so popular that a handbook, *Badger and Porter's Stage Register*, listed the different lines, and their routes and schedules. In the issue for 1825, the following was listed:

Duxbury and Boston accommodation stage, leaves Duxbury Monday, Wednesday, Friday mornings—arrives in Boston in time to dine. Leaves Boyden's City Tavern Tuesday, Thursday, Saturday at 11 a.m.—arrives Duxbury same afternoon. Travel through Pembroke, Hanson, Scituate, Weymouth, Quincy, Dorchester. Fare Boston to Scituate 75¢, Boston to Duxbury $1.37. Proprietors Simon Boyden & Co. Boston. Sirret and Whiting, Scituate.[1]

An advertisement (c. 1894)

The stage which connected Duxbury with the railroad at Kingston, stands before the Alexander Wadsworth house (1867). Oscar Peterson, driver; Peleg Brooks, in tall hat; and Ed Sampson behind him.

We tend to romanticize stagecoaches, but it was a rough, tiresome, sometimes hot and dusty, sometimes muddy and cold, way to travel. The term stagecoach originally applied to a coach which traveled from station to station over a number of stages of the road. Horses were usually changed about every ten miles. With four horses pulling the coach, it averaged four to five miles an hour. Until 1887, travel was prohibited on Sundays, except in unusual circumstances.

For many years the *Old Colony Memorial* carried advertisements for various stage lines which gave the times and localities of stops for changing horses and boarding new passengers. These *halfway houses*, as they were called, were located at regular intervals along the route. Along the shore route were Leonard's Tavern in Scituate, the Old Ordinary in Hingham, and Weston's Store in Duxbury. Going to Boston meant staying overnight. All the lines going into Boston converged in the vicinity of Brattle and Elm streets, where agents had their offices in nearby taverns.

There were connections by stage as far west as the New Bedford–Taunton area. In 1842 a stage line advertised,

New arrangement New Bedford, Plymouth, and Duxbury Stage leaves . . . New Bedford on Tuesday, Thursday, and Saturday at ten 1/2 o'clock A.M. Arrives Duxbury six o'clock. Returning leaving Weston's Store in Duxbury on Monday, Wednesday, Friday at six A.M. arriving in New Bedford to dine.[2]

Duxbury's best-known driver, Jacob Sprague, known as "Jake," was popular all over the South Shore. He drove first for a Plymouth line and then owned his own line in Duxbury, where he lived on Harrison Street. In the 1840s he ran a line from Duxbury to Hingham, where passengers could connect with one of the Boston-bound packets. There was keen competition between the packet lines as well as the different stage lines. Stage drivers competed to provide the fastest, most punctual service, so there were some hair-raising, bone-jarring rides.

Jake Sprague was a bluff, jovial man. Benjamin Foster, who later became a driver himself, said that as a boy he helped in changing the horses when Sprague stopped at John Nash's store in South Scituate. If there was a single twist in the reins, Jake would yell, "Auger in those reins, Ben!"

Like other drivers, Jake often supplemented his wages by doing errands. Pauline Winsor Wilkinson wrote,

> I remember going to his house with a sample of green silk from which a dress was being made, and asking him to get eight yards of guimp for it, about so wide, and the next night when he returned he brought an exact match. He said he could remember about forty errands without a memorandum, but beyond that he had to write them down.[3]

After the railroad lines were completed, travel by stagecoach diminished. The stages still served to connect the railroads to surrounding villages, but they were so much slower than the trains that they could not compete on longer trips.

Railroads

As a maritime community, Duxbury did not easily accept the idea of a railroad. For years townspeople were content to take the stage to Kingston where they could catch trains on the Old Colony Line. The struggle to build a railroad to Duxbury began in the 1846 annual town meeting. That meeting voted to take part in investing in the South Shore Railroad. John Hicks, Gershom Bradford Weston, and William Sampson were among a group who received a charter to build the line from Braintree to Cohasset, then on through Scituate and Marshfield to Duxbury. Weston took part in the preliminary surveys, working up and down the line in all kinds of inclement weather. This exposure to the elements impaired his health for the rest of his life. However, the railroad never reached as far as Duxbury; it ended at Cohasset because other towns showed no interest in the project.

In 1847 another group, including Samuel Stetson, the Reverend Josiah Moore, and Samuel Knowles, was granted a charter from the state to build a Duxbury

Millbrook Station (c. 1900) on Railroad Avenue, where Goodrich Lumber is.

branch railroad north from Kingston. This effort also ended abruptly because there was so little interest. Other efforts, in 1861 and again in 1866, also failed, but finally in 1867, a charter (finalized in 1868) was granted that proved successful. Incorporators from Duxbury included Joseph Cole, Amherst Frazer, Samuel Hall, Bailey Loring, and Nathan Whitney. Three towns were involved, Scituate, Marshfield, and Duxbury.

H. G. Reed, a civil engineer from Scituate, took charge of the preliminary surveys. The line was to be 15.83 miles long. The projected cost was $304,093, but the three towns only subscribed $75,000 each, or $225,000 in all, with the Old Colony putting up the rest of the money. On December 7, 1870, the contract for construction of the Duxbury and Cohasset Railroad went to Mr. Reed for $168,000. The entire job was completed

South Duxbury Station on South Station Street (c. 1900), diagonally across from the Clipper.

in less than eight months, but the roadbed sagged so badly in swampy areas that passengers had to disembark and then reboard further on, where the ground was firmer.

One of the main reasons for hurrying the completion of the work on the railroad was that it was supposed to be ready in time for the dedication of the ground for the Standish Monument. In August, the first train, consisting of two engines and twelve cars, arrived in Duxbury, four hours late. Newspaper accounts reported that this was the "day of days," filled with festivity, despite heavy showers and wilting heat.

Rolling stock of the Duxbury and Cohasset was rented from the Old Colony Line. It was never a financial success: the first year the road showed a net profit of $1,433.98, the second year there was a $2,000 loss, and the third year there was another small profit. The line was unable to pay any interest on the debt. In 1877, suspecting fraud, Henry Nelson, representing the railroad committee of the Town of Marshfield, initiated an investigation. Following a public hearing, the railroad was exonerated. No fraud was discovered, but the railroad was absorbed into the Old Colony network the following year.

For sixty-eight years, from 1871–1939, there was a railroad running through Duxbury. By opening the town to the *summer people,* it made a tremendous impact, both socially and economically. Summer people brought in much-needed business and their property increased the town's ratables.

The railroad provided jobs for townspeople—baggageman, flagman, conductor, freight agent, and engineer. Perhaps the most well-known engineer was Henry Fish, who wrote on Duxbury history after retiring. Men were assigned locations by seniority. Russell Freeman, a ticket agent, had to travel by motorcycle from Duxbury to the

Egypt Station in Scituate before he attained the seniority needed for a position in Duxbury. Many members of the Freeman family were connected with the railroad. Al Freeman, after being "called on the carpet" for being late one day, wrote a poem, the last verse explaining,

> The grade was long and steep.
> The cars full of coal and slate
> and THAT'S the reason
> Al Freeman's late![4]

Another Freeman, Walter, used to take the mail from the South Duxbury station in a hand cart to the post office at Hall's Corner.

The railroads made the public more time-conscious, not only about meeting schedules, but also as they paused to listen to the train whistles. One train was known as the *South Shore Heifer* because of the peculiar sound of its whistle. The 8:30 A.M. and 5:30 P.M. to and from Boston were the businessmen's trains; the 10:30 A.M. and the 2:30 P.M. were used by shoppers going to and from Plymouth.

The trains were met by "barges," used to "ferry" passengers around town and to and from the railroad stations. Three of the best-known horse-drawn wagons, named *Pet*, *What Cheer*, and *Martha Washington*, carried eight to twenty-four people. Helen Eaton wrote that in her childhood,

> The only traffic was a big yellow barge with steps that let down at the back which used to meet the trains at South Duxbury Station and bring us to Grandma's.[5]

Cushing's Livery and Stable on Standish Street at Hall's Corner had two carriages for hire, as well as barges to meet the train. Stephen Currier remembers:

> As a young boy with my mother, three brothers and sister, I would take the train each summer from Newton to the South Duxbury Station. A barge would come

A "barge" ferried vacationers from the railroad station to hotels, boarding houses and summer places. *(Anna B. Millar and Barbara B. Gifford)*

from Levi Cushing's Stable which was at Hall's Corner. My brothers, sister and I would take off our shoes and run barefoot down sandy Standish Street to our cottage on "the Ridge" off Marshall Street. Mother would follow at a more sedate pace in the barge with all the luggage.[6]

In 1937, a resolution was introduced at Duxbury town meeting to dissuade the trustees of the Old Colony and the New York, New Haven and Hartford Railroad (of which the Old Colony was now a branch) from discontinuing service to Duxbury. Service continued for two years, but ended on June 24, 1939. After the Second World War, the tracks were torn up, but the roadbed still passes through many backyards.

JOAN C. SCHLUETER

~ *Timeline*

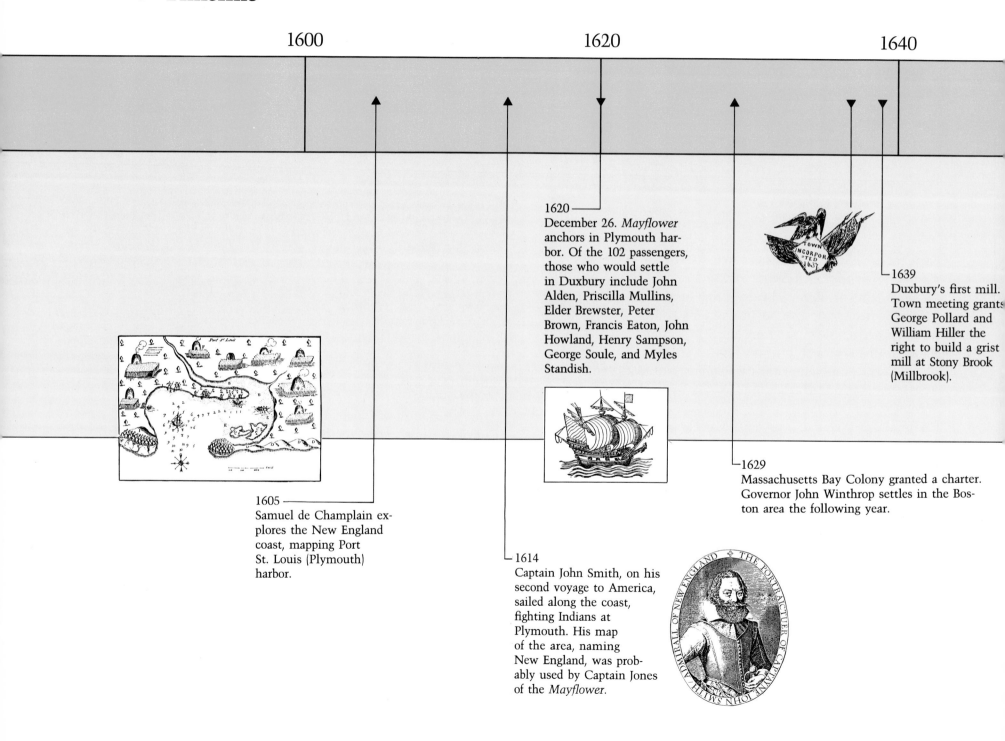

1600

1620

1640

1620 —
December 26. *Mayflower* anchors in Plymouth harbor. Of the 102 passengers, those who would settle in Duxbury include John Alden, Priscilla Mullins, Elder Brewster, Peter Brown, Francis Eaton, John Howland, Henry Sampson, George Soule, and Myles Standish.

1639
Duxbury's first mill. Town meeting grants George Pollard and William Hiller the right to build a grist mill at Stony Brook (Millbrook).

1629
Massachusetts Bay Colony granted a charter. Governor John Winthrop settles in the Boston area the following year.

1605 —
Samuel de Champlain explores the New England coast, mapping Port St. Louis (Plymouth) harbor.

1614
Captain John Smith, on his second voyage to America, sailed along the coast, fighting Indians at Plymouth. His map of the area, naming New England, was probably used by Captain Jones of the *Mayflower*.

1660   1680   1700

1662
Death of Massasoit.

1656
Death of Myles Standish.

1687
September 22. John
Alden, oldest surviv-
ing signer of the
Mayflower Compact,
dies.

1706
Town votes for a new
meeting house (the sec-
ond). Common lands sold
to defray the cost. Robert
Barker and others object.

1712
November 25. "Six men going off the
Gurnet Beach in a whale boat at Dux-
berry after a whale, by reason of the
Boisterousness of the sea, oversetting the
Boat, they were all drowned, viz. Wil-
liam Sprague, Ebenezer Bonney and
Thomas Baker of Duxbury; . . . ."

1653
John Alden builds a larger, two-
story house in Duxbury, the only
house still standing built by a
Mayflower passenger.

1690–91
Duxbury selects the Reverend
Ichabod Wiswell to be Plymouth
Colony's representative to
England to seek a royal charter.
The mission fails. Plymouth
Colony is absorbed into Massa-
chusetts Bay.

1675–1676
King Philip's War. Indians attack on
broad front. Benjamin Church successfully leads combined force of
English and native Americans. Philip
is killed.

PHILIP. KING of Mount Hope.

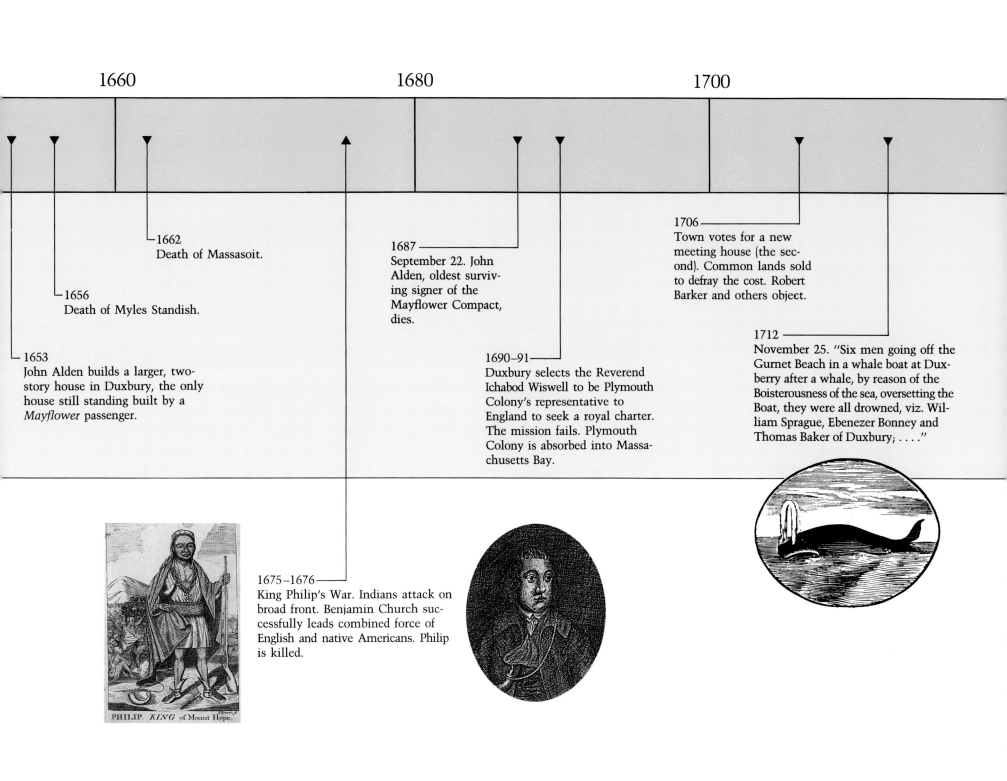

～ *Timeline*

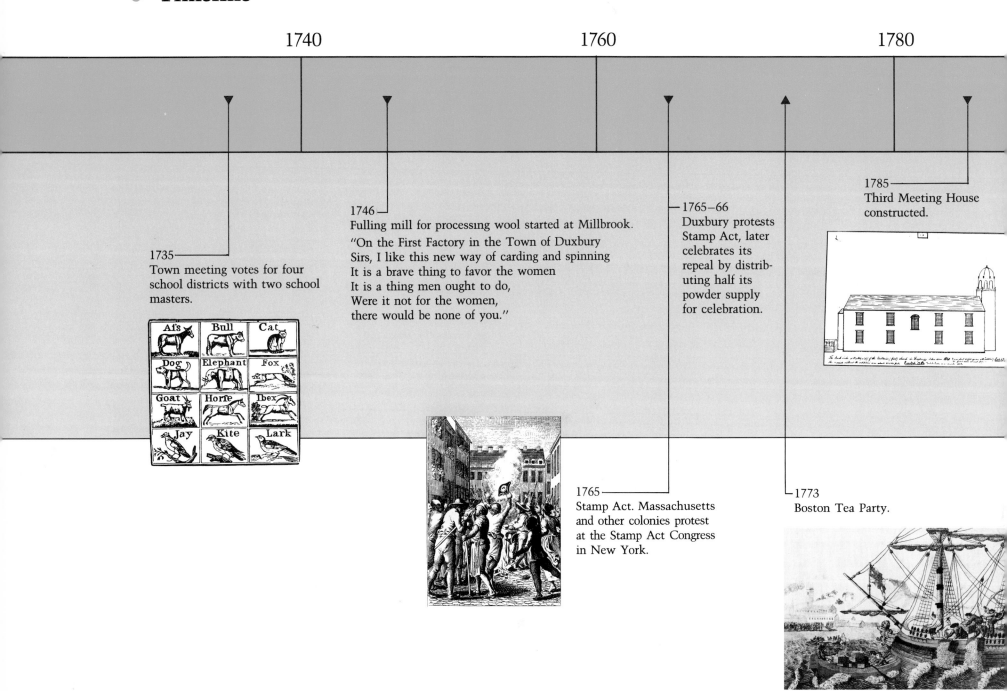

1740

1760

1780

1735
Town meeting votes for four school districts with two school masters.

1746
Fulling mill for processing wool started at Millbrook.

"On the First Factory in the Town of Duxbury
Sirs, I like this new way of carding and spinning
It is a brave thing to favor the women
It is a thing men ought to do,
Were it not for the women,
there would be none of you."

1765–66
Duxbury protests Stamp Act, later celebrates its repeal by distributing half its powder supply for celebration.

1785
Third Meeting House constructed.

1765
Stamp Act. Massachusetts and other colonies protest at the Stamp Act Congress in New York.

1773
Boston Tea Party.

AMERICAN REVOLUTION 1775–1783

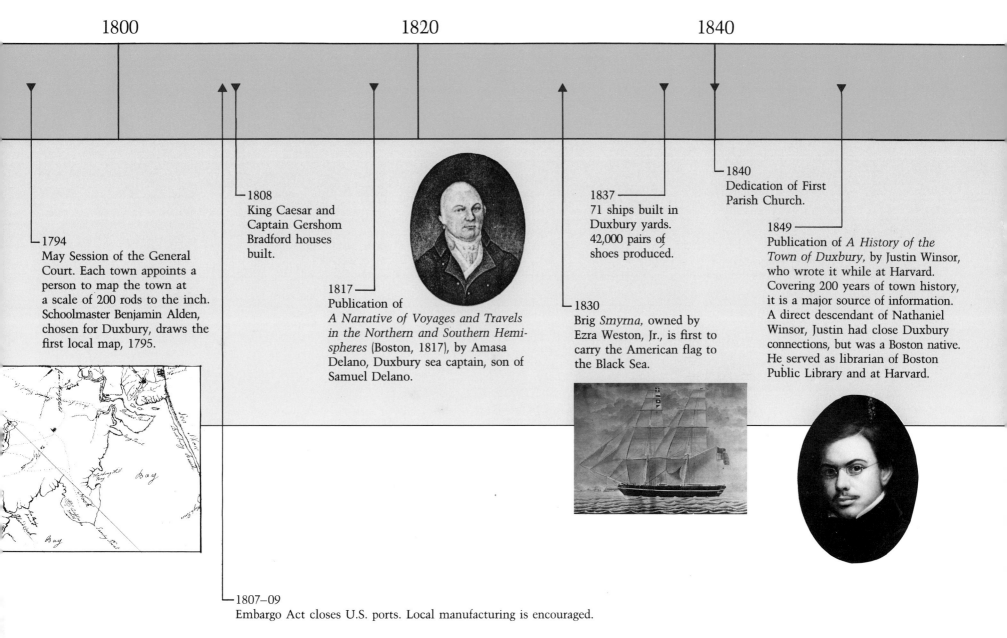

1800

1820

1840

1794
May Session of the General
Court. Each town appoints a
person to map the town at
a scale of 200 rods to the inch.
Schoolmaster Benjamin Alden,
chosen for Duxbury, draws the
first local map, 1795.

1808
King Caesar and
Captain Gershom
Bradford houses
built.

1817
Publication of
*A Narrative of Voyages and Travels
in the Northern and Southern Hemi-
spheres* (Boston, 1817), by Amasa
Delano, Duxbury sea captain, son of
Samuel Delano.

1837
71 ships built in
Duxbury yards.
42,000 pairs of
shoes produced.

1830
Brig *Smyrna*, owned by
Ezra Weston, Jr., is first to
carry the American flag to
the Black Sea.

1840
Dedication of First
Parish Church.

1849
Publication of *A History of the
Town of Duxbury*, by Justin Winsor,
who wrote it while at Harvard.
Covering 200 years of town history,
it is a major source of information.
A direct descendant of Nathaniel
Winsor, Justin had close Duxbury
connections, but was a Boston native.
He served as librarian of Boston
Public Library and at Harvard.

1807–09
Embargo Act closes U.S. ports. Local manufacturing is encouraged.

WAR OF 1812 1812–1814

~ *Timeline*

1880

1900

1920

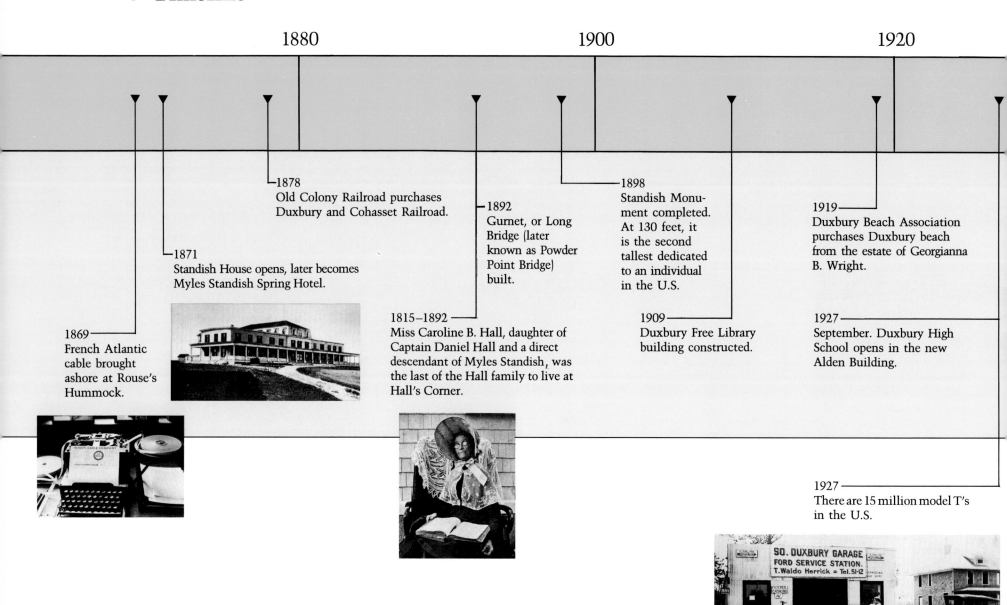

1869
French Atlantic cable brought ashore at Rouse's Hummock.

1871
Standish House opens, later becomes Myles Standish Spring Hotel.

1878
Old Colony Railroad purchases Duxbury and Cohasset Railroad.

1892
Gurnet, or Long Bridge (later known as Powder Point Bridge) built.

1815–1892
Miss Caroline B. Hall, daughter of Captain Daniel Hall and a direct descendant of Myles Standish, was the last of the Hall family to live at Hall's Corner.

1898
Standish Monument completed. At 130 feet, it is the second tallest dedicated to an individual in the U.S.

1909
Duxbury Free Library building constructed.

1919
Duxbury Beach Association purchases Duxbury beach from the estate of Georgianna B. Wright.

1927
September. Duxbury High School opens in the new Alden Building.

1927
There are 15 million model T's in the U.S.

CIVIL WAR 1861–1865

WORLD WAR I 1917–1918

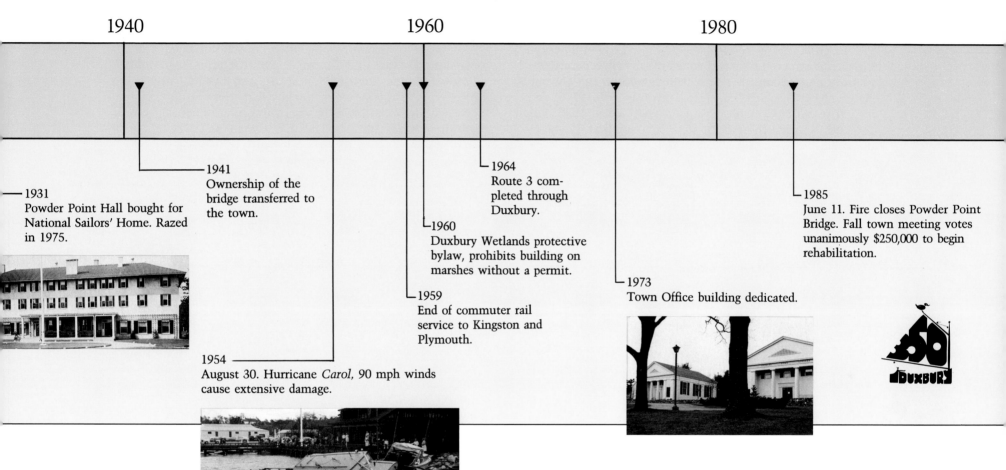

1940

1960

1980

1941
Ownership of the bridge transferred to the town.

1964
Route 3 completed through Duxbury.

1931
Powder Point Hall bought for National Sailors' Home. Razed in 1975.

1985
June 11. Fire closes Powder Point Bridge. Fall town meeting votes unanimously $250,000 to begin rehabilitation.

1960
Duxbury Wetlands protective bylaw, prohibits building on marshes without a permit.

1959
End of commuter rail service to Kingston and Plymouth.

1973
Town Office building dedicated.

1954
August 30. Hurricane *Carol*, 90 mph winds cause extensive damage.

1980
Massachusetts voters approve referendum which limits property taxes to 2.5% of assessed valuation. (Proposition 2½).

WORLD WAR II 1941–1945   KOREAN WAR 1950–1953   VIETNAM WAR 1961–1975

Benjamin Smith, Yeoman

A tomb buried in the hillside at the corner of Tremont and Depot streets holds the bones of several generations of a family named Smith. The legend carved on the door of the crypt begins with Benjamin Smith, born in 1755, and ends with Lillie Collamore Smith, who died in 1935. Six of the eleven buried there once slept in a small story-and-a-half house, still standing about an eighth of a mile down Depot Street. As current owner of that now much enlarged house, I have tried to imagine its first owner. That he was poor and prolific seems self-evident, that he was rep-

resentative of Duxbury's heads of households is equally evident. He was, like almost everyone else in town, white, Protestant, and English by descent, a man who earned his living by the sweat of his brow. It was the only kind of livelihood possible in a semi-rural, pre-industrial community where almost all labor was manual.

Biographical fragments of Benjamin Smith dot the path through a forest of early records. Readers have to plot dramatic encounters and imagine dialogue.

Molly Matson

1755
Born in Plymouth, son of Benjamin Smith, mariner, and Sarah Tinkham Smith.

1776 *August 5*
First child Mary born in Duxbury to him and wife Sarah. (No record of their marriage found.)

1776 *December 10*
Mustered into Capt. Bildad Arnold's company of minutemen as a private. He served fifteen days in R.I.

1778 *January 16*
Daughter Sarah born.

1780 *March 11*
First son, Jacob, born.

1781 *April 10*
Smith signed a note to Jebdiel Weston for seventy-six pounds ten shillings with interest.

1782 *February 17*
Daughter Patience born.

1784 *April*
The court ordered Smith to pay the judgment or be commited

to gaol until the sums of the note to Weston were paid.

1784 *May 25*
Son Benjamin born.

1784 *July 10*
The judgment against Smith was "fully satisfied being levied on real estate."

1786 *July 5*
Daughter Lucy born.

1789 *April 6*
Daughter Judith born.

1790 *1st Census*
Smith listed as head of a household of three free white males (including himself) and six free white females.

1792 *January 4*
Son John born.

1794 *March 7*
Daughter Hannah born.

1797 *May 11*
Daughter Polly born.

1799 *June 25*
Son William born.

1800 *2nd Census*
Smith listed as head of a family that included five free white males and seven free white females. All the children seem to have lived; one female sibling unaccounted for.

1805 *January 11*
His wife, Sarah, died.

1807 *June 22*
Smith married Jemima Whitman.

1809 *December 14*
Smith sold an undivided half part of his land and house to his son, Benjamin Jr., for $540. If repaid with interest within seven years the deed would be void.

1810 *3rd Census*
Smith listed with a family of four free white males and six free white females.

1820 *4th Census*
Smith's family reduced to two males and two females. Smith was placed in the occupational category of manufacturing.

1825 *September 15*
His second wife, Jemima, died, age sixty-six.

1828 *February 28*
Smith borrowed $71.73 from Seth Sprague.

1830 *November 22*
Seth Sprague recovered judgment against Smith for failing to repay. The court appointed appraisers to assess the value of the property.

1830 *December 4*
Appraisers reported, "The amount of the aforesaid sums being One hundred and three Dollars & ninety two cents the amount of this Execution with all fees and charges."

1831 *February 5*
Benjamin Smith died of consumption, age seventy-six.

1831 *November 26*
His son, also Benjamin Smith, Master Mariner, satisfied Seth Sprague's judgment against his father, thus clearing the property of debt.

*A Town
for Summer*

Summer People

They came at the end of the nineteenth century in their Reos and Simplexes, after innumerable blowouts en route. They came on the Old Colony Railroad from Boston for $1.50 round trip. They were met at the three Duxbury depots by barges and schooners—wonderful horse-drawn vehicles, not the nautical kind—their huge domed trunks piled high. These were the summer people, who had arrived for a week, a month, or for the season.

Although Duxbury had already been discovered as a sportsman's paradise for gunning and fishing, it was the railroad which brought the town within reach of city-bound residents longing for refreshment by the sea.

Out on Standish Shore, which was sparsely inhabited, the Duxbury Shore Company, realizing the area's great potential as a summer resort, built a small hotel, the Myles Standish House, off what is now Marshall Street. It became so popular two wings were added and every amenity was considered for the comfort of the guests. It flourished for the next twenty years and catered to the elite from Boston and New York. Word of mouth brought others to the area and soon summer cottages appeared on what is known as *The Ridge* along Ocean Avenue. Stephen Currier resides where his great-grandfather started coming as early as 1876.

Fifteen years later, the Powder Point School for Boys, capitalizing on its ideal location, which boasted a view of the Bluefish River and Duxbury Bay, decided to take guests when the boys were on vacation. During those years and even later, smaller establishments became popular. All up and down Washington Street there were inns and many, many boarding houses.

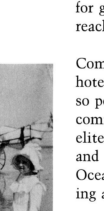

Mrs. Edward Elms and her three daughters.
(Anna B. Millar and Barbara B. Gifford)

In 1908, Florence Stacey and Josephine Sahr, former Radcliffe classmates, visited a mutual friend, Sally Dawes, whose parents, Captain and Mrs. Josephus Dawes, lived on Tremont Street. During their stay, the girls saw much of Duxbury and Miss Stacey was captivated by Abrams Hill. There were only four or five houses standing there then, one of which was the house where the Atlantic Cable came ashore in 1869. However, at the time of their visit, the hill had been divided into house lots and Miss Stacey, being a foresighted young lady, wasted no time purchasing five of these. By 1910, she had built a summer cottage with room for guests to whom she enthusiastically revealed the delights of Duxbury.

Her friend, Josephine Sahr, along with Josephine's aunt and uncle, Dr. and Mrs. Theodore Erb and infant daughter, arrived from Boston. Thus began the Erbs' love affair with the town and in 1913, they also purchased a home on Abrams Hill. Today the house is occupied by the Erbs' granddaughter, and her mother lives in the renovated guest house. The seeds of another summer colony had germinated.

It soon became apparent Duxbury was rebounding from the depression caused by the termination of its shipbuilding. An entirely new financial security was beginning to take root here. Duxbury became such a way of life for these vacationers that it was advantageous for families either to purchase fine old sea captain's houses, when available, or to build their own summer houses. All of this activity became a new industry for the community.

(top) Summer house of Oliver L. Briggs, the first on Powder Point (c. 1870); (bottom) "The Ridge," Victorian summer cottages on Standish Shore.

Swimming off the pier at the Charles Clapp lower house (c. 1900).

Generations of "new" families, along with the Standishes, Aldens, and Winsors, were settling in. Today, along with the Curriers, others can boast of almost one hundred years' continuity. Mrs. Robert G. Millar's great-grandmother, Mrs. William Gardner Benedict, vacationed on Powder Point before 1900, and she later stayed with her son after he built *The Channels* at the end of King Caesar Road in 1907. Unfortunately, this house was razed in 1955. Each Sunday, great-granddaughter Anna recalls having to put on her very best dress and sit through a long and tedious midday meal. With a beautiful Duxbury summer day beckoning, the little girl who loved the out-of-doors found this an extraordinary waste of time. The Millar's own house is built on property owned by her other grandparents, Mr. and Mrs. Edward E. Elms, who had built *Elmstead* in 1915. Great-great-great-granddaughter, Laura Benedict Millar, now six, is the youngest member of this family.

Young and old lived for the season which would bring them to Duxbury. Earlier there may not have been dune buggies, but there were horse-drawn buggies taking families for a day's outing over the wooden bridge. Swimming, sailing, and tennis were sports enjoyed then, just as they are today, with croquet another summer pastime. Social life centered around the large hotels and, of course, the Yacht Club which had its inception at the Standish House. The tempo of the day was three-quarter time, rather than the frenzied pace of the present.

With byways now highways, this little south shore hamlet once hidden amid the sand dunes and marshes is no longer seasonal. Its many charms have been discovered. The summer people aided in Duxbury's revival and later became four-season residents. Their caring and sharing of time and talent have lured many to our historic town.

MARGERY L. MacMILLAN

Growing Up in Duxbury

The first of the pictures that come to mind when I think of growing up in Duxbury is of Mrs. Devereux at Point Elementary School, wielding a fistful of foot-long wooden rulers over the knuckles of my right hand. In those days, opening exercises in the elementary schools consisted of standing at attention for the Pledge of Allegiance to the flag, sitting down with closed eyes and heads bowed over desks for recitation of the Lord's Prayer, and then sitting up with hands folded on top of the desk for a Bible reading. Stern warnings were issued against opening eyes during the prayer; for, as Mrs. Devereux explained, angels were watching and would be very displeased if we peeked through our fingers to see them, and indeed ancient tradition does support the belief that angels were guardians of public worship.

Unfortunately, this particular morning I did peek, and saw not an angel, but the menacing eye of Mrs. Devereux, who, as soon as the exercises were over called, in front of the entire four grades in the room, "Bobby Merry, come up to my desk at once!" Grabbing the handful of rulers she kept on the desk for this purpose, she whacked me over the knuckles several times. Damage to my fingers was repaired in a few days, but damage to my ego remained much longer. Yet Mrs. Devereux loved us all, and regularly dissolved in tears as each fourth grade graduated and moved up to the Village Grammar School.

We were sure also that our parents loved us, but the principles of duty and discipline, seasoned with a modicum of fear, permeated all our relations with them. Punishment proceeded out of this love, and we were warned that our animal nature, like that of the horses and pigs and cattle which we associated with daily, had to be trained and ordered into a pattern that would fit us for civilized society. Permanent consequences for our bad attitudes and misbehaviors were indicated: "You have made your bed, now you must lie in it." Chiefly, it was discipline that groomed us for adult life. Shakespeare's *Seven Ages of Man* were emphasized, and we were frequently admonished to "act our age."

I recall vividly the first time I put on long pants. It was a Sunday afternoon, and all the family were away. We had bought them several days before, and now that my voice had changed, and I had a light fuzz on my face, long pants were in order. So I put them on and went into my mother's bedroom, in front of her full-length mirror. It was a grand and glorious feeling. I had gone through the diaper stage in infancy, the knee-pants stage in boyhood, and now I had become a young man! Girls followed similar progressions through hair styles: first, a fuzzy stage in infancy; then a Dutch cut with bangs; then pigtails at, say ten; and finally flowing hair, carefully coiffed.

Daily household and farmyard chores were allotted according to age and ability, and in our family of nine children, girl and boy responsibilities were divided as well. Girls had inside chores, like making the beds, cooking meals, and mending clothes. Boys had the gathering of wood for fires, the care of horses, cows, and pigs in the barn. Horses were a heavy chore, with weekly grooming and stall cleaning, and wagons and harnesses to be kept in condition.

It was an age when life had specific limits, an order perceptible in the seasons, and in nature in general, and to deviate could spell disaster. Hay had to be gathered before late summer rains fell, firewood needed to be cut and split in early fall, and ice had to be cut and stored when the ponds were frozen to the proper thickness.

Some of our chores extended to neighbors such as Mrs. Jackson, who hired me to tend her coal furnace for

The author about to leave North Hill on his milk route in 1926. *(Robert E. Merry)*

$10 a month. At Mr. C. G. Allen's house, Cora, his housekeeper, gave me my most unusual task, killing the chicken for their Sunday dinner! Every Saturday she had me combine the removal of the furnace ashes with the execution of her bird. It was a weird experience in the darkened cellar, first sifting out the ashes, then proceeding to dispatch the chicken, wearing its cloth hood.

Chopping kindling for the kitchen stove often coincided with the arrival at Duxbury Station of the 5:30 P.M. commuter train from Boston. A cloud of steam would hang above it as it passed the John Alden House

116

and crossed the meadow and the Bluefish River marsh. When the fireman stoked the boiler for the last of the run to Plymouth, the red glare would reflect on the steam, and I could hear the whistle blow for the grade crossing at Harrison Street and know that all was well.

Probably the largest employer in town, the railroad had not only freight agents, section foremen, crossing guards, engineers, firemen, and conductors, but even employed us teenagers to burn the grass along the right-of-way every spring to forestall fires from the locomotive sparks. Standish Hotel boasted it met as many as twelve trains a day bringing guests from Boston. In 1920, I can remember a special carrying a full train load of Duxburyites to the Tercentenary of the Landing of the Pilgrims, when President Warren G. Harding re-dedicated Plymouth Rock in its present location.

The railroad seemed so important to Duxbury life that an outcry arose on notice of its abandonment, in 1939. A vice president, arriving at the subsequent hearing in Boston, merely asked for a show of hands as to how many people in the room had come by train. Not a single hand went up, as they had all come by car. All he said was, "I rest my case."

Duxbury's summer people were different from most resort visitors, who would come, enjoy the breezes and the beach, and then go home. Ours took a real interest in town affairs, lent their expertise to town problems, treated Duxbury as a second home. Indeed, many had Pilgrim ancestry, or were more recently related to the captains of Duxbury's shipbuilding era. When the town in winter consisted of only some 1,500 people, in summer it might increase to nearly 5,000.

To meet this demand, very necessary to the economic well-being of the town, all sorts of tradesmen thrived in what I have called the peddler's era. My father owned two enterprises and sponsored a third: a retail

Watering Trough

In front of the Drew House where the flagpole now stands, the Rural Society had erected a stone watering trough set on a solid piece of granite. One hot July morning, Hortense Merry's ice wagon had been delivering ice to Powder Point for several hours, and the horses, foam-flecked beneath the traces, moved faster than usual, anticipating a cool drink. By the time they approached the trough, the wagon had gathered considerable momentum, and hit the trough, knocking it sideways off the supporting base. Who should pay for this accident, the Rural Society or Mr. Merry? The Rural Society at the monthly meeting voted the repairs with some indignation, for the bill came to a staggering $1.76.

Jack Post

meat business that operated out of the basement of our house on Washington Street, a milk business that was based on North Hill, and an ice business located on Round Pond.

Housewives would order groceries by phone in the morning from Sweetser's for delivery in the afternoon. Fruit and vegetable trucks from Peterson's Farm near the Marshfield border would come by; and even the Marshfield Wet Wash would call for and deliver clothes which housewives would then hang out in their yards to dry. An elaborate system of cards was worked out, whereby a housekeeper would place in her window the card of the peddler whose goods were needed. All of this resulted in a substantial increase in business which kept us going the rest of the year. The summer people were indeed an important part of life in Duxbury.

ROBERT E. MERRY

Hunting and Fishing

Gray-gold October. A season of new light before, perhaps just days away, that permanent melancholy cast of the coastal winter settles down in tones of brown and purple. Across the great marsh a flight of eider ducks, low and erratic, close to the open water as they turn toward the Powder Point Bridge. In the tidal pool, hidden by the long lashes of marsh grass, swim a dozen black ducks. In just a few minutes, a flock of Canada geese sweeps out from the trees into the broad expanse and soars off, a V-silhouette against the bright sky like a stroke of delicate Oriental calligraphy.

To describe our marsh and coast in such solitary moments as beautiful is hugely inadequate. Aside from color and form, it is the fecundity of this fragile estuary that has delighted and amazed sportsmen for a dozen generations. The colonists wrote about it, and certainly the Indians had enjoyed the land for eons before that. From the shellfish, bottom and game species of finfish, to the myriad waterfowl that use the expanse as a staging area in the flyway, the Duxbury coastal wetlands have been far more than a sportsman's playground. Indeed, during some of the darker economic periods, the bay and marshland was an important life-support to the community.

The barrier beach itself, of course, has changed greatly since the days when colonists left herds of cattle to feed on the grassy plains that stretched nearly the entire seven miles. Not-too-old-timers can remember a much higher profile to the dunes, as viewed seaward from the bay.

As the beach migrates toward the mainland, the silting process has shoaled the bay, as most fixed-keel sailors of the region can testify. It is difficult to imagine the Ezra Weston three-masted ship, *Hope*, sliding down the ways into Bluefish River today, bobbing there in the inlet in all her 800-ton glory. Yet the fish and wildlife of the estuary remain rather remarkably unspoiled.

Interior of a gunning stand which stood in the vicinity of Massasoit Road. (*Anthony Kelso*)

118

While herring, mackerel, and eels have been taken from time to time for their commercial value, the real fishing fleet of Duxbury worked offshore. The staple catch of these early fishermen was cod and mackerel taken from George's Bank and the Grand Banks. Along the shore of the bay, several ancillary businesses—curing racks, salt-evaporation, packing and storing facilities—bespoke the seriousness of the Duxbury fishing fleet. During these years, as late as the Civil War, the annual fishing revenue ran between $60,000 and $80,000.

Sport fishing developed much later, and the grand prize of local waters has been the fabled striped bass. The story of their modern decline is both complex and controversial, but decline they have since Jonathan Bradford's day. It was Bradford who commented in his journal after a fishing trip off the Gurnet that the bass were so thick one could cross the bay "drishood" by walking over the fish.

Through the ages, the coming and going of most migratory species has been in identifiable cycles. But still, observes Billy Bennett, one of the town's lifelong outdoorsmen, "there seem to be less and less fish in each cycle." When Bill was a boy, he had hardly ever heard of a striped bass. Then, from about the early fifties on for less than a decade, bass were so abundant throughout the bay that every trip would produce at least three or four good-sized fish. In about the same era, he added, there were so many black duck around that gunners could limit at eight every time. Needless to say, both these prize game species are in a worrying downtrend of their cycle.

Though there is a Bluefish River in our town, there have been periods when local fishermen in the waters would regard bluefish as total strangers. In the later 1960s, many local fishermen would make the trip down to the south side of the Cape seeking the frenzied, exciting bluefish. By about 1970, blues were encountered around Race Point, and within a couple of more seasons, had come across into Duxbury Bay and in along the beach. So erratic are these toothy marauders, that swimmers have been chased out of the water when schools come in and stage a spectacular feeding frenzy. In recent years, schools of blues have driven pogies (menhaden) up onto the shore there to die and rot. One bather in 1985 was not intimidated. Having been warned from the water by the Coast Guard who spotted a school of blues moving down the shore, the man ran up to his car, returned with a plastic laundry basket, and waded in after the school to take a few home to the table—hardly recommended in the book of *Compleat Angling*.

Duck-shooting, still a part of the scene, is nothing like the old days when some gunners might fill a barrel with waterfowl in a morning on the flats or the beach. While we may see plenty of Canada geese these days, twenty years ago they were rare.

"It was a big thing to see a goose out there," says Billy Bennett, who adds, "Today, there's much less pressure, fewer guys out hunting. Years ago it would be just loaded out there. You'd hear hunters crashing and banging all morning."

TONY CHAMBERLAIN

The Gunning Stands

In John C. Phillips' *Shooting-stands of Eastern Massachusetts*, he says of Duxbury beach marsh: "This great bay is one of the best wild-fowling grounds on the coast of Massachusetts. Ducks are hard to decoy, as a rule, but many geese are shot from the several stands."

In the decades between 1900 and 1930, Hunt's Camp, considered to be one of the best, was located half way between the Long Bridge and High Pines, and had a blind about 70 feet long. It kept a gunner there the whole fall, using about 140 live geese, 50 ducks, and around 125 wooden blocks. The greatest year was 1921, with a bag of 620 geese and 499 ducks, a Massachusetts record.

South of High Pines, Barney Williamson's 150-foot long stand was used to kill up to 300 geese a season. Another, known as Dirty Spoon Camp, was owned by the Cushing brothers and R. P. Freeman of South Duxbury. There were several other blinds north and south of the Long Bridge, including the Peters' stand, a house set on posts over the water, from which mostly black ducks were shot.

On Clark's Island a famous goose stand started by Arthur Train, Winthrop Winslow, Fisher Ames, and Dr. C. Rockwell Coffin kept a team of live decoys on the crest of the island above the stand. Migrating geese would light there when the bay was too rough. Usually the bag went to 150 geese a season, but in 1911 it hit a record 328. Dr. Coffin reports standing on the bluff that year after a bad storm and counting 5,000 geese in flight, but with the wind northeast, they would not decoy to the stand.

No traces of these original gunning stands remain.

Jack Post

Sailing and Racing in Duxbury Bay

*E*arliest Pilgrim settlers, on fishing or clamming expeditions, spread sail to help them on their way when the wind was astern. Use of the winds, tides, channels, and shoals obviously has existed as long as man has tried to sustain himself in the area, but the records of sailing as we know it today, for recreation and pleasure, appear first in the late nineteenth century. At that time, Duxbury was one of the earliest sponsors of organized yacht racing.

Of the early days, George A. Green wrote,

The beginning was in 1875 or 1876 when a few of the pleasure boats owned along the village shore and at Kingston and Plymouth and some lobstermen's spritsails from Cut River and Clark's Island got up some races. Of the pleasure boats, I remember centerboard Cats rigged with Jibs, the *Pearl* from Standish Shore, owner Cook; the *Comet*, owned by Nathaniel Thayer, Jr.; sloops *Mary B.*, owner Austin Hutchins; the *Wanderer*, owned by Nathan Watson (later much talked of for skipper of one of the defenders of the America's Cup). . . .

The only real records I found are the dance order and admission tickets for the Dedication Ball which occurred July 13, 1877.

The first Commodore was Austin Hutchins, Vice-Commodore William J. Wright . . . A syndicate built the first Club House on the old wharf at a cost of $600.00 . . . Hutchins was a good Commodore, put things through regardless of expense, and hired a Tug Boat for the Judge's boat at the first real regatta. Hub punch was served on board, as liquors were barred at the Club House. (This rule is still standing except for a few special exemptions.)[1]

Catboats at anchor form a sunflower pattern on the bay. (*Donald Muirhead*)

121

A union regatta was held in Duxbury in 1879; the first to have a neutral board of judges. Then the club went into a decline, but the Standish Shore Association, which had built a clubhouse in front of the Standish House, held a regatta in 1883 and in 1885 acted as a link between the old Duxbury Yacht Club and a revived and incorporated club.

The first 15-footer was built in Boston, apparently about 1908, others in Kingston at Shiverick's on the Jones River. These boats were 25 feet overall with a small bowsprit, keel, and centerboard. Potters, Ellisons, and Thomas Lawson of the Standish Shore were early winners in this 12- to 15-boat class. C. Chester Eaton and the Amesburys did well later in this fleet which was popular until 1927. The large class of 18-footers dwindled to three, and in later years the Ellison boat was used, without a mast, as a nice quiet motor boat.

The 14-foot catboats were also Shiverick-built, a class of about ten boats which raced for many years with Curriers, Huttons, and J. Burns near the top. Henry Erving's *Kotick* and Robert M. Walker's *Katinka* are still sailing around the bay with these sailors at the helm.

In 1916, the 17-foot Bay Birds appeared in the records, gaff-rigged, jib and mainsail centerboarders. Early sailors in this class included Helen Maxwell, Louise Coburn, Charles Sabine, and Horace Soule. The Bay Birds were popular with husband-and-wife crews.

After World War I, there was an influx of *new* summer people, many of whom had sailed and raced in other places, couples in their thirties with families of small children. Welcomed by older sailors, they gradually became the mainstay of growing interest in sailboat racing on Duxbury Bay.

In 1923, it became obvious that there was a need for a small, simple boat for children to sail. The club picked the twelve-foot gaff-rigged catboats designed and built by John N. Beetle of New Bedford. The price was to be $200, but when orders grew to forty, it was reduced to $180. The fleet, called Bugs in Duxbury, was added to from time to time; there are still fifteen or so of this class around the bay, although none of the originals.

Most of the Bug skippers moved on to the Duck class, designed by John Alden specifically for Duxbury. They were eighteen feet overall, with a modest spinnaker. The first twenty-four were built by G. W. Chaisson of Swampscott in 1925. Later on, others were built by William Taylor, who started the yard where Long Point Marine is today, and by Shiverick. The latter group seemed to be faster than the old boats. An investigative committee discovered that the new boats were built much closer to the architect's specifications than the older boats. By 1950, more than eighty racing numbers had been assigned in Duxbury.

The class was a great success for thirty years, particularly enjoyed by married couples. They mostly took racing very seriously, but there was one spouse who always took along a book of poetry to read aloud to her husband if things got dull. Wives were encouraged to go channel-sailing at low tide during the week, even if they had to miss a tea party, to find out where the currents were running. One year, the last race of a very tight season was a disaster. The leading skipper, on the port tack trying to cross his best friend, who was on the starboard tack, didn't make it. He withdrew immediately. When they all got onto the float, the wife of the loser was in tears; the friend's wife was in tears; as was the wife of the new winner. In spite of episodes like this, all had a marvelous time. Ray Hunt was supreme for the few years he sailed in this class. Other leaders in the early years were the Benedicts, Coffins, Huttons, Kelleys, Lawsons, Lunds, and visiting sailors from Plymouth.

Duxbury Bugs, in junior race (1924). Albert Pratt leads the race in #30, followed by Mary Elizabeth Lowe in #23 and Helen Hunt in #17. (*Mr. and Mrs. Frank B. Lawson*)

By 1927, the fleet of gaff-rigged 15-footers began to seem quite antiquated, and a new class, Pilgrims, was organized for the following year. They were 26 feet, 9 inches overall, with the tallest racing masts in the bay. Ray Hunt was again supreme, winning race after race. Commodore Harry Hunt's daughter Helen also did well. Two boats of this class are still in the shed at Long Point Marine.

After the Pilgrim class, there were no new additions to the fleet until after the Second World War. From the 1930s to the 1950s (except during the war), racing continued at about the same level. The names Boynton, Chandler, Clifford, Danner, and Hoyt were replacing the old names at the top of the racing fleets. As the older Duck class skippers became less active, they turned more to cruising boats, mostly auxiliaries, but some motor boats.

The 1954 hurricane *Carol* decimated the Duck class, but some may have considered it a blessing in disguise. Most of these boats were thirty years old, and there were many new and exciting boats sailing in other waters. After trying out the Ray Hunt-designed 110s and 210s, the International 14s, and light-displacement Thistles, Duxbury sailors turned to the new, larger, reverse-shear, decked-over edition of the Thistle, called Highlander, built by Douglass and McLeod of Painesville, Ohio.

These molded plywood boats had a modern rig, huge spinnaker, heavily weighted centerboard, and a hinged rudder for coping with shallow spots in Duxbury Bay. They were very fast and would get up on a plane under the right conditions. Although an innovation for Duxbury, these twenty-foot boats were chosen. Eight were raced in 1955 and the fleet grew to fifteen. The first

with a fiberglass hull belonged to the Everdell family in the early sixties, all superb sailors. The Highlanders provided Duxbury with the best racing it had had for years. The Highlander National Championships were held in Duxbury in 1955 and again in 1968 when Jack Clark became champion.

There were those who thought the Highlanders too big, a crew of four being required to be competitive, and some sailors were still looking for a Duck replacement. Mercuries were tried in 1959, but they were too small. Pioneers were introduced in 1963 and were quite popular for twelve years, but the double bottom, which was filled with styrofoam, leaked, and they became very logy. In the meanwhile, the old wooden Bugs for the children were being replaced with Turnabouts, which are now mostly built of fiberglass.

In 1976, the fiberglass Flying Scots, similar to but slightly smaller and lighter than Highlanders, were chosen to replace the ailing Highlanders. These are great boats, ideal for Duxbury Bay, and the fleet has grown to more than thirty. It took a few years to convert some of the Highlander skippers, but as their old wooden boats developed more and more troubles, they became very happy in the Scots. Duxbury finally has a worthy successor to the long-popular Duck class.

Now, the racing fleets are nearly all fiberglass, and sadly the Bug class is dying. It is getting harder and harder to find enough good boats for the annual Old-Timers Race for which they are so eminently suited. This race, for the Harry Hunt Trophy, was started in 1949 for sailors who had reached their fifty-fifth birthday. Alvah Boynton was the first winner. Bill Ellison has been racing for it for over twenty-five consecutive years and is still going strong.

Except for Bugs, the most continuously sailed class in the bay is the Frostbite Society's Interclub Dinghy,

Fifty years ago, to help Duxbury celebrate its Tercentenary, the Navy sent a four-stack destroyer from Boston, the *U.S.S. Schenck #159*, Captain George Nold in command, with 100 or so sailors on board who were to form a marching unit in the Fourth of July parade. The commodore and vice-commodore of the Duxbury Yacht Club and several ladies sailed a cruising ketch down the bay to greet the *Schenck*, at anchor outside of Saquish. While the two commodores went on board, the destroyer put a launch overboard to take soundings to make sure the ship could swing with the tide. Just after the launch motor was started, there was a *pop* and the launch caught fire. The women waiting on the welcoming ketch were very relieved when another small boat was lowered from the destroyer to rescue one man from the water and extinguish the blaze. The launch was too damaged to be used for transporting the men to the parade, so the much-chagrined captain had to be brought ashore to telephone the Navy Yard for another launch.

The next day being a race day, Captain Nold was invited to sail a Duck. He appeared never to have set foot in a small sailboat, but he accepted. The owner went along as crew, and with a great deal of coaching and cajoling, abetted by lucky wind shifts, the captain won. His junior officers on the nearby spectator boat gave him a rousing cheer.

Duxbury Ducks preparing for a race (1926). View looking towards Mattakeesett Court. (*Mr. and Mrs. Frank B. Lawson*)

designed by Sparkman & Stephens; these boats have been used by the society ever since it was organized in 1955. This hardy group is still the least provincial of the Duxbury racers, going to regattas up and down the New England coast.

Frostbiters begin their season in late September with an "All hands on the dock" start from the old Bluefish River fire station for a race around Bug Light and back. They end their season in late April with a huge regatta of boats from all over New England—Interclubs, Lasers, 420s, and later, the colorful Windsurfers.

Lasers were popular cartop boats during the 1970s, but recently the smaller and less expensive Windsurfers have pushed the Lasers and Sunfish aside. The 420s, an international class especially popular with teenagers,

carries a jib, mainsail, and small spinnaker, with a trapeze for the crew. The 420s are 13 feet 9 inches over-all, self-righting and fast. In the summer, they sail the same course as the Scots.

There is a revived interest in catboats in Duxbury. More than forty are moored around the bay, ranging from the old fourteen-footers to the big, twenty-four-foot Marshalls. These have formed an interclub group, "North of the Cape," for cruising and racing.

After 350 years, young and old Duxbury sailors are enjoying Duxbury Bay as much as ever. We can't think of any other place we would rather sail and race small boats.

BEN & PEGGY LAWSON

The Wright Estate

Duxbury High School is on the site of what was one of the town's most beautiful and opulent estates. Today the only visual reminders are tall shade trees and graceful granite entrances along St. George Street. The land was originally the homestead farm of Philip de la Noye, ancestor of Duxbury's Delano family. In the 1820s, the farm was sold to Gershom Bradford Weston, son of Ezra Weston, Jr. and heir to the Weston shipping fortune. He needed a home more befitting his status than the modest dwelling which stood on the farm, so around 1840 he built a mansion costing $60,000.

A newspaper described Weston at the time as "generous, hospitable, fond of good living, more fond of having his own way, and pretty sure to have it. Mr. Weston is a cordial friend and a constant enemy."[1] On May 30, 1850, the house and outbuildings burned to the ground. They were uninsured. The mansion was rebuilt by 1855, but its drain on Gershom Weston's resources forced him into a foreclosure sale to his brother Alden. Gershom finished out his days in reduced circumstances, living in a small house on Pine Hill Avenue which had been purchased for him by old friends in the Massachusetts State Senate.

Alden Weston put his brother's grand estate up for sale. An advertisement in the Plymouth *Old Colony Memorial and Plymouth Rock* newspaper described it:

> An elegant residence, with barn and outbuildings, and about 20 acres of land, situated in Duxbury, Mass. The house is large, is heated by a furnace, has water closet and other modern conveniences. The grounds are beautifully laid out with orchards and ornamental trees, hedges, and shrubbery. A very desirable country residence for any person wishing one. Will be sold cheap.[2]

George and Georgianna Wright purchased the estate in 1868 for $9,500. The Wrights had made their fortune in cotton. As they were moving into their new home, originally built with shipping money, the last of the Duxbury ships were being built along the shore. An era had ended in Duxbury and a new one had begun. *Summering* was in its heyday, and the Wrights added glamor and excitement to the village.

They renamed their estate *Pine Hill*, and for a time called it *Liberty Hall*. While also maintaining homes in New York City, Brookline, and on Dartmouth Street in Boston, they were considered year-round residents of Duxbury. Noted for lavish entertaining, they gave the dance in 1869 which concluded festivities in honor of the landing of the French-American cable. The governor, the mayor of Boston, and other dignitaries waltzed and toasted the night away in the brightly lit mansion.

For the town's 250th anniversay in 1887, tents were pitched on the grounds of the estate, the house was opened to the community, and field sports were played on the lawns. Even after the Wrights died, the estate was used for town-wide celebrations, the 1937 Tercentenary, for instance, at which lunch was served in tents on the lawn and the wide front verandah was used for the reading of proclamations.

Improved and expanded from its Weston beginnings, the mansion had twenty rooms, one of which included a $7,000 Italian marble fireplace. There were four stables on the grounds, a garage, greenhouse, octagon-shaped summer arbor and pergola in a sunken garden, an ice house, cow barn, water tank, boathouse, and gunning camp. The estate had its own private electrical and water systems, including three hydrants. The Wright's steam yacht *Lucile* was anchored in the Back River near a salt marsh hummock renamed Fire Island.

Pine Hill covered over fifty acres of land between Lovers Lane and Onion Hill Road. The latter owes its

The Wright's steam yacht *Lucile* was too big to negotiate the turns in the Back River, so they had a straighter channel dug.

shape to the Wright's cinder race track which they used for exercising their thirty-two horses. The family also owned four houses along Pine Hill Avenue in which their guests and employees lived.

The Wrights were benefactors to Duxbury. They employed a staff of eighty people, some of whom were given houses and remembered generously in family wills. In 1912, they paid in excess of $10,000 in real estate taxes to the town. They also gave the land, building, and money for the town's first library. But the Wrights also benefited from their extensive land holdings in town. They owned Duxbury's outer beach and laid out plans to divide it into 250 cottage lots. They paid one-third the cost of Powder Point Bridge in 1892 so this development could be realized. The storm of 1898 was sufficiently discouraging to their plans so only three cottages were ever constructed. They owned a sizeable section of Powder Point which was divided into lots and on which

Liberty Hall, the Wright estate on St. George Street, before demolition.

George Wright, Sr. died at *Pine Hill* on March 6, 1897 at age seventy-two. He left his entire estate to Georgianna, who in 1900 married her husband's nephew and administrator, William Wright. "Willie," as he was called, loved horses. A section of what had become St. George Street was the first in town to be black-topped so he could race his horses and sleighs on it. There was a private cemetery on the estate reserved for Willie's horses.

William Wright died of heart failure in December 1912, the *Old Colony Memorial* stating, "He was greatly loved by all and had done a great deal for this town and its people, and was representative for the town some years ago in the Legislature. He did more real good than anybody ever knew about."[3]

Georgianna Wright lived until March 31, 1919. That year's town report states that Duxbury had lost "its generous giver and steadfast friend. She was thoughtful of the interest of the library to the last and among her bequests, she left to the library nearly three hundred books."[4]

Pine Hill was left to Harvard College, her son's alma mater. In 1939, Harvard sold the estate to Eben Ellison and Percy Walker, prominent Duxbury citizens who did not want to see the property cut up into building lots. Ellison later bought out Walker, but never lived on the estate. Over the years, caretakers and occasional tenants cared for the property. In 1966, Eben Ellison's children, William P. Ellison and Harriet Rogers, gave the Wright estate to the town of Duxbury as the site of a new school. William Ellison said at the time, "This is a beautiful spot. It should belong to the town."[5] It was an expression in keeping with the philanthropic spirit of the Wrights.

ANTHONY KELSO

summer houses were built. They also owned the cranberry meadows off Temple Street, and the reservoir there is still called Wright Reservoir.

Two of the four Wright children died tragically. George, Jr. was killed in Boston in an 1888 accident. It was in his memory that one of the former guest houses, stocked with books, became a town library, and that Harmony Street was renamed St. George Street. Florence Wright, the youngest child, died of meningitis at age twenty-four in July 1901. The surviving children, Anna and John, married but neither had children.

Duxbury Free Library

To a newcomer arriving in Duxbury in the early autumn of 1953, the setting, the appearance, and the general surroundings of the Duxbury Free Library greatly differed from the scene we know today. The present Alden Upper School, on the hill, housed grades six through twelve, while the Alden Lower School served as the elementary school. The site of the intermediate school was a declining, yet still verdant apple orchard. Train Field offered but one baseball diamond for the spring season. The corner of Alden and St. George streets, now the location of the Percy Walker Pool, provided the setting for police headquarters in an early nineteenth-century house, being conveniently located almost directly across the street from the then town offices. The Onion Hill area was still undeveloped, and across from the library, the yellow majesty of the Wright estate, *Pine Hill*, loomed above a vast expanse of lawn amidst overgrown and abandoned formal gardens of box and exotic shrubbery. In this setting, with the summer people having evacuated the town, stood the Duxbury Free Library, in much the same posture as when it was dedicated on May 22, 1905.

Entrance was made directly from St. George Street (no parking problems on that quiet byway) up a broad concrete sidewalk, thence up the broad rhododendron-flanked stone steps to the massive front door. Passing through the vestibule, with its stacks of *Illustrated London News*, one approached the circulation desk to be greeted by the welcoming smile of Minnie Burke Figmic, then in her second year as the sixth librarian in town service. To the left, in what is now the Walter C. Beckjord Reading Room, stood a gigantic table on which, to the browser's delight, were placed Mrs. Figmic's carefully selected, and highly eclectic new acquisitions. To the right of the circulation desk, in the

An early library bookplate.

west wing (now the Helen Bumpus Gallery), was a double level of poorly-lit stacks, installed by direction of Mrs. Figmic's predecessor, Fisher Ames, during the austere wartime year of 1942. This area had its own peculiar charm, however, for the upper level, protected only by a token pipe railing, was reached by a retractable ladder, counter-balanced by weighted ropes which rattled down into basement depths when the ladder was lowered for climbing. For the cognoscenti bent on a good "read," the best location was (and is) the Oval Room, then at the back of the building, where comfortably seated in an over-size Windsor chair, one might enjoy the late afternoon sun coming through the ceiling-height windows, or later, in the depths of winter, the snugness of the room as the wind and snow whistled by outside.

Even the basement had its charm. The library had served as a collection point for books for the armed services through two world wars, and many of these remained on the shelves, bound copies of *The Rudder* for the years 1898 though 1915, for example. There were tightly rolled Liberty Bond posters, c. 1918, together with "Remember Pearl Harbor" appeals, c. 1942. This was, in a sense, a synthesis of the town of Duxbury in the last few historical moments of its *summer* years. It has been a distinct privilege to have savored, however briefly, the aura of a quieter and less frenetic period in time.

Duxbury has ever maintained the characteristics of a literate society: a library developed through the generosity and foresightedness of its citizenry; an active, concerned, and intelligent newspaper; and a selective and eclectic bookstore, which is now in its third location, and fourth ownership. The unique campus-like relationship of the library to the core of the Duxbury School system is a further manifestation of this profound quality which has evolved naturally as the town has grown

The Duxbury Free Library with the Bumpus Gallery on the right. (*Fran Nichols*)

during the past three decades. The physical bounds of the library have surpassed the estimates of growth established twenty years ago and must soon be eased by new strategies and techniques to maintain its present service. With worrisome cost factors being felt by all town services, the library has had to continue to combat increased demands with a lessening portion of the tax dollar. As the town stretches toward physical maturity and the twenty-first century, the cooperation of an enthusiastic staff, discerning overseeing by incorporated and elected trustees, and the continued generosity and support of the town must be maintained to continue the norm established over the past century. In a nation faced with the problem of illiteracy which equals, if not exceeds, the concerns of drug abuse and nuclear holocaust, nothing less will suffice.

JAMES F. QUEENY

Physicians

The first person to provide medical care to the earliest settlers was Deacon Samuel Fuller, a "physition and chirurgeon" who was a passenger on the *Mayflower*. Although he was not the official ship's doctor, and apparently had had no formal medical education, he was preferred by Bradford and his brethren. He cared for the Plymouth settlers, "a great help and comfort to them," until his death in the epidemic of 1633.[1]

Comfort Starr, Duxbury's first doctor, came from Cambridge in 1638 when he bought a dwelling house and land from Jonathan Brewster. Although he had received a grant of 120 acres between the North and South rivers in 1638, and was admitted as a freeman in Duxbury the following year, he left Duxbury for Boston where he died in 1659.

Duxbury's next doctor, Samuel Seabury, came from Boston to settle before 1660, when he bought Comfort Starr's house and land. After Seabury's death in 1661, he was succeeded by his son Samuel. Samuel Jr. was a prominent citizen, serving the town as treasurer and representative to the colony court, and as an ensign in King Philip's War.

Another early Duxbury physician was Dr. Thomas Delano, son of Philip de la Noye, who had come over on the *Fortune* in 1621. Dr. Delano built a small house on the Bay Path (now High Street) far from the shore in West Duxbury, where he lived with his wife Rebecca, daughter of John and Priscilla Alden.

Dr. Eleazar Harlow (c. 1717–1800), prosperous and well-liked, was plagued by tragedy. The great-grandson of William Harlow, a cooper who had come from England, he lived in the Millbrook area where he was a partner of John Southworth in operating a grist and fulling mill. He also had extensive interests in the Maine fur trade, so his medical practice may have been secondary. When

Dr. John Porter (1795–1865) served as Duxbury's "beloved physician" for forty-five years.

131

Dr. Harlow's first two wives died, he married the widow Dabney of Boston. In 1766, his house burned and a daughter and step-daughter died in the fire. His wife escaped by jumping from a second-story window into a snowbank. Once again, in 1797, when the doctor was about eighty, he lost his house and all its contents in a fire, but he spent his remaining years living peacefully with his son Gideon in a house which still stands in the Crooked Lane neighborhood.

Dr. John Wadsworth (c. 1706–1799), great-grandson of early settler Christopher Wadsworth, was a "Practitioner of Physicks." A self-taught physician who apprenticed under a Dr. Haynes in Marshfield, he married Mary Alden in 1734. Their daughter Salumith married Ezra Weston in 1770. An ardent patriot, Dr. Wadsworth

The Nurse Association

The Duxbury Nurse Association, founded in 1918, offered vital health care to the community. At a meeting on September 21, 1918 at the Unitarian Parish House, the association was organized with Mrs. Roger Spaulding as president and five vice-presidents, four directors, and committees for Advisory and Child Welfare, Bed Clothing, Nursing Supplies, and Automobile. Mrs. Spaulding was instrumental in bringing Duxbury's needs to the attention of the community. A graduate nurse herself, she had children in the local schools and had learned of health problems through her husband's practice.

In 1969, service by the Plymouth Community Nurse Association was extended to Duxbury, through a contract with the Duxbury Board of Health. The agency was well-received and services have been continued.

was a captain in the militia at the beginning of the Revolution. Energetic and eccentric, he was believed to possess extraordinary powers, so was consulted "concerning stolen property, absent friends and coming events."[2]

When Rufus Hathaway (1770–1822), an itinerant artist, married Judith Winsor, her family encouraged and paid for him to enter the medical profession, so he apprenticed to Dr. Winslow in Marshfield and then became Duxbury's only physician. His house and office were on Washington Street.

Dr. James Wilde graduated from Harvard in 1832 and practiced in Duxbury for forty years. He lived on St. George Street. His name is mentioned in town reports for examining Civil War recruits, for providing medical attendance at the Alms House, and for serving on the School Committee, Board of Health, and Board of Trustees for Partridge Academy. The first-known folding bed, made for Dr. Wilde by his father, is on display in the King Caesar House.

Another doctor who lived on St. George Street at about the same time was Dr. John Porter whose home and office were where the Percy Walker Pool now stands. "Everyone knew and loved Dr. Porter, who had a large practice, going far and near, his old horse jogging on often while the doctor took a nap. He made long calls, often staying for supper. His wife, too, was very prominent, being very kind to the sick or poor."[3]

Dr. Edward Perry Wadsworth practiced in Boston but also saw patients at his house at the end of Bayberry Lane. He gave each of his seven children a house and funds for its maintenance. Two of these houses still stand on Washington Street.

Dr. Ira Chandler moved from Chandlerville in Tarkiln to the Nook where he built a house on Standish Street. He became well-known as an herb doctor.

Dr. Nathaniel Kingsbury Noyes (1865–1945)
practiced in town from 1892 to 1933.

Dr. Nathaniel Kingsbury Noyes (1865–1945) was born in Manchester, New Hampshire. After receiving his M.D. from Dartmouth Medical School in 1889, he practiced in Duxbury for over forty years from 1892 to 1933. He was an active member of the Board of Health, served as a captain in the Medical Corps in the First World War, and was school physician until 1931. His house, office, and barn were on Washington Street in the area of Long Point Marine. In the early days of his practice, Dr. Noyes made house calls by horse, wagon, sleigh, and on snowshoes, making many trips to the Gurnet on horseback. In 1905, he bought the first Ford in southeastern Massachusetts.

Dr. Roger Spaulding from Cambridge, a graduate of Harvard College and Harvard Medical School, practiced in Duxbury from 1904–1957, first as a summer resident. His house stood opposite Dr. Noyes' with whom he served as school physician when Dr. Connie King was in the service. Dr. Spaulding delivered almost two thousand Duxbury babies in their homes, but used Massachusetts General Hospital for patients requiring hospitalization.

Dr. Connie King came to Duxbury in 1932. Born in Alabama in 1907, he was a graduate of the University of Tennessee Medical School. He had an extensive local practice from 1934 until 1948. Chief of Anesthesia at the Jordan Hospital, he was also medical agent for the Board of Health, a cemetery trustee, and school physician except during the war years. His office on Cedar Street would successively become the offices of Drs. Walter Deacon, Lansing Bennett, James Peters, Jr., Donald Muirhead, and Leo Muido.

Dr. Deacon, who took over Dr. King's practice, served as school physician, and was succeeded by Dr. Sidney Wiggin, Dr. Arthur Kuntz, Dr. Donald Muirhead, and Dr. Leo Muido.

In more recent years, Duxbury physicians have included Dr. George Starr, renowned decoy carver and collector who practiced on Washington Street, and Dwight Fowler, who practiced on Cove Street. Dr. Starr served as agent for the Board of Health from 1948 to 1982. He was succeeded by Dr. Donald Muirhead.

Since 1838, there have been dentists in Duxbury. A dental clinic was established at the high school in 1929.

In recent years there have been many specialists, radiologists, orthopedic surgeons, allergists, obstetricians, internists, surgeons, pediatricians, and others who have offices in Duxbury and are staff members at the Jordan, South Shore, or Boston hospitals. They have brought modern medical practice to Duxbury.

JEAN HUDSON PETERS

Duxbury Stores

When Duxbury citizens got about on foot, each neighborhood had its own general store, usually operated in conjunction with the post office. The proprietors often lived above the stores, which served as neighborhood centers for the exchange of mail, merchandise, and information. Customers might barter for the items they needed: a basket of eggs for a yard of percale. They would bring their own containers: jugs to hold molasses or milk and cream, and homemade bags, sometimes made of handwoven material, for carrying their purchases.

Often merchants would come to the householders. Stores delivered daily and there were peddlars who followed regular routes through town. Charlie Gleason, a "dry goods" man, would drive around once a week with an assortment of items like needles and thread, yard goods, hair nets, buttons, bows, and candy. Another peddlar, Jacob Shiff, a familiar and respected figure, eventually owned a successful shoe store in South Duxbury.

Nancy M. Houghton

Interior of Peterson's Store (1901).

(top) The village drugstore, originally run by Nelson Stetson, then taken over by Paul Peterson in 1907, is located on Washington Street. (right) Washington Street and Sweetser's Store in the early 1900s.

The Theatre

heatre in Duxbury has been, and is, primarily of the do-it-yourself variety. "For pleasure, not for pay," has been the motto. Sometimes performances are given for the benefit of a worthy cause. An undated, except for "July 25 and 26," flier survives, advertising "Entertainment to aid St. John's Episcopal Church at Mattakeesett Hall." The flier lists the *programme* as an overture, several original sketches, "coon songs," a petite comedy, solo and Spanish dances, "feats of legerdemain," and a "Comedietta," after which "the Hall will be cleared for DANCING." This probably took place around the turn of the century.

Aside from its ingredients, the entertainment's historic interest lies in the participants, including several members of the William Seymour family—James William Davenport Seymour, John Russell Davenport Seymour, Miss May Davenport Seymour, and William Seymour himself. The Seymours were theatre professionals performing in an amateur capacity "at home" for their own pleasure, for the amusement of their neighbors, and in this case, for the benefit of St. John's Episcopal Church.

The Davenport/Seymour families lived at least part of each year in Duxbury through several generations. Fannie Davenport and Harry Davenport were the most famous, Fannie on the world's stages, and Harry, later, as a ubiquitous Hollywood character actor. Fannie built a great estate on Washington Street across the way from her sister, Mrs. Seymour.

William Seymour's granddaughter, Joan Field, launched a summer stock company in Duxbury shortly after World War II. A Broadway actress, she came back to Duxbury with director/producer Albert Moritz and approached the citizenry for financial backing. Money was needed to support the endeavor until it could support itself, and individuals were needed to paint scenery, collect props, sell tickets, and act, inasmuch as few actors could be brought in from New York. Those who were would be paid meagerly. (This writer was one of those meagerly paid a few seasons later.)

Duxbury Playhouse, the former Bay Farm barn, which housed a professional summer theatre in the late 1940s and the Plymouth Rock Center of Music & Drama in the early 1950s.

135

Both money and talent were forthcoming, and the Duxbury Playhouse opened in the old GAR Hall on Washington Street, upstairs on the second floor, which had a tiny stage onto which both exits and entrances had to be made directly from outdoor staircases. *The Women* was the most ambitious play produced there with Roberta Cutler playing Crystal in the famous bath-tub scene.

Meanwhile, up the street, Franklin Trask of the Priscilla Beach Theatre was launching another semi-professional troupe in Mattakeesett Hall. He didn't fare well, however, competing with so many Duxbury families who had not only their money, but also their members, in the Duxbury Playhouse. Following Trask's retreat, Joan Field moved her company of players into the more commodious Mattakeesett Hall.

Modest success engendered major ambition. Increased financial support from Elbert Harvey, Margaret Metcalf, B.F. Goodrich, Jr., Russell Eddy, and others allowed the Field/Moritz enterprise to acquire the old Bay Farm buildings at the corner of Bay Road and Park Street. The enormous old barn was turned into a rustic but beautiful theatre, dependencies became galleries and rehearsal halls. Cid Ricketts Sumner cut the ribbon for the opening and Duxbury residents flocked to the Duxbury Playhouse, Theatre, and School, which was the "in" social spot for several summers.

Ticket sales and student fees could not support such a sizeable operation, however, so in spite of substantial and continuing contributions from numerous Duxbury *angels*, The Duxbury Playhouse closed at the end of the summer, 1950.

Concurrent with the Playhouse development, David Blair McClosky had been creating an ambitious venture called Plymouth Rock Center of Music and Drama, which gave its first productions in a hall at the Kingston Public Library in 1945. They moved to Memorial Hall in Plymouth in 1947. With the demise of the Playhouse, McClosky and his wife, Barbara, both well-known voice coaches and singers, moved their company into the Bay Farm complex, with the blessing and support of many of those good people who had backed the Field effort. Plymouth Rock Center of Music and Drama had its first Duxbury season in 1951.

For the next five years, they provided highly professional performances of operas, operettas, and plays. Critics came from as far away as the San Francisco *Chronicle* to review productions. In the crucial fifth season, a major backer was lost, so the Center closed in 1955. Shortly thereafter, all but one of the buildings were demolished. The only visual reminder of what was once a vital theatre center is a magnificent copper beech which stands in the middle of the yard.

Preceding these semi-professional activities, and succeeding them, were two Duxbury institutions: the American Legion Minstrel (later Variety) Show, and the Duxbury Yacht Club Show. Both were annual events drawing on local talents, young and old, as the Yacht Club Show continues to do.

In 1932, Eben Briggs, Walter Prince, and George Newitt drove to Plymouth to see if George Phillips would allow his daughter Harriet (age 17) to direct the first minstrel show planned by the Duxbury Post of the American Legion. Phillips was famous for his minstrel productions.

Father said *yes*. Harriet Phillips (later Crocker) came and conquered, directing all but two American Legion shows over the next thirty-six years. When Mrs. Crocker's health failed in 1968, the shows stopped. They had ceased being minstrel shows when blackface became unacceptable, switching to straight variety—though many of the popular musical portions were retained, most notably the tambourine overture. There must be hundreds of men and women in Duxbury who were in one of Harriet Crocker's tambourine routines. It was part of growing up. If they didn't participate in the American Legion Show, they slapped, shook, and rattled in the Yacht Club Show which carries on the tradition.

For more years than anyone can remember, the Yacht Club has presented a variety show each summer, with casts as large as 125, which means if you add all those working behind the scenes and out front, approximately one-quarter of the club membership might have been involved. Original music, lyrics, and libretto are written each year by local talent, though in the dim past, some musical comedy material was adapted.

Open to the public, the show has over the years raised thousands of dollars, which for a time were given to the Boston Children's Hospital, but in recent years have been added to other monies the Yacht Club gives to Duxbury High School annually for scholarships. Cherished awards presented each year at the close of the show are the Yacht Club Theatrical Award, which is given to a person who has worked on the production, on stage or otherwise, and has made an outstanding contribution; and the Lee Daniels Awards, one to a junior member of the cast and one to a senior, both to mark special performances. Lee Daniels directed the shows for a number of years.

In the 1980s, theatre in Duxbury means to most people the Bay Players. This very active group celebrated its 30th anniversary in 1986, having presented three major productions each year since 1964. Too many people have been involved in Bay Players to single out any for special mention.

Two Duxbury teachers, Donald Prigge and Larry Dunn, were instrumental in starting the group, first experimenting with an English comedy, *Miranda*, performed "in the round" in the auditorium of what was then Duxbury High School in the fall of 1955. The enthusiasm engendered by this effort led to formal estab-

Duxbury Playhouse production of *Tammy* with Joan Field (left), Roberta Cutler (center), and Dorothy Pease (right). The men are actors from New York. The play was written by Cid Ricketts Sumner and Al Moritz from Mrs. Sumner's novel. (*Roberta S. Cutler*)

lishment of the organization of Bay Players on April 26, 1956, with *The Happy Time* as their first production.

The demands of lavish productions, especially the musicals, and the high standards which they seek to achieve, has opened membership and participation to residents throughout the region. Bay Players remains a Duxbury entity, however, making many contributions to the community beyond those of providing live theatre experience. In 1970, for instance, to honor a distinguished member, Bay Players established the Everett Marston Theatre Award, which is given each year to a graduating Duxbury High School senior.

Do-it-yourself theatre has served Duxbury well. There is every expectation that it will continue.

ROBERT D. HALE

The French Atlantic Cable

On July 6, 1868, the government of France granted the French Cable Company a charter, giving it the exclusive right for twenty years, to construct and operate a submarine cable from Brest, France to the coast of the United States, upon the condition that no soil foreign to France or the United States be touched by the cable in transit.

As soon as the charter was issued, the French Cable Company was organized and within eight days, $6 million of capital was raised. On the day the subscriptions were closed, an advance payment of $1 million was turned over to the Telegraph Construction and Maintenance Company, the same company that had successfully, after four earlier failures, laid the transatlantic cable in 1866 from Ireland to Newfoundland. This company was the only one large enough to undertake the project, which called for a cable not only 1,500 miles longer than the Ireland–Newfoundland project, but larger as well. The cable was 1¼ inches in diameter and when completed, weighed close to 6,000 tons.

Great care was taken in selecting the best route, along which meticulous soundings were made, a route ultimately running from Brest, under the Atlantic, to the southern edge of the Grand Banks, thence to the French island of St. Pierre, off the south coast of Newfoundland, then down past Cape Breton Island and Nova Scotia, ending at Duxbury. The average depth of the submarine plateau for the French Cable was considerably less than that of the cable from Ireland to Newfoundland; furthermore, by avoiding the northern edge of the Grand Banks, the track was entirely free of any danger from ice and did not cross any anchorage area for fishing vessels. The *Great Eastern* was chartered for the project. It was the same vessel used in laying the earlier transatlantic cable, the only ship in the world large enough to carry the entire cable in her three huge tanks.

The telegraph office at the Cable House.

The landing of the French Atlantic cable, July 1869. (*Massachusetts Historical Society*)

After eight months of preparation, the expedition set forth from Brest for St. Pierre on June 21, 1869. The *Great Eastern* was accompanied by two consort ships, the *Chiltern* and the *Scanderia*, while a third ship, the *William Corey*, went ahead to St. Pierre to run in the heavy shore end, and so be ready for splicing to the main cable. Each of these ships carried a section of cable and was fully equipped with grappling irons, buoys, and picking-up tackle, as well as a paying-out machine similar to that on board the *Great Eastern*.

For the first three days all went well, but on the fourth, a gong mounted on the wall outside the testing room sounded an alarm. The ship was stopped and the engines reversed, as tests showed evidence of a fault in the cable a short distance astern. With the hauling-in machinery in operation, the fault was soon located and proved to be a minute hole that penetrated the layers of gutta-percha. It was cut out, a new splice made, and the paying-out operation resumed.

Another fault was discovered on June 26, with no more serious trouble than the first, but on June 29, the weather suddenly changed to a heavy gale. During the storm another fault showed up on the testing instruments, and again the engines were reversed, and the hauling-in commenced. As the wind increased in intensity, the gauge on the stern indicated that the strain on the cable was increasing at an alarming rate. Then when the ship heaved up on a huge wave, the cable snapped, fortunately just inside the mechanical brake. With quick action of the crew, the brake caught before the broken cable-end could run over the stern. Since the gale was too severe to risk hauling-in any longer, the broken end was secured to a huge buoy and set adrift. Two days later when the storm had moderated, the buoy was picked up and the fault repaired.

After running through another gale without trouble, the fleet finally arrived off St. Pierre and spliced the cable to the heavy shore end. With their part of the task completed, the *Great Eastern* and the *William Corey* headed for home, while the *Chiltern*, paying out the final section of the cable, headed for Duxbury, with the *Scanderia* accompanying her. Most of the remaining course ran through the relatively shallow waters of the Continental Shelf, so when the cable broke once more, the crew had no difficulty repairing it quickly.

On July 23, 1869, the fleet anchored about half a mile off Duxbury Beach, opposite the small knoll known as Rouse's Hummock. The cable ships were soon surrounded by small craft of every description, and a delegation from Duxbury came aboard to congratulate the captain and crew. Late in the afternoon, the heavy two-inch shore end of the cable was ready for landing. They hauled enough scope from the hold of the *Chiltern* to reach the shore. They carefully coiled the cable on a platform of planks lashed to two large sea-boats, until the entire contraption was ready to be towed to the beach. As the boats grated on the sand, salutes were fired from the ships, and the thousand people who had gathered to witness the final linking of the old world with the new burst into cheers. With a sudden rush to the landing place, many eager spectators helped to run the cable up over the beach to the little hut which had been built beside the hummock to receive it. There, tests found that the cable was in perfect condition. Soon

signals were sent and received from Brest, including one to Emperor Napoleon III announcing the successful completion of the enterprise. It was the first direct line of submarine communication between Continental Europe and the United States, a distance of more than three thousand miles.

In anticipation of the landing of the cable, Duxbury Town Meeting voted for a mammoth celebration to be held July 27, 1869. They invited the Governor of Massachusetts, the Mayor of Boston, and a host of lesser celebrities. When the day arrived, the Plymouth Band was on hand, two cannon of the Second Massachusetts Light Battery were belching fire and smoke in salute, a huge tent had been erected on Abrams Hill to shelter six hundred banqueting guests, while thousands more crowded around to watch the festivities.

Meanwhile, work crews had been struggling to finish laying the cable across the marshes to the tent, so that greetings could be exchanged with France during the ceremonies, a task which seemed impossible. At about six o'clock in the evening, the laborers triumphantly appeared with the end of the cable and ran it right into the tent. Amid band music and deafening salutes of artillery, people jumped onto the tables and cheered the final completion. More jubilation took place at a party in the elegant Wright House that evening, and in the next few days, the cable was entrenched in Cove Street and on down to the Duxbury Bank Building at the corner of St. George and Washington streets, which was then renamed the *Cable House*.

Originally a busy office, the Duxbury terminal gradually declined in activity as new and more efficient communications took over, until it was closed at the end of World War II after a long and useful term of service.

FRANKLIN K. HOYT

Clam Digger, Duxbury, Mass by J.J. Enneking (1841–1916) was painted on the Standish Shore.
(*Mr. and Mrs. Abbot W. Vose*)

Winslow Farm, Eagles Nest. (*Fran Nichols*)

Harvesting Cranberries. (*David C. Bitters*)

Hautboy Castle, summer home of Mr. and Mrs. Horace H. Soule, Sr. Watercolor by Charles Russell Loomis. Two buildings which once housed workers at Ezra Weston's shipyard were moved across the marshes to form the rear section of this house, which stood on Fort Hill Lane. (*Mrs. Horace H. Soule*)

Frostbiters. (*David C. Bitters*)

Start of catboat race in Duxbury Bay.
(*Carleton Knight, Jr.*)

145

Bluefish River Bridge.
(*Joan B. Hacker*)

4:20 a.m. June 11, 1985. The Bridge Fire.
(*Judith Klutzow Blanchard*)

146

Dawn over Duxbury Bay. (*Deni Johnson*)

Shirley family bicyclist,
Fourth of July parade (1976).
(*Carleton Knight, Jr.*)

Sweetser's General Store, by Marie Fox (1986).
(*Mr. and Mrs. John Turner*)

148

The Bridge

About 4 A.M. on Tuesday, June 11, 1985, someone living on Powder Point awoke to see billowing clouds of smoke, and to realize that the bridge was burning about a quarter mile from shore. The fire department quickly responded and soon put out the fire, which had destroyed about twenty feet of the planking, with not much damage to the pilings. That was repaired easily enough in July; but a state inspection led to a much more serious closing, when it was discovered that the underpinnings of almost the entire bridge were so eaten away that the whole structure was considered unsafe and was summarily closed to all vehicular traffic.

The Gurnet, Long, or Powder Point Bridge, as it has variously been called, was first opened to the public in October 1892, a gala occasion for Duxbury. Two years earlier, the Plymouth County Commissioners had been petitioned to lay out a highway and bridge across Duxbury Bay from Powder Point to Gurnet Beach. Conservationists and many residents objected strenuously, but proponents of the bridge won, and work began on the 2,200-foot-long structure supported on heavy pilings with (at first) a draw over the deep channel area.

In October 1892, the *Boston Herald* reported: "Gurnet Beach is a long, narrow slip of white quartz sand which extends southeasterly from Green Harbor, Marshfield, for almost seven miles, ending at the high promontory of the Gurnet at the entrance to Plymouth Bay. A mile or so of the beach is in Marshfield, and the promontory lies in Plymouth, while the intervening section belongs to Duxbury. To reach it formerly took eight miles of travel that traverses Marshfield. The bridge cuts this long trip down to less than half a mile. Duxbury is a great place of summer resort, and the demand for shore property is heavy. The bridge throws several miles of desirable property into the market, and allows good communication with the railroad."[1]

A postcard of Powder Point Bridge. (*Russell Edwards*)

A regatta, a clambake, martial music, and speeches helped celebrate the bridge opening. Gershom Bradford described the festivities as follows:

"We gathered at the Point end of the bridge, under the direction of Thomas Knight, principal of Partridge Academy. First there were bag, 3-legged, and potato races. Then there was a 'greased pole,' a quaint device consisting of a round spar horizontally extending over the water. It was well smeared with fat. The competitors were expected to work their way out the pole, seize the little flag stuck in the end. Boy after boy tried to keep his balance but failed and fell into the water. At last a smart lad tried a new trick: he RAN out, grabbed the flag, and won amid cheers.

"The big event was the bicycle race. Can you imagine high excitement over a bicycle race? How simple were our needs for fun! The era of the little wheel behind had passed, and we had progressed to wheels of equal size. They were called 'safeties,' because there were no more 'headers,' and in fact we spoke of them as 'wheels' rather than bicycles."[2]

In the early years of the bridge, its draw opened occasionally to permit boats with masts to pass into the Back River. But the draw had a different charm for small boys who would climb it, then dive into the channel with a mighty splash, swim to the ladder, and go at it again. Some fondly recall the draw, no longer in place on the bridge, for one day the chain holding it broke, the draw crashed down and was never raised.

Then and now, the bridge has drawn fishermen by the score, crowding each other and jostling for place over the swift flowing channel, even occasionally catching a fish if the mackerel are running or heading for the shallow water to avoid the blues. No fisherman seems to mind if there is no action. The bridge makes a pleasant place to while away a summer afternoon.

Cars parked along Powder Point Bridge
(c. 1917).

The bridge is a cherished landmark now, reputedly the longest wooden bridge on the eastern seaboard. Although built to reach a planned development on the beach, a scheme fortunately thwarted in the nick of time, happily it now ends at an open strand, free and clear of any structures for most of its seven miles. The bridge has been repaired and rebuilt a number of times, and is once again under construction following the fire and the subsequent condemnation in late 1985. It will be back in use soon, a source of pride and joy to the people of Duxbury and their friends.

BRADFORD H. BURNHAM

The Myles Standish Monument

With flags flying and brass bands playing to lead the way, on October 7, 1872, 10,000 people trudged from the Duxbury Depot to the crest of Captain's Hill. Many had come to Duxbury by special trains from Boston to witness the laying of the cornerstone of the Myles Standish Monument. Almost as many enthusiastic citizens had the year before attended solemn ceremonies at the consecration of the monument site.

Designed by architect Alden Frink, the granite shaft rises 116 feet from the foundation to the parapet. The statue of Myles Standish, fourteen feet high, was the work of S. J. O'Kelly of Boston. O'Kelly molded the heroic model in plaster. From the cast, the statue was cut of Cape Ann granite by Stefano Brignoli and Luigi Limonetta of Bayeno, Italy. The commanding figure of the Pilgrim captain holds the charter of Plymouth Colony in his hand, as he looks to the east across the bay.

The arch over the bronze doors was made from stones contributed by the New England states; the keystone was a gift from President Ulysses S. Grant to represent all of the United States. The Commonwealth of Massachusetts contributed money for the iron staircase, the bronze doors, and ornamental windows. All the other funds for construction were raised by the Standish Monument Association through private subscription. When fund-raising became a problem, work on the granite shaft was stopped at a height of seventy feet for a number of years. It was finally completed in 1898, twenty-six years after the cornerstone had been laid with such enthusiasm.

The Standish Monument Association gave the monument and surrounding area to the Commonwealth of Massachusetts in 1920. Now known as the Standish Monument Reservation, it is administered by the Massachusetts Department of Environmental Management.

In 1924, lightning struck the statue of Myles Standish, destroying the head and right arm. Two years later, Boston sculptor John Horrigan cut a replacement head from a solid block of granite and repairs were completed in 1927. In 1980, however, the monument had to be closed as the spiral staircase was deemed unsafe. Funds were appropriated in 1986 to refurbish and restore the well-known landmark in time for Duxbury's 350th anniversary.

Frances D. Leach

(top) Massachusetts Historical Society; (bottom) *Fran Nichols*

Cranberries

Cranberries grow wild all along the northeastern seacoast of the United States. About the year 1816, Henry Hall of North Dennis noticed that sand applied to wild cranberry vines improved their growth and greatly increased the size and amount of the fruit. This small beginning has led to an industry global in scope and quite sophisticated in culture. The name cranberry is alleged to have come from crane berry, since the blossoms on the woody stems resemble the head of a crane.

Captains of sailing vessels making long ocean passages noticed that the crew was free from scurvy, caused by a deficiency of vitamin C, when the sailors' diet included some cranberry sauce each week. Cranberries were easily stored in water-filled barrels, remaining fresh for several months in the cool hold of the ship, the natural wax coating on mature berries keeping them from rotting. They required only sugar and boiling water to make a good sauce.

Duxbury, with its many ships sailing on the high seas, provided a market for the commercial cultivation of cranberries. Around 1845–46, Stephen Gifford tried raising them as a crop to sell. It would be interesting to see how Mr. Gifford drained his swamp, cleared it of brush and trees, pulled the stumps with oxen, and made the land fairly level on which he planted each vine by hand. Today, large tractor-type *skidders* take bundles of whole trees and transport them to a place where they can be cut into logs. Large hydraulic excavators pull stumps as easily as a gardener pulls weeds. Bulldozers load the stumps onto trucks that take them to large pits later covered with fill and reforested.

When the land is cleared, bulldozers level the surface for planting. A two-inch coating of sand is spread on the bog's peat soil, then vines cut from another bog are spread on the sand and disked into the earth. Two men with a machine can plant two to three acres in a day. Hand-planting in Mr. Gifford's time would take a crew of fifteen to twenty men a week or more to do the same job. Mr. Gifford's hand-planted 1845 bog is still bearing fruit at the corner of Church and Temple streets.

In 1937, twenty-five Duxbury growers produced a crop of approximately 36,000 bushels on about 600 acres. At present, ten growers in the town produce about 54,000 bushels on around 150 acres.

Duxbury is blessed with many swamps and an abundance of fresh water, essential in cranberry growing. Rainfall is in excess of 48 inches per year. Cranberries flourish in acid peat soil, which Duxbury has in abundance. The application of readily available sand keeps the root system from being bound together, and the cool, dry, air temperatures during the growing season keep the fruit from scalding.

The community benefits from cranberry bogs are often overlooked—the stocking of fish therein, the attraction to birds and other wildlife, and the maintenance of the water table that the town draws on for its domestic water systems.

Spring

Spring marks the beginning of the crop year. To watch dormant cranberry plants come alive is fascinating. After the middle of March, when there is usually little danger of desiccation of vines by temperatures below twenty degrees and drying winds, the water is drawn from the bogs, ditches are cleaned to aid in drainage, and the work of repairing and setting out the irrigation system begins. As the tender buds swell, they are susceptible to frost kill. Being close to a large tidal bay effectively reduces frost damage, especially when high

tide occurs from midnight to 4 A.M. On the other hand, *kettle holes*, low swampy pockets made by glaciers thousands of years ago, are where cranberries grow, and these can be many degrees colder than the surrounding terrain. To overcome problems of frost damage, provide water during dry periods, and allow even application of materials beneficial to the bog, an irrigation system is necessary. Sprinklers spaced fifty feet apart (fed from grids of plastic pipe buried six inches below the bog surface) allow a spray of water to completely cover the bog. Temperatures as low as twelve degrees have been recorded without doing damage to the vines. Latent heat within the ice-encased fruit and stems provides a small coating of unfrozen water beneath the ice, and the ice itself becomes an insulation from the cold air.

Abundant fresh water is essential for good cranberry culture. Growers have sometimes spent more money

The thriving community of Duxbury residents whose ancestors came from the Cape Verde Islands off the west coast of Africa began in the nineteenth century with young men who had initially been recruited for whaling vessels sailing out of New Bedford and Providence. Brought to America, many of them decided to remain, becoming stevedores or fishermen with their own small boats.

Gradually some moved inland to work the cranberry bogs that were being developed in Plymouth, Carver, and Duxbury. They either brought their wives over from the Islands, or went back to marry and then returned to establish homes and families here. Names such as Fernandes, Veiga, and Amado became familiar in town and remain so.

Robert D. Hale

Wright bog, off Temple Street (1880). Duxbury women prepare to plant vines in a grid pattern. It took a crew of fifteen a week to complete the job.

on water sources and irrigation than on all the rest of the bog development. Pre-emergence herbicides are applied in early spring to inhibit grasses and weeds. Sanding is undertaken when necessary.

As spring turns to summer, terminal buds put out fruiting pods—the pink underside of the flowering pistils. At this time, growers bring in bees. Most growers use one beehive for each two acres of bog, with perhaps 50,000 bees in each hive. If the bloom is exceptionally heavy, more hives are added. With the temperature rise,

insect pests' eggs laid the previous fall on the underside of the cranberry leaves hatch out and can, if not checked, defoliate a bog in a few days. The earliest pest is usually the black-headed fireworm.

Damaging insects often infest a bog during bloom when the bees are most active, so the grower has to apply insecticide at night when bees are in their hives. To prevent insecticide residue remaining on the bog, which would imperil the bees, the grower has to flush it with fresh water for several hours. Bees do not like to get wet, so will stay off the bog while the sprinklers are in use. Any and all materials applied to the bog must be in accordance with state regulations, and Ocean Spray will not accept delivery of any crop without a written accounting called the Pesticide Report.

The fear that pesticide residue from bog spraying might contaminate ground water appears to be unfounded. Studies by Dr. Karl Deubert of the University of Massachusetts indicate that acid cranberry soils are excellent mediums for breaking down pesticides before they reach groundwater levels. Also, under each bog is a seal of hard iron ore, used in colonial days to make cast-iron cooking utensils.

The summer growing season produces many weeds which have to be controlled without damage to the vines or the crop. One method is to allow the weeds to grow considerably higher than the vines and then mow them off with a three-bladed clipper. The most recent method is to apply a herbicide to the weeds above the vines, which inhibits photosynthesis. This must be accomplished with great care to prevent damage to the vines. None of these bog activities is harmful to wildlife. Young ducklings hatch and feed on the algae in the ditches. Canada geese nest on the edge of the reservoirs. Fish guard their nests in gravelly shallows. The cranberry complex of swamps, streams, reservoirs, bogs, and woodlands provides excellent shelter for wildlife. Their increase in these areas shows that a healthy environment is present for all of us.

Fall

August is the month for harvest preparation. The equipment must be tested and weeds clipped so they won't clog the harvesting machines. Harvest season ranges from mid-September to the first of November. When the berries are colored enough to be considered *blending* berries, they qualify for a bonus. Crews work as long as possible each day, rain or shine, wet-picking all week, including Sundays and holidays. Wet-picking consists of flooding the bog area so that the buoyant berries aren't bruised when they are beaten off the vines under water; the water acts as a cushion to prevent damage to the fruit. During wet-picking, yellow legs, plovers, egrets, and other shore birds come in from salt marshes to feed on insects floating on the bog water. Hawks of all types also appear to enjoy the rodents disturbed by the flooding. And occasionally, snapping turtles come in with the high water.

The berries are gathered by a floating wood or canvas boom which encloses and compresses them around a conveyor that carries them up an incline to a bulk truck, which then transports them to either the Middleboro or Carver receiving plants. A few growers pick the crop dry. Dry-picked berries are usually sorted and packaged to be sold as fresh fruit.

Long ago it was discovered that the skin tension of a good berry would allow it to bounce over a small barrier; bad berries would not have this quality. Accordingly, a separator was developed on this principle. Even so, a few misshapen or poorly colored berries might get by, so sharp-eyed human sorters stand at the conveyor belts to pick them out. Each handler of bulk berries attends to this screening process. This is an improvement over the days when each grower had his own *screenhouse*, where the berries were sorted, packaged, and sold fresh.

Scandinavians in Duxbury

The peak decade for Scandinavians coming to America was from 1880 to 1890. Although most settled in the Midwest, a few found their way to Duxbury, having first lived in other parts of the country.

Aaron Nelson was the first to settle in Duxbury, with his wife and children. He was so enthusiastic about the West Duxbury area, and the possibilities for growing cranberries, that he spread the word in several Swedish churches. The minister of one, Emil Swanson, bought land in Tinkertown from Mr. Nelson in 1908. In 1912, he bought a farm on High Street, and moved his family there. Several families followed. Several bought homes on High Street; others settled in Tarkiln. At least a half dozen were cranberry growers. Names like Nelson, Berg, Teravainen, Swanson, Bitters, Nielson, Alquist and Olhson were added to the school enrollment.

The Scandinavian families were fairly large, and they not only added their numbers to the West Duxbury Methodist Church, but their musical and cooking abilities. A good cup of coffee with delicious coffee bread could be shared in many houses at four o'clock every afternoon. Some Scandinavian customs are kept by the descendants of the original settlers, some of whom still occupy the original homesteads in Duxbury.

Priscilla Swanson Harris

A handbeater dislodges the cranberries. (*Stanley Merry*)

Berries dropped on the bogs by the dry-picking method are floated to the surface by flooding the bog. While the dry-picked fruit is what is seen in bags as fresh fruit, the crop saved by flooding is usable for making sauce and jelly. The wet-picking methods were developed when the demand for processed fruit exceeded that of the fresh. The wet method is easier, faster, and satisfies the requirements for juice and jellies. The cranberries are frozen as soon as they are received by the handler.

After the harvest is completed, the equipment is stored away and it's clean-up time around the bogs. Vines are pruned, flumes are repaired, ditches are cleaned, dikes checked, bogs fertilized, and herbicides applied.

Winter is the time for vacation, and the time for taking stock. Brush and trees may need to be cleared from around the bogs to allow for better air circulation and more sunlight. When freeze-ups are indicated, each bog must be flooded so that a layer of ice will prevent desiccation of vines from drying winds. There are times when water inundation can be harmful. A thick coating of snow over ice can prevent sunlight from reaching the vines, impeding photosynthesis and resulting in oxygen deficiency. In these circumstances, the water has to be drained off and the area reflowed.

When ice on the bogs is thick enough (about four inches) to support the equipment, sanders are rushed in to spread screened, clean sand, which will settle onto the vines without abrasion when the ice melts. This ice sanding dismays skaters who use the frozen bogs as a community rink, but it is a necessary part of cranberry culture, improving chances for a good crop the next year.

It should be noted that the miracle of the cranberry's popularity results from the efforts of the management of Ocean Spray, many of whom reside in Duxbury. They have developed cranberry juice mixes, sauces, and jellies, and methods of packaging which make this natural fruit readily available around the world. Ocean Spray is a cooperative of over seven hundred growers in the United States and Canada. It markets approximately 82 percent of the entire crop of cranberries, and in 1985 became one of the Fortune 500 companies.

In almost any large wetland area of Duxbury, the marks of ditches and dikes are visible evidence that someone, perhaps many years ago, built a bog there. Then as now, it has been a principal means of livelihood for those so involved and an incalculable asset to the community.

STANLEY H. MERRY

156

Clams

In spite of its humble appearance and lowly position in life, the clam has played an honorable part in Duxbury history. For years before the first white settlers came, native Americans were coming each summer to these shores to gather shellfish. They named one particularly productive area *Saquish,* meaning "place of many clams." Even that prestigious Pilgrim historian, William Bradford, found room for a clam story: "In the end, they came to that misery that some died with cold and hunger. One in gathering shellfish was so weak as he stuck fast in the mud and was found dead in the place."[1]

Clams and other shellfish kept the early settlers alive in lean times, but shellfish, and particularly clams, became popular after the Civil War when people in inland communities developed a taste for clam chowder. By the turn of the century clam chowder had become New England's best-known regional dish.

During the Depression, local residents, like their Pilgrim forefathers, depended on clams for food. Many men, out of work but not wanting to admit it, would wait for the tide to go out to dig a pailful for lunch, for there was little else to put on the table. Wives and children would dig, too, and try to trade the clams for provisions at the grocery store. How fortunate it was that clams were nourishing and provided essential vitamins and minerals.

There are two varieties of clams in Duxbury: the first and most common is the round, hard-shell variety, *Venus mercenaria;* the second, the beloved steamer, or soft-shell clam, *Mya arenaria.*

Regulations concerning the digging of steamer clams set a legal length of two inches, for which the clam warden and professional diggers carry metal testing rings. The daily limit is six quarts per family; the months to dig are

Plowing clam beds (1937). The man with the plow is Peter Hagman. (*Alvin Marks*)

157

April and May, September and October. No digging is allowed on Sunday, and no one can dig on the flats set aside for seeding and growing.

The quahog, or hard-shell clam, is second to the steamer in popularity. These clams are round with much harder shells. They seldom lie deeper than six inches below the top of the clam bed. There are two varieties of hard-shell clams: *little necks*, which must be two inches in diameter; and *cherry stones*, which must be at least a half-inch wider. Some quahogs can grow very large indeed, often six to twelve inches around their fattest part, weighing two to three pounds each. Too tough to be eaten raw, they are suitable for chowder or ground clam dishes.

In 1954, scallops were so plentiful trucks lined up at Mattakeesett Court for loading.

Since the early 1900s when the first raw little necks were served at the Savoy Hotel in London, they have become highly regarded as a first course for formal dinners or as an hors d'oeuvre with champagne or cocktails. However, the very best way to eat them is to wash them on the spot, take an oyster knife out of your back pocket, and start in on a bucketful, right by the sea.

Sea clams and razor clams are less popular in Duxbury. Sea clams live in fairly deep water, so they can be reached only when the tide is unusually low. The razor clam is an elusive creature, burrowing down in the sand out of reach of the ordinary digger. They were once so numerous they were shelled and sold for bait at five cents a pound.

Bitter cold winters have discouraged oyster growers in Duxbury Bay, as one hard freeze can wipe out an entire bed. Recently, however, new methods of seeding have been partly successful. It is hoped that breeding stock can be developed along with relays for *put and take* programs, by which new seed is added to older clams to enable continued growth and harvesting, as well as the establishment of permanent beds.

In the 1950s, scallops, with their beautiful shells and lovely taste, suddenly appeared in large numbers in Duxbury Bay. So plentiful were they that the whole town turned out to scoop up the treasure. Stores closed mid-week, children skipped school, dowagers appeared in blue and pink slickers, and huge trucks with New York license plates filled the Snug Harbor parking lot. The most humble dinner tables were loaded with the delicacy. Duxburyites who happened to be here at the time will never forget the plain, unplanned good times of the "Scallop Days."

While clamming still offers its special sense of humor, the attitude now is more scientific. Donald Beers, Duxbury's Harbormaster and Shellfish Constable, has been trained at school and college in modern methods of shellfish propagation and keeps abreast of the latest developments coming from marine laboratories here and in the south.

A supervised clam transplant program began in Duxbury in the 1950s. Several beds were marked off for propagation, and a half-dozen bushels of white soft-shell clams (which are more popular commercially) from Captain's Flats were mixed with those from a mud clam bed. The latter were darker, because the surrounding mud was darker, but they were also plumper and firmer. The result of the mix was whitish clams which were larger, fatter, and better tasting.

In 1981, clam grants in Duxbury Bay were leased to Duxbury residents. Two knowledgeable friends and I were licensed to plant seed quahogs on an acre off Standish Shore. We paid a fee of $250 to a surveyor, $25 for a clam grant, and $850 for 10,000 clams for a test planting. At high tide we towed seven five-by-eight foot plywood trays out to our grant, anchored them, filled them half full of sand and planted the baby clams. Within a half hour they burrowed down in the sand, so we tacked plastic webbing called conweb over the trays. Within a year they were an inch long and used to spout a welcoming salute as we came on the grant—a miniature Versailles in Duxbury!

By Labor Day of 1985, our first crop was almost ready but we decided to delay the harvest until later in the fall, when the clams would be larger. Unfortunately, on September 27th, Hurricane *Gloria* struck at dead low tide when the clam beds were exposed. Fierce gusts blew the netting off the trays and the clams were scattered far and wide. The predators, horseshoe crabs, starfish, green crabs, and moon snails, feasted on the exposed clams, leaving the area covered with empty shells. Clam farmers are as helpless as wheat farmers when nature goes on a rage.

The future for clams looks bright because trained

Rum-Running

In prohibition days, Duxbury, with its twisting tidal channels known only to local boys, often gave nightmares to pursuing Coast Guard cutters that could get stuck on the mud flats.

They say one night a rum-runner was followed into the bay by the Coast Guard. The quick-thinking smugglers launched a raft bearing a light at the opening of a blind channel off the beach and watched the Coast Guard follow it. To the Coast Guard's chagrin, the channel shoaled and they were fast aground. The rum-runners guided their boat to shore and unloaded their cargo.

They say one load was so large that no smuggler had room to store it, until one volunteered space in a garage owned by summer people. As caretaker, he knew it would be safe there since the owner was president of the Women's Christian Temperance Union.

They say that much of the success of the rum-runners was due to their excellent communication system. The prime radio operator, when a boy, was a friend of the cable operator's son. The father was delighted to teach the boys, but was later heard to say about one of them, "If I'd known how he was gonna use it, I never would'av taught him."

---

young marine biologists will surely strengthen, improve, and extend the life of our shellfish. A whole new business of aquaculture might grow up on the shores of Duxbury Bay, providing health and delicious nourishment for young and old. With its two vents, its mantle, its foot, and its valves, the Duxbury clam is as efficient, and about as pretty, as the first Ford car . . . except nobody has ever wanted to change it.

JEAN POINDEXTER COLBY

Duxbury's Mayflower Heritage

Gravestone in the Old Burying Ground.
(*Tori Foster*)

"*I*n the name of God, Amen." These are the opening words of the May-flower Compact, written by the Pilgrims in the cabin of the *Mayflower* on a cold November night in 1620 before they went ashore at Provincetown after a long-overdue and tempestuous voyage from England. They had expected to arrive months earlier, and not here, but in the "northern parts of Virginia" at the mouth of the Hudson River, claimed by England. Plymouth in Massachusetts Bay lay outside this jurisdiction. Consequently, the new colonists had no laws, rules, or regulations by which to govern themselves, and dissension had already broken out among them. Being a law-abiding people, they created the Mayflower Compact to fill the need—the first document in the history of mankind "of the people, by the people, and for the people." On this was founded our American way of life, the most valuable heritage the Pilgrims could have left for future generations.[1]

The first several years after landing at Plymouth the settlers lived communally as they struggled for survival, but in 1627—an important date for Plymouth and Duxbury—Isaac Allerton, on behalf of the Pilgrims, concluded an agreement with the London Merchant Adventurers by which the colonists became the owners of their own lands. They proceeded to allot property around the bay. Most likely, 1628 is the date of the first settlement in Duxbury.

Captain Myles Standish led a small group which included Alden, Brewster, and Prence around the shores of Plymouth Bay. In 1632, Elder Brewster gathered "the parish at Morton's Hole," which became Duxbury. The town was not incorporated until 1637 when the Reverend Ralph Partridge arrived from England to become the first ordained minister of the church. A town could not be legally incorporated until it had a church with an ordained minister supported by the town. Of the twenty-five (or twenty-three "recognized") families of Plymouth who had arrived on the *Mayflower*, about half had come to live in Duxbury by the time it was incorporated. To this day, many streets and landmarks bear testimony to their names.

For almost one hundred years the occupations of the town's inhabitants were limited to farming and fishing. Then, as they struggled through King Philip's War and other wars before the Revolution, Duxbury gradually became involved in the major issues of the day.

During the Revolution and before, Duxbury was a Whig town. The people protested the Stamp Act of 1765 vehemently and later erected their own liberty pole on Colonel Gamaliel Bradford's hill, proudly displaying the slogan "Liberty or Death." The pole would serve as a rallying place for many years after.[2] When a fort was built at the Gurnet in 1776, Duxbury residents furnished a share of the supplies. Later generations appreciated what their Pilgrim heritage implied.

Having kept its militia active, Duxbury was able to send a company of about forty militiamen under the command of Major Judah Alden to the siege of Boston during the Revolution. Later, two more companies were sent out. When the militiamen departed, the women took over the men's work as well as their own.

After the Revolution, descendants of the original settlers had new worlds to conquer. Some communities looked westward and others toward the north, but Duxbury looked to the sea. Shipbuilding became a major industry. Ezra Weston, Sr. and Jr., father and son, built ships in several yards, increasing in activity to become some of the most important shipbuilders in America. Other builders also answered the increasing demand for Duxbury vessels, until at one point there were twenty active shipyards employing over nine hundred men, nearly a third of the town's population.

Sargeant Blanchard and Harvey Reynolds at the head of the Duxbury Town Band, Memorial Day (c. 1900).

Although the energy and reputation of the town had been centered on shipbuilding, this was also the period of the "flowering of New England," when writers and educators were encouraged. Small private schools were opening in many New England towns. In Duxbury, the Honorable George Partridge, a civic leader and educator who was a collateral descendant of the Reverend Ralph Partridge, left funds in his 1828 will to "provide a higher degree of instruction" in the town. Opening in 1845, the academy served Duxbury well into the next century.[3]

When the Civil War started, Duxbury, an abolitionist town, was quick to respond, sending 236 men to join the Grand Army of the Republic. As on former occasions, the family names of many Duxbury volunteers were those of the Pilgrim forefathers. After the war ended, a monument was erected at the Mayflower Cemetery in honor of those who had served.

In 1872, another monument, this time in honor of the Pilgrim Captain Myles Standish, was begun at the top of Captain's Hill. Other construction projects included bringing the railroad through town and the laying of the French Atlantic cable. Summer people began to arrive, bringing new life to the town.

In 1917, all matters were subordinated to the major purpose of prosecuting the war against Germany. As in the past, the town was quick to respond, organizing to sell Liberty Bonds and War Savings Stamps, as well as collecting clothing and supplies for the Red Cross.

Unfortunately, that did not turn out to be "the war to end all wars," and in 1941, World War II started. Once more Duxbury tightened its belt, marshalled its forces, and met the challenge, this time with both men and women serving in the armed forces.

Duxbury today boasts a wide variety of civic groups. Those who are interested in historical and genealogical societies may belong to any one of several local, state, and national organizations from the Duxbury Rural and Historical Society and the Pilgrim Society in Plymouth, to the Society of Mayflower Descendants, Ancient and Honorable Artillery Company, or Order of the Cincinnati. Many residents of Duxbury bear the Pilgrim genes, but not Pilgrim names. They continue to carry forward the spirit of the founders. With the words of William Bradford in their hearts,

> . . . as one small candle may light a thousand, so the light here kindled has shown unto many, yea, in some sort, to our whole nation . . .[4]

we know the spirit of our Pilgrim forefathers lives on.

VERNA ROSS ORNDORFF

Ruby Graves

Ruby Graves was a real lady and charming storyteller. Generations of children can recall with pleasure their visits to her Surplus Street home where she fed them cookies and entertained them with tales of long ago.

One favorite tale was about her grandfather, Rufus B. Holmes, who had spent many years at sea. Once his ship was wrecked on Pitcairn Island. The natives were laboriously making a bark cloth called *tapa*. They were using crude wood rollers that were not durable, so Grandfather took pieces of iron from the wrecked ship and made them into rollers to make their work easier. In appreciation they presented him with a pair of silver leg bracelets. Miss Ruby's eyes would sparkle as she continued, "When Grandfather returned to Duxbury he had those 'heathen ornaments' fashioned into two teaspoons marked *RHC* for Rufus and Clara Holmes." Then she would proudly display them to her enthralled audience.

She loved to tell of the time she and her companion-housekeeper, Mrs. Mildred Fralic discovered several cases of preserved rum cherries which her mother had put up at least twenty years earlier. They didn't dare eat them, so they emptied them behind the barn. "Then . . .," she continued, "we had the happiest dogs in the neighborhood!"

Still surrounded by friends, she celebrated her 100th birthday in 1972.

Ruby Graves and Paul Peterson (c. 1900).

Beatrice R. Richards

World War II in Duxbury

*D*arkness—for those who lived in Duxbury during the period of the Second World War (1941–1945), the experience of a town in darkness governs their memories.

Duxbury's wartime life was primarily influenced by the fact that the town directly faced the Atlantic Ocean and that Germany lay across that ocean. Civil Defense regulations were much more stringent for coastal locations than for areas somewhat inland. The fear of air raids, lurking submarines, or spies landing upon the beaches was ever-present.

To move about Duxbury after sundown was an adventure. The town was very dark, so a moonlit evening was greatly appreciated. While Civil Defense rules varied, depending on the perceived danger and battle successes in Europe, reduced light was the rule. Blackout curtains covered windows, car lights were painted or taped so that only tiny slivers of light escaped, and street lights were shielded with metal guards. To drive along the town's streets after dark was to embark on a risky venture. However, because both cars and bicycles had to feel their way along the streets, speeds were generally prudently low and gasoline rationing greatly reduced the number of automobiles. Occasionally, a total blackout was signaled. Families reached for flashlights, feared they might step on family pets in the pitch darkness, and went to bed early.

In other ways, wartime life in Duxbury was similar to the way it was all across America. Gasoline rationing meant great reliance on trains with steam boilers fired by coal. Bicycles were the best mode of local transportation, and in most families, every person had a bike. Although they were hard to obtain, three-speed English Raleighs with thin tires were much desired. Rationed foods were supplemented with produce from family Victory Gardens,

Station for spotting airplanes, probably located at the foot of Linden Lane. (*Duxbury Free Library*)

local seafood, and squab from the farm on St. George Street. Civil Defense airplane watches were maintained at several locations, including the Butler's pier at the end of Linden Lane. Red Cross bandages were folded at Hall's Corner in the building now occupied by the Deli and at the Old Sailor's Home. In a barn that stood at what is now the intersection of Depot Street and Prior Farm Road, scrap paper and metals were collected for bailing and shipped to regional collection centers. Water and sand were stockpiled in attics against the possibility of air raids. Many years after the war, one local family located a very heavy trunk in the attic. What treasure did it contain? Silver, valuable books—what? Imagine the disappointment when the lock was broken and they discovered it full of sand!

The war seemed closest on the water and at the beach. Most large boats and yachts had been loaned to the Coast Guard or Navy; others were laid up in boat yards for the duration. Fishermen who used the water regularly were required to be finger-printed and to have registration papers. While small sailboats still dotted the bay and the Duxbury Yacht Club races continued, fuel for small outboards did not exist. Undisturbed by the noise of boat engines, seals became frequent visitors along the shoreline.

Parents still took their children to Duxbury Beach during daylight hours, but the area was, essentially, a war zone. It was off-limits to all civilians from sunset to sunrise. Patrols walked its length. At various times, these were from the Army, Coast Guard, or Coast Guard Auxiliary. Gun emplacements (though no guns) and fox-holes dotted its length. Overhead, blimps and yellow biplanes (known locally as *yellow perils*) from the Weymouth Naval Air Station maintained submarine watches. Occasionally, one saw a pillar of smoke from a damaged ship, miles at sea. The shoreline was cluttered with flotsam and jetsam of naval engagements—life jackets

and life rings, and broken and burned pieces of ships. Probably the area was used for the testing of military flares, for casings and small, white silk parachutes were regularly found by children playing along the beach. Occasionally, wartime activities came even closer. Imagine the surprise of two boys, Dunkin and Faneuil Adams, when they heard the crash and clatter across the roof of their home on Abrams Hill. Rushing to their bedroom window and peering into the thick fog, they could make out the faces of crew members of a blimp just above the house. The shattering noise came from the mooring chains of the blimp which, off-course in the fog, had barely avoided a more serious collision with their house. Understandably, it is a memory the boys never forgot.

Duxbury was not immune from visible signs of war. Active military units were billeted in town. The Army and Coast Guard maintained barracks at Sprague Hall on Washington Street and in a group of Quonset huts in the parking lot on the west side of the Duxbury Beach bridge. Military uniforms and southern accents brought the wartime atmosphere to rural Duxbury.

The units had various responsibilities. Both services were, at various times, responsible for night patrols with dogs along the beach. The fear of submarine landings was ever-present, though, in fact, they never materialized. In addition, the historic Atlantic Cable with its U.S. terminus at the Cable House was reactivated to be ready in case of an emergency, and Army troops were used to protect the building. Dorothy Wentworth recalls that "it was an extraordinary sight to see an armed uniformed guard pacing the street sides, turning the corner smartly. The changing of the (palace) guard in London never impressed us . . . more than the changing of the guard at the Cable Office."

Duxbury also had its own armed services unit. In early 1942, the United States Navy and Coast Guard did

Group photograph of Flotilla 600. Second row center are Lt. (J.G.) Graham T. Winslow, Commander, and to his left, Joseph Lund, Vice-Commander. (*Duxbury Free Library*)

not have the resources to maintain coastal patrols along the eastern seaboard, so the Coast Guard set out to recruit volunteers and to borrow civilian boats. Duxbury Flotilla #600 USCGR (United States Coast Guard Reserve) was born.

The Flotilla, founded May 17, 1942, was commanded by Graham T. Winslow of Standish Street. Approximately 125 men and one woman from Duxbury and neighboring towns made up the unit. Many were Boston businessmen who normally lived in Duxbury only in the summer months; so some of the weekly training sessions took place in Newton and Boston. The usual arrangement was for these volunteers to take a 12- or 24-hour shift of Coast Guard duty per week.

Initially, from June 1942 to December 1943, the unit was responsible for boat patrols. Using locally-loaned vessels, the crew patrolled the shore from Green Harbor to Manomet. All sighted shipping activities were reported to Coast Guard headquarters in Boston. Patrols are remembered as being rough, choppy, very dark, and boring. The patrols slept at Gurnet in Coast Guard barracks, and drew, so they felt, more than their share of latrine cleaning and floor waxing. However, the men on these patrols did have the satisfaction of knowing that they were guarding the beach and entrances to Duxbury, Kingston, and Plymouth harbors.

From June 1943 to January 1944, beach patrols were added. Two men and a dog would set out from Gurnet, headed north to a telephone shack just south of the beach parking lot. There, they would telephone back to headquarters at Gurnet and then resume the hike back. Again, it was frequently bitter cold and incredibly dark, so Flotilla members were glad to reach their barracks for a hot cup of coffee and warm bed. Later in the war, their barracks were located in the Army Quonset huts at the end of the bridge.

As 1944 progressed and the outcome of the war in Europe became clearer, the need for the Flotilla diminished. For a brief period, the watch was kept in the Winslows' living room. Some members were assigned to the base at Constitution Wharf in Boston on special duty to guard the pier and liners like the *Queen Mary*, which were being used as troop transports.

By the war's end, Flotilla #600 was a closely-knit group who had shared adventure and tedium together, which in the post-war years, they remembered in semi-annual reunions.

ELIZABETH BOYD STEVENS

Church bells rang wildly and whistles blew joyfully to announce the official end of World War II. In these days of continuous strife it's difficult to realize how relieved we all were and how hopeful of better things to come.

It seemed like a dream from which we soon must awaken, but the tremendous fact that the war was over dwarfed everything else. For many families there would be happy reunions as sons and husbands came home to carry on normal lives again. For others there would be no homecoming, which to those was the real meaning of war.

It was of those mothers and wives I was thinking as I drove to Duxbury in the early evening. Boston had been quiet through the long hot afternoon, but there was a feeling of impatience everywhere.

While a cool breeze swept over the meadow, bright with goldenrod, and the red August sun sank slowly, the long-awaited news that the Japanese had accepted full and unconditional surrender came clearly over the air.

There were no cheering crowds, but instantly, out of every Cape Cod cottage and shingled saltbox, tumbled excited children crying, "The war's over!" Some of them wore pajamas and some waved flags. Others were lined up in pig-tailed platoons beating on tin pans and blowing horns.

Then the church bells in all the tall white spires began to ring out the glad news. Flags were quickly unfurled along the elm-shaded streets. Fire engines shrieked and automobile horns added to the tumult. Radios blared and dogs barked.

Lights burned brightly behind the tiny-paned windows as friends joined friends in sharing the joyful tidings. And all through the evening, grateful people knelt with bowed heads in the quiet village churches where their ancestors had sought comfort in other crises in the nation's history.

Finally, the lights blinked out, one by one. The children went reluctantly to bed with memories to thrill their grandchildren in the years to come. The night wind whispered over the fields where crickets chanted rhythmically. Overhead, stars burned brightly in the dark sky. Peace had come once again to a New England town.

Alison Arnold

Modern
Duxbury

Town Government

When Duxbury celebrated its tercentenary in 1937, it was a small rural community with a year-round population of less than 2,000, but with a substantial increase in that number each summer. We now find ourselves, fifty years later, with a population in excess of 16,000 and a summer influx that's hardly noticeable. The most dramatic period of rapid growth occurred during the twenty-five years from 1948 to 1973, although growth has continued since then, but at a slightly slower pace. During this twenty-five year period, the population increased from less than 3,000 to more than 10,000, or nearly 250 percent. The school population grew from less than 500 students to approximately 3,000, an increase of more than twice the population percentage increase. Total town expenditures in 1948 were less than $500,000. By 1973, we were spending $15 million.

A review of Duxbury's annual town reports provides a detailed record of how town government responded to growth. In addition, they indicate the outstanding foresight of its officers and committees in attempting to control the future. The records of Duxbury's open town meetings clearly demonstrate that town officials were recommending changes in anticipation of growth, not just in response to it. It is also clear that town meeting generally responded positively by adopting general and specific bylaws and providing structural changes in town government, so that the town would have the tools it needed to meet the challenges of unparalleled growth.

In 1937, the Board of Selectmen were also the assessors, the Board of Health, the Finance Committee, the Board of Public Welfare, and the Building Inspectors, among other things, and had very little in the way of full-time help. In their 1941 report to the town, the selectmen stated that the work of the

The first horse-drawn tub was purchased in 1902, shown with Hortense E. Merry at the reins, Frederick B. Knapp on the rear step and "Bess." (*Howard T. Blanchard*)

board had been chiefly of a routine nature. Such a statement cannot be found in subsequent reports, and the actions taken by town meeting after that time, to enable others to perform some of their functions, demonstrate the increasing burdens and complexities. In 1941, the town meeting voted to elect a Board of Public Welfare in the following year; its members would serve without pay and hold no other public office, thus relieving the selectmen of these duties. In 1948, the Finance Committee was established, and the Boards of Selectmen and Assessors were separated beginning in 1970. Next, the selectmen were directed by town meeting to appoint an independent Board of Health in 1978.

An era ended in Duxbury just prior to our entrance into World War II, when Sidney Soule stepped down from the Board of Selectmen after serving thirty-five years. Walter Prince was elected to replace him. During the war, the old Abbott House, on the corner of Alden and St. George streets, was used in part by the Red Cross, the U.S. Army Patrol, and various defense committees. This building also housed the police department and the district nurse. The town had purchased this property in 1936, but the 1937 annual town meeting voted to sell the building and retain the land. The town was unable to do so and continued to use the building until 1975, when it was torn down in order to build the Percy Walker Pool.

In 1944, the town adopted its first protective bylaw, and 1945 saw the first brief report from the newly appointed Board of Appeals. The town adopted a new comprehensive protective bylaw in 1973.

To minimize tax rate fluctuations, the town meeting voted to establish a stabilization fund in 1946. During that same year, the town sold the Alms House on Depot Street and moved the highway department to the rear of the present Town Office Building.

Firefighters

The first records of the Duxbury Fire Department are dated 1834 when the first Hunneman hand engine was purchased, although firefighting began much earlier with house and forest fire prevention.

Hunneman #1 was manned by Company #1 and housed at Cedar Street. It was supplemented by Hunneman #2, called *Victory*, manned by Company #2 and housed at Surplus Street, near Bumblebee Lane. The town reports first list the Fire Department in 1857—29 members in Company #1, 27 in Company #2. In 1906, a chief was selected. The Company #1 meeting of January 1936, chaired by Captain Eben Briggs, reported that a Fireman's Band had been formed which would begin rehearsals in the Town Hall. This meeting also celebrated Hortense E. Merry's 20th anniversary as chief, for which occasion the engine company had purchased a box of cigars.

The earliest fire records were for 1909 when the department handled 11 fires: 5 in the woods, 3 in houses, 1 grass, 1 watertower, 1 unknown. The 1950 report submitted to the selectmen requesting an increase in the department budget reported 75 general calls in 1949.

The fire department has grown with the town. During 1984, 1225 emergency calls were handled, including 189 buildings; 87 outside fires; 35 vehicles; and 680 medical calls, an invaluable addition to the duties of the department. Also, 4,000 brush-burning permits were issued and supervised.

The department handles this volume with a limited work force, but with more men on full-time duty, and more efficient equipment. The two stations are well-located so that calls can be answered quickly and efficiently. Above all, Duxbury's fire department always maintains a very high rating among comparable units in the Commonwealth.

Howard T. Blanchard

Town meeting as drawn by M. Wilber for the *Clipper*. (*Clipper*)

A special town meeting in July 1947 adopted the town's first set of general bylaws. These have been amended and recodified several times over the years and special bylaws have also been adopted, including a personnel bylaw in 1955, an anti-loitering bylaw in 1972, and a leash law in 1979. In 1980, the town turned down a proposed new Town Charter on referendum.

Until 1948, a moderator was elected under Article One of each town meeting. Since then, a moderator has been elected at each annual town election. At a special town meeting in 1948, motions to increase the Board of Selectmen and Assessors from three to five members were defeated. About this time, the Planning Board, which for years had been groping for a definitive purpose to better warrant their existence, was beginning to get much more ambitious. In 1950, they recommended an appointed building inspector, one-acre zoning, a representative town meeting, and a town manager. The 1967 town meeting voted to increase planning board membership from five to seven, as they were now a very busy board indeed.

In 1950, the Memorial Office Building Committee recommended a new town office building to replace the converted residence on St. George Street. They recommended it be built on the site of the former Partridge Academy and be designed to resemble it. Twenty-five years later, the present Town Office Building was completed and dedicated in 1975.

The selectmen began reviewing plans in 1953 for the Expressway to be built through Duxbury. Work actually started within the town in 1962 and it was opened one year later, exerting the greatest influence on our changing environment, and coinciding with our most rapid period of growth.

In 1955, the town meeting voted to petition the Legislature to have the town take over the Duxbury Fire and Water District. Three years later, three Water Commissioners and two members of the Finance Committee were appointed to investigate enterprise accounting for the Water Department, which actually operated on that basis for the next few years, but was not successfully re-established until 1981.

In 1956, Charles Crocker retired from the Board of Selectmen after serving for twenty-three years. Meantime, the town meeting continued to respond to the real and anticipated growth that was by now accelerating even faster. In 1959, the town voted $1.3 million for a new junior/senior high school (now the Intermediate School) on St. George Street. The following year, the town purchased the land for the Chandler Street School,

The Police

Before the twentieth century, Duxbury had no official police department, and even in the early 1900s, the selectmen made their own chairman chief of police, with several elected constables. Two constables, Charles Pierce and Andrew Delano, followed later by Joseph Bolton and Warren Prince, occasionally overlapped each other's terms of office, but in general, managed to accomplish the necessary work. Special officers handled criminal matters, but constables were elected to handle civil warrants.

Things began to change when James O'Neil was appointed constable in 1925. In 1931, he became Duxbury's one-man police force. A police station was built in part of the old South Duxbury school, and funds were appropriated for a motorcycle and a cruiser. O'Neil became permanent chief, with temporary officers on call when needed. During 1931, the force answered 256 calls resulting in 19 arrests.

After 1932, with the appointment of Earl Chandler as first full-time patrolman, the department settled into a long period of gradual expansion. Chandler became chief and was succeeded by Lawrence Doyle.

Henry McNeil, chief since 1946, was a prime mover in the expansion and modernization of the department. After thirty-seven years of service, he was succeeded by Daniel L. Skelly, who resigned in 1986 to become Chief of the Capitol Police in Boston. The selectmen then appointed Enrico Capucci, former chief of Shirley, to the post.

In 1967, the department moved into its own building that included a lock-up, radio systems, and offices to handle a workload of over 15,000 calls a year, with a total force of twenty-six full-time officers.

Jack Post

although the funds to build it were not voted until 1972. A permanent fire department was established by the 1961 town meeting and two years later, town meeting appropriated the funds to purchase the town's first ambulance.

The Conservation Commission was established by the 1963 town meeting, and in 1970, the town meeting voted unanimously to adopt a conservation policy and make a commitment to conservation. The town now owns approximately fifteen hundred acres of conservation land. The town also purchased the Bay Farm in 1972 and North Hill in 1977.

A number of undertakings began in 1965, over a three-year period, which markedly demonstrated the tremendous growth that was then occurring in Duxbury. The town voted and built a new police station, Central Fire Station, Middle School (which is now the high school), a sub-fire station at Ashdod, and an extensive addition to and remodeling of the library. In 1974, funds were appropriated for substantial additions to both the high school and the intermediate school. Beginning in 1978, the sub-fire station at Ashdod, in addition to the Central Fire Station, was fully manned.

Primarily as a result of all this construction, the town's debt reached a peak of nearly $15 million in 1976. This will have been reduced to approximately $5 million in 1987, if the town doesn't borrow any more money.

Even as we celebrate Duxbury's 350th anniversary, the pressures of growth on the town's environment are continuing. We assume that the structure of town government will continue to respond positively as it has in the past. Due to the constraints imposed by Proposition 2½ on the town's ability to levy taxes, innovative approaches and serious long-range planning will be necessary to meet Duxbury's future needs. The three most pressing concerns for the immediate future are: the school budget, which is growing at a faster rate than revenues; insurance, both the cost and the ability to obtain necessary liability coverage; and the cost and disposal of solid waste, which is a problem far beyond Duxbury's capacity to resolve on its own. To meet these and other challenges, the organization of town government may have to undergo structural changes, but residents are confident, based on the past, that town government will meet the future successfully and wisely.

JOHN P. LEONARD

Preserving Duxbury

The first grants of land given to Duxbury men, presumably in 1623, were single acres; but in 1627, a second land division provided for *great lots* of twenty acres for each man, and twenty for each member of his family, with his grants "fronting on the bay as far as possible."[1] These lots were free; today, 360 years later, an acre of land averages over $100,000, with waterfront property, if available, selling for four or five times that.

Duxbury's housing needs grew steadily from the seventeenth through the twentieth century, and then explosively as the town changed, with the completion of the expressway, from a remote sleepy seaside village to a Boston suburb. Although largely a summer resort from 1870 through World War II, it has today been transformed into a year-round community with some summer residents. The latter, many of whom boarded here at one time or another, bought their own houses and began living here permanently.

Town land-use boards have long been occupied with planning, conservation, and regulatory efforts. In 1926, the town elected its first Planning Board (Franklin Brett, B. F. Goodrich, Charles Bittinger, Mrs. Josephine Shaw, and Miss Agnes Ellison), whose purpose lay "in constant attempts to bring to the attention of the Selectmen of the Town and its citizens measures for improvement of the roads, widening and straightening of bad corners and curves, making for road safety, as well as improving the appearance of the town; and offering suggestions as to laying out of new roads that will develop unused tracts of land, and open up desirable residential properties."[2] Yet, at the same town meeting, it was voted unanimously to postpone indefinitely the adoption of a zoning bylaw, which had been issued in pamphlet form to the voters in August 1925.

Cover of the 1969 report.

173

The August 1927 Town Report gives certain regulations set by the Planning Board for proper roads and set-backs for all new buildings, and recommends reserving certain areas for business centers. In 1936, the town report states, "the public intention is to keep Duxbury, so far as is practical, the same quiet old New England village, preserving its natural beauties of varied landscape, and making such accessible with good roads and paths, and by so doing to attract the type of resident who appreciates such things, and seeks such restful features."

The Planning Board noted in 1938 "unfortunately, Duxbury is unusually lax in having no definite or reasonably complete bylaws, with the result that many detrimental and unrestricted courses can be followed by property owners in the character of their buildings." The next year they were still bemoaning the lack of a regularly accepted set of bylaws.

By 1943, preparations were finally made for bylaws, which were adopted at the 1944 town meeting, and approved by the attorney general. Minimum lot size was 20,000 square feet, with 100-foot frontage, effective June 12, 1954. In 1948, the town established the office of Building Inspector, and a building permit requirement. The permits increased from 64 that year to 85 two years later, when the town adopted regulations for subdivisions. In 1952, the lot size was upped to 30,000 square feet with 150-foot frontage, and two years later enlarged to 40,000 square feet, with the 200-foot frontage which stands today. This resulted in multi-bedroom, single-family dwellings requiring costly public services, particularly schools, and leading inevitably to rising taxes.

Two comprehensive plans were published in 1959 and 1969. Dwelling unit permits went from 44 in 1963 to 74 in 1966, 150 in 1968, and to the historic peak of 200 in 1972. The school population nearly doubled from 1085 pupils in 1959 to 2080 in 1969, then continued to grow at a ten percent annual rate through the early 1970s. Assessments on houses rose to 100 percent, so in effect taxes were rising at a rate of fifteen percent a year. High taxes were hard on older people, and there were few apartments for them to move into. Duxbury had only two such buildings, one of six units in an old captain's house on the corner of Harrison and Washington streets, and a 32-unit garden apartment on Route 53. At several town meetings, voters, fearful of the experience of neighboring towns where unsightly buildings had proliferated as soon as zoning was changed, turned down proposals for multiple-occupancy buildings.

It was felt that further steps should be taken to manage the growth of the town. An ambitious land acquisition program, begun in 1969, resulted in almost fifteen hundred acres being preserved, both upland and wetlands. In 1971, a Land Use Committee was formed, which included a selectman, members of all other town committees, representatives of the League of Women Voters, the Rural and Historical Society, and the Conservation Commission. It hired a firm of town planners who studied Duxbury, talked with town officials, and in 1973 came up with the Comprehensive Plan Statement. This, together with the General Plan of 1962 and the 1969 Comprehensive Plan, set guidelines for Duxbury's future growth.

The result was a new zoning bylaw, the first in the nation to be based on impact zoning, in which the town was given the tools to sit down and negotiate with planned unit developers. The town allows the developer to build at higher densities, to cluster his units, or to build multi-family housing. In return, the developer agrees to consider the town's ecology, to mix housing types in a way that would have favorable impact on the school budget, and to allow for open space. The planned unit developments also carry a restriction of two bedrooms, thereby discouraging large families. These developments and clusters permit higher density with common open space. Shorter, privately-maintained roads save the town maintenance and service costs.

The plan addressed both the problem of too-rapid growth and the town's inability to apply qualitative controls to subdivisions by right. It is a major land use consideration. It states that the existing residential character of Duxbury is in keeping with the New England tradition of residential land use concentrated in small village centers and separated by farm land and open space. It is in this spirit that further development in Duxbury is intended to reinforce its residential character through clustering, to vary housing density in neighborhood groupings, thus encouraging a variety of housing types, and to maintain the historically significant New England architecture in town.

Young couples continue to buy in Duxbury, due to its excellent schools and its beauty and historic attractions. In some cases, they are buying the large multibedroom houses vacated by *empty-nesters*, who move on to the newer one- or two-bedroom condominiums; but they are also buying the new planned-development houses, most of them west of Route 3A.

So Duxbury, with a still-growing population, is developing at a rate of only eighty percent of its lowest potential growth. Building permits for dwelling units declined thirty-nine percent in 1985. This is still a residential community, and will continue to be. The long-range planning and concerns of the town have resulted in diversified housing which accommodates the diverse needs of the residents and encourages a more balanced community.

PRISCILLA SANGSTER

Percy Walker

Percy Walker really was a legend in his time. Who else could claim such feats as establishing a town water system for Duxbury, pushing through the zoning laws, and all the while building a flourishing real estate business. Mr. Duxbury? The slightly ironic title was becoming to him.

Water in Duxbury came from wells, often pumped by windmills which failed when the daytime breezes subsided in the evening. Complaints were strident, for Mr. Walker had sold many of the properties thus left dry. He was asked to do something—and he did. He inaugurated a campaign for a water system that eventually passed the town meeting and benefitted the entire community.

More important was the first zoning to protect Duxbury from the fate that has engulfed many seaside communities: the tendency to cut the waterfront into tiny subdivisions. In 1942, Percy Walker joined the Planning Board, then purely advisory, and built it into an effective means of regulating growth in the town, thus maintaining Duxbury's rural charm and non-commercial atmosphere.

He worked closely with the Rural Society when his brother Herbert E. Walker was president for seven years from 1893 to 1899, and for twenty-eight more from 1921 through 1949. Then Percy took over for seven years himself—a family dynasty that helped develop the concept of conservation and did much to develop Duxbury's awareness of its heritage.

"Mr. Duxbury" has indeed bequeathed to us a town to his—and to our—liking.

Jack Post

Conservation

*I*f Duxbury's 1987 residents fret over what seems like an endless succession of housing developments marring the landscape, they can take comfort in knowing their sentiments have been shared by prior generations. They may also take comfort in knowing that some two thousand acres will never be developed. The reason: visionary leadership that dates back to the late 1800s, leadership which fostered a climate of conservancy before the average citizen truly understood the concept.

At that time, Duxbury was experiencing economic reversals as the closing of the shipyards resulted in a local depression. The town's economy was changing from production-oriented to service-based, as Duxbury's inherent attractions became a drawing card for revenue. The pleasing landscape might well have become the basis for population explosion, but the town was blessed with a small contingent of individuals sharing a collective desire to beautify Duxbury, to preserve its elegance, to restore what had been damaged by careless use, and to look to a future that needed no crystal ball to decipher. These individuals were, among others, the creators of the Rural Society. The society is chiefly responsible for Duxbury's unique character, for that society's concerns led to land use and acquisitions consistent with the early goals of the conservation movement. By the time President Theodore Roosevelt was speaking to the American people about the values of conservation, Duxbury's own Rural Society had already taken steps toward preserving land and water resources.

Many residents today assume that growth pressure in Duxbury is a new event, caused chiefly by the completion of Route 3 in 1963. But between 1930 and 1980 Duxbury's population growth consistently outstripped that of nearly

176

all other towns in the metropolitan area. It experienced 350 percent higher population in 1980 than at the 1930 U.S. census; the rest of the region grew at a rate of less than half that. During the war years, Duxbury grew 39 percent in one decade, while its Boston-area neighbors collectively grew at a mere 2 percent rate. Clearly, Duxbury was already expanding and its residents could see what was coming. They adopted a zoning bylaw in 1944, far earlier than many other towns. The Route 3 experience taught that zoning alone could not protect the town's natural resources. Faced by increased pressures, the town itself began to take measures toward conserving resources and controlling growth. State officials, realizing that cities and towns were growing far beyond their ability to provide services, enacted a series of statutes to facilitate better zoning and allow sizeable land acquisitions that would keep fragile or resource-significant properties off the development market. Duxbury's leaders seized upon the opportunities. In 1963, a Conservation Commission was approved. In cooperation with the Planning Board and with the backing of an active group of concerned citizens, Duxbury embarked on a land acquisition campaign second to none in the Commonwealth, with the result that the town now ranks among the highest in protected lands.

Dr. Lansing Bennett, whose tireless work and famous town meeting presentations will always be remembered, was chairman of the commission. During his tenure, over a thousand acres of conservation land were acquired. These acquisitions were selected on the basis of their natural resource characteristics, already defined in earlier land use planning reports commissioned by the Planning Board. The intention was to create an extensive greenbelt adjoining stretches of wetlands, and so properties central to the watersheds of Island Creek, the South River, and the Back River and its tributary, West Brook, became prime candidates for acquisition. A move to establish wetlands protection in the zoning bylaw was made, with officials keeping fragile lands in the forefront of acquisition plans.

Central to virtually every purchase was the protection of a key resource: ground water. Dependent solely on wells for its water supply, Duxbury could not afford the risks of contamination. Combined work by the Rural and Historical Society, the Conservation Commission, and the Massachusetts Audubon Society would eventually result in an almost one thousand-acre preserve within the core of the town. That acreage, combined with many other tracts, forms the basis for an aquifer protection plan for which the town must be eternally grateful, and over which it must be forever vigilant. Duxbury's aquifer formation is unique. It is confined within the town so that ground water consumed here is ground water originating here.

The Conservation Commission has periodically acquired, through gifts of small parcels, one of the key natural resources along the entire eastern coastline, the Great Salt Marsh. Duxbury Beach, managed by the privately owned Duxbury Beach Reservation, and the adjacent salt marshes rank among the twenty most important shorebird stopover sites by federal standards. The entire marsh is now protected by the local wetlands zoning bylaw. Of the roughly seventy-five acres, the commission owns more than ten.

The late Edmund Dondero cautioned residents during a 1973 zoning bylaw debate that "Duxbury is no longer the best-kept secret on the South Shore." To the degree that ongoing growth disturbs us all, let it be said that early attention to resource conservation paved the way for an unparalleled protective land use program. The goal was not to stop growth, but to maintain a beautiful community. At that, Duxbury has unquestionably succeeded.

JUDI BARRETT

The Natural Shore

Something stirred the flock of sanderlings. There was an unrest throughout the group and in a split second they were together in the air and on the wing. The young ones weren't sure about this move but they flew with the group in perfect alleles: together, in one motion, a tightly woven patch of small shorebirds headed north from South America. After a feeding stop along Cape Hatteras they continued their flight. The older birds knew there was a synchronic movement taking place, or at least they depended on it. They knew that when they arrived at the barrier beach along the Atlantic coast, called Duxbury, there would be a collection of big crab/spiders laying eggs in such profusion that birds and horseshoe crabs had a well-insured future. Sure enough, they skated in along the tenuous sands and found in the shallows of the bay hundreds of the crabs and millions of their eggs. They ate well and fattened before heading into the Arctic for nesting.

The glacial and storm-formed strand called Duxbury Beach has been taken from the eroding bluffs left by the last glaciation. These sands have been windblown and storm-tossed until (for today at least) they lay as we know them. The marsh side has served huge flocks of migrant birds for the past ten thousand years. Brant float in the shallow water eating the eel grass that grows as one of the few underwater flowering plants. Sanderlings, semi-palmated plovers and sandpipers dash across the flats and probe the sand looking for arthropods and other small animal food items. Sea ducks and loons of various species have used the foreshore and its crabs and molluscs for food for the same time period. Fishes of small sizes attract the loons as well as grebes, cormorants, and mergansers. In the fall, spectacular flocks of swallows form along the strand to take advantage of the bayberry fruits before departing for the Florida keys and the islands of the Caribbean. Offshore there are tuna, bluefish, mola

Roseate terns in flight. (*David C. Twichell*)

mola, and huge blooms of sand launce, each of these pulsing to a seasonal rhythm that allows for the species to exist in the linear flow of time, each species eating and being eaten in numbers sufficient to abet its prey and predators, but not in such numbers that they themselves begin to disappear. Cycles, individually crucial, species-wise important, and inter-specifically necessary, all flow together like a myriad of currents, ebbs, eddies, and flows.

These rivers of life meet and feed each other and Duxbury Beach has long been a superb stage for this theater. The performance never ends, but when man made himself a player about five thousand years ago, a ripple was felt throughout the cast. The new predator was ruthless. He took beyond his needs and affected populations as the other animals never had. Today the population and sizes of fishes, birds, and mammals in the North Atlantic are nothing like they were in the past. Lobsters are smaller and fewer. The fishes, almost to a species, are in the same distribution. Whole bird populations have been wiped out. Nesting turtles are all but gone from our shores. Atlantic salmon and other migrants have been obliterated. What remains can be seen on those special places like Duxbury Beach.

Birds are a good barometer as they are easily seen and often heard. There are many people who watch them, list them, and remember them. There are bird lists from Duxbury Beach that cover the entire past century. It is from these and more current sightings that we get an idea of the value that these fragile lands have for wildlife. Wildlife is transient. Sanderlings use the beach for a week or two in spring and again in fall, but the beach is essential to them for those time periods. There isn't any other place like Duxbury Beach to go to. The coincidence of movement and production cycles are in synch only in certain places, and it is these that the birds (and others) need—not just space.

Joe Lund was instrumental in creating the High Tide Shorebird Sanctuary for protection of the tern colony. (*David C. Twichell*)

The beach provides the food and isolation that a feeding, fattening, resting bird needs before returning south. For southward moving birds, the next flight might be one thousand miles or more. For a bird that weighs about two ounces, there is an overwhelming need to pack on fat to prepare for the journey. It is in very few places that we find congregations of birds in such numbers that it seems primeval.

These creatures are not lesser beings, but as Henry Beston suggests, are other nations traveling through the world from a different vantage. They use large expanses of the planet, traversing those sections of little value to them in long hops and settling on those small specific areas that enhance their being. They are truly cosmopolitan in nature and each of the spots they visit are important to their well-being as individuals and as a species. Duxbury Beach is one of the areas that provides sustenance and shelter for these nations.

DAVID E. CLAPP

Duxbury Beach

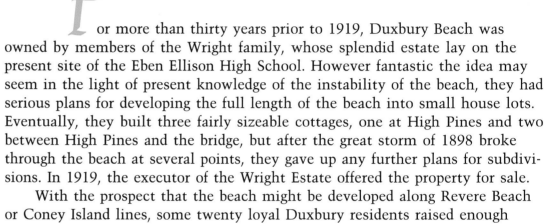

For more than thirty years prior to 1919, Duxbury Beach was owned by members of the Wright family, whose splendid estate lay on the present site of the Eben Ellison High School. However fantastic the idea may seem in the light of present knowledge of the instability of the beach, they had serious plans for developing the full length of the beach into small house lots. Eventually, they built three fairly sizeable cottages, one at High Pines and two between High Pines and the bridge, but after the great storm of 1898 broke through the beach at several points, they gave up any further plans for subdivisions. In 1919, the executor of the Wright Estate offered the property for sale.

With the prospect that the beach might be developed along Revere Beach or Coney Island lines, some twenty loyal Duxbury residents raised enough money to buy the property. Title was taken in the name of the Duxbury Beach Association, a common law trust organized to acquire and protect the beach for the benefit of Duxbury.

At the time, there were about eighteen houses or shacks and three large shooting stands on the property south of the area now marked by the park gates. Some had been on the beach so long owners claimed to have acquired title to the land under their houses by undisturbed occupancy for more than twenty years. All but three of the houses and all the shooting stands have been removed or destroyed. Walter Prince took charge of floating the three Wright houses across the bay to relocate them on Landing Road in South Duxbury.

In 1926 and 1931, the Association's title to the beach was confirmed by the Massachusetts Land Court, an action which required negotiation and litigation over ten years, the purchase of marshlands bordering the beach, and the spending of thousands of dollars financed by shareholder subscriptions.

Duxbury Beach. (*Fran Nichols*)

180

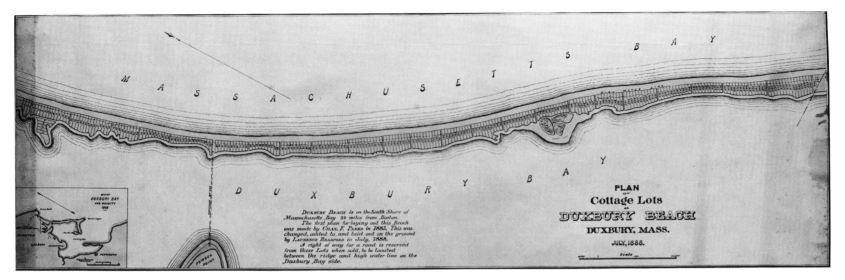

The Wright's plan of cottage lots for Duxbury Beach.

During the early years, the only practical access was over Powder Point Bridge. By the mid-1920s, automobile traffic and use of the beach was rapidly increasing. Every pleasant Sunday, the entire bridge and all adjacent Powder Point streets were completely lined with parked automobiles, greatly limiting use of the beach by Duxbury people, and creating not only a nuisance but a real danger of catastrophe.

In 1928, a bill was introduced into the Massachusetts legislature providing for acquisition by the Commonwealth of several beaches, including Duxbury Beach. Commissions visited Duxbury, and the town in its turn organized in opposition to the plan, expressing disapproval in town meeting, 112–46. This attempt at state ownership was defeated.

In 1931, a study was made by the town which recommended that parking on the bridge be prohibited and that two parking areas be constructed, a smaller one on the beach end for Duxbury residents, and a larger one at the north end for general use, with the town policing both. Town meeting approved these recommendations unanimously, an arrangement which has since received continuous cooperation from both the town and the Duxbury Beach Association. To defray increasing costs, seasonal stickers are required for Duxbury resident parking, and daily parking fees are charged at the northern area for the general public.

The bridge itself was originally a Duxbury project, dedicated October 21, 1892 and maintained by Duxbury, Plymouth County, and three neighboring towns; but in 1941, Duxbury took over entire control (and expense) in order to retain exclusive rights.

During the war years, the beach saw relatively little use except for occasional training exercises. A movement for a military road was discouraged and abandoned. After the war, the question of state acquisition of the beach arose several times, the most important test occurring in 1950 when the Governor proposed to create a Recreational Authority to take over Duxbury Beach, among others.

Mass meetings were held in Duxbury, and mass transportation to legislative hearings in Boston was arranged. Signatures were collected and so much opposition generated that proposals for the Recreation Authority and the purchase of Duxbury Beach were both defeated.

In 1968, the state Department of Public Works threatened to take the beach by eminent domain under a plan by the Massachusetts Area Planning Council, but again alert opposition by the town of Duxbury and friends of the beach resulted in an adverse report and abandonment of the project.

Beginning in 1973, substantially all of the beach, except the Duxbury Beach Park area, has been leased annually to the Town of Duxbury. Under this arrangement, the town issues beach vehicle permits, provides police protection, and provides the conservation officers to patrol the beach throughout the year.

In 1975, ownership of the beach was transferred from Duxbury Beach Association to Duxbury Beach Reservation, Inc., a Massachusetts charitable corporation. The purposes of the reservation are to preserve the ecology of the beach as a barrier beach for the protection of Duxbury, Kingston, and Plymouth, and to make the beach available as a recreational beach for the benefit of the residents of Duxbury and the general public.

In 1978, a severe northeast storm caused extensive damage to the beach where the ocean washed through to the bay, and large parts of the dunes were washed away in several areas. The reservation undertook an extensive beach restoration program in cooperation with the Town of Duxbury, funded in part by assistance from the federal government.

The reservation carries on an annual beach maintenance and restoration program which includes fertilizing existing dunes and beach grass, planting new beach grass, installing sand fences to trap sand for dunes growth, and installing post and cable fencing to control traffic over the right of way to Gurnet and Saquish.

The beach has a tendency to recede and move westward and is often endangered by severe storms and high tides. This makes it difficult to maintain parking areas and to foster beach grass which is vital for the protection of the dunes. Duxbury citizens demonstrate their concern for the beach in a practical way each spring when entire families turn out to help in the beach grass planting program.

Management of the beach necessitates balancing the needs and demands of divergent user interests including ecological preservation, general recreational use, controlled beach vehicle use, and the public right of way, which provides the only access by land to the Gurnet and Saquish areas of the Town of Plymouth. Duxbury Beach Association and Duxbury Beach Reservation, Inc. have worked in close harmony with the Town of Duxbury to preserve and maintain Duxbury Beach as a priceless asset for the benefit and enjoyment of the citizens of Duxbury and the general public.

FREDERICK T. PRATT & ROBERT G. MILLAR

Bug Light

At the mouth of the waters which open into Duxbury, Kingston, and Plymouth bays sits a squatty, iron-clad, spark plug-shaped navigational aid officially named the Duxbury Pier Lighthouse. This beloved landmark, known as the *Bug Light*, was originally built to aid the heavy commercial traffic from Plymouth and to augment the land-bound lighthouse on the bluff at the Gurnet. One hundred twelve years after it was built, the United States Coast Guard discovered just how beloved it was when they attempted to replace it with modern equipment.

In 1871 when the Bug Light was erected on the ledge off Clark's Island, the United States Lighthouse Service had jurisdiction, with the entire coast of Massachusetts falling into District Two.

The Lighthouse Service, eventually a division of the Department of Commerce, was established by the federal government in 1789 at the first session of Congress, making it one of the oldest public works in the country. Until that time, lighthouses and other aids to navigation were built and maintained privately. Bug Light fell officially into the category of attended lighthouses and is considered of moderate size and common design. Cast iron caissons form the base over concrete; surmounting those are the storage rooms, keeper's quarters, lamp room, and light (or lantern). The entire structure, sunk firmly in the shallows, rises thirty-five feet above the high water mark.

Bug Light has stood as a landmark in the bay since 1871. (*Fran Nichols*)

Bug Light's flashing red beacon—a navigational signal to be kept to the starboard as boats enter the harbors—is provided by approximately fifty storage batteries which supply the current. The keeper of the Gurnet Lighthouse initiates Bug Light's fog horn, while radio signals activate the continued sound.

Although Bug Light continues to be an aid to navigation, the structure has been neglected. By 1980, its light was no longer effective and the fog horn worked only sporadically. The structure was rusted and although the base was as sound as ever, the walkway and ladders were rickety and windows broken. Estimated repairs were set by the Coast Guard at $400,000.

In 1983, while attending a meeting in Boston, Duxbury Harbormaster Donald C. Beers, III, was approached casually by a member of the Coast Guard who wondered if Mattakeesett Court (Duxbury Town Landing) would be clear and large enough to land the helicopters and store the equipment scheduled to be used for the dismantling of the lighthouse. Initial plans were for the top section of the lighthouse to be removed (at the railing) and replaced with a thirty-foot fiberglass tower topped with solar light and fog horn.

It was Don Beers who suggested that the plan first be presented to the selectmen and area citizens, at least through publicity in local papers. When notification still wasn't forthcoming, the harbormaster wrote an impartial letter, published in the *Duxbury Clipper*, outlining the Coast Guard's plans and reasoning. Dismantling of Bug Light was set for the twentieth of June.

The Massachusetts Historical Commission deemed other spark plug-shaped lighthouses more worth saving and neither the Duxbury nor Plymouth historical societies were in positions to save "the Bug." Nevertheless, a grass roots effort sprang up immediately.

Fundraising for Project Bug Light began while the committee worked to convince the Coast Guard that the lighthouse could be saved, and saved for under the $400,000 figure. Duxbury's Earl McMahon, a retired electrical engineer with a degree from the Massachusetts Institute of Technology, had the expertise the committee needed. After fruitless meetings with the Coast Guard, McMahon, his committee, and local officials met with Rear Admiral Richard A. Bauman. They presented a cost analysis and suggested that if the Coast Guard refurbished the bottom of the lighthouse as planned, Project

Twin lights at the Gurnet, two octagonal towers constructed in 1843. They remained operative until 1924, when one was removed, the other modernized.

Bug Light would do the rest. A reprieve was granted on the spot.

Major repairs were completed by the summer of 1985. For approximately $20,000, Project Bug Light restored the landmark, thanks to the time and talent of Kingston, Plymouth, and Duxbury volunteers. Area professionals replaced fire doors, windows, the walkway, roof, and ladders. After sandblasting, the base is now marine red and the upper half white, for increased visibility. Under a leasing arrangement with the Coast Guard, the non-profit group will maintain it for five years, at which time the option may be renewed.

Whether for lobstermen and commercial draggers returning after a hard day's work, sailors home from a cruise, or Frostbiters in their annual around-the-lighthouse regatta, Bug Light still stands, warning and welcoming as it was meant to, a tribute to the men and women who love it.

LESLIE DAVIS GUCCIONE

184

Education in Duxbury

Since 1946

Throughout most of the last forty years, the main concern of Duxbury schools has been keeping up with growth. In 1946, the public school population of Duxbury, 342 children, fit into three little one- or two-room schools for grades 1 through 4 and the high school on the hill, now Upper Alden (without the 1952 addition). By 1986, the Duxbury school system housed 3038 children in three full-size elementary buildings, an intermediate school, and a high school.

Population boomed all over the country after World War II, with a fifty percent increase in the birth rate. It boomed even more in Duxbury, and the question was not only where to put all the schoolchildren, but how to get teachers for them. In 1947, John Whitehead noted in his superintendent's report, "This is a time when securing any teachers is a problem."[1] The teacher shortage had made itself felt earlier, during the war, when the School Committee was forced to compromise its policy of never hiring married women as teachers. Helen DeWolf, a second grade teacher at the Village School in 1941 and 1942, remembers her amazement at being rehired just before her wedding. But even as he offered her the job, Walter Prince of the School Committee warned, "Now, we don't expect you to get pregnant and go faintin' all over the place."

In 1948, construction was begun on a K through 6 elementary school to serve the whole town. The School Committee report for that year noted that the building would be nearly full to capacity as soon as it was completed. In fact, in September 1949, the new school opened its doors to *more* pupils than the building was planned for.

The next year, Dr. Everett Handy moved from Westminster College in Pennsylvania to begin his twenty years of service in Duxbury as superintendent

Dr. Handy giving diplomas to the Class of 1951. (*Everett L. Handy*)

of schools. At that point the budget was $141,791.69, the school population was 605, and the total staff of the school system, including janitors, was 46.

A constant characteristic of Dr. Handy's superintendency was foresightedness. "The housing problem will again become acute in the elementary school in September 1953," he predicted his first year. "There may be a problem in the high school in September 1952."[2] Taking advantage of his foresight, the town added a new wing to the high school in 1952, and the next year began construction on a new wing of the elementary school.

The continual question was how to improve the education program without increasing costs. "We didn't have Prop. 2½ in those days," says Dr. Handy, "but we always had an economy-minded FinCom." One answer to the problem was the campus plan for the school system, taking advantage of the public library and the natural science resource of the woods and marsh. Much later, in the 1970s, the town pool would also fit into this plan.

As the shortage of teachers continued, Dr. Handy conducted an ongoing search, up to Maine, down to Connecticut, even out to Cleveland. He also amended the former school policy of never hiring women teachers with children. (Helen DeWolf, rehired in 1954, was one of the first teacher-mothers.) Single teachers were difficult to retain because "they wanted more than an occasional PTA meeting for their social life," as Dr. Handy puts it. Married male teachers found it difficult to support a family on a teacher's salary.

By this time the schools had to cope with another pressure besides growth: rising expectations from Duxbury students, parents, and other citizens. One third of the Duxbury High School Class of 1950 went on to college, but by 1955, 58 percent of the high school students were preparing for either two- or four-year colleges. In 1957, Sputnik launched a spate of intense criticism of American education, felt in Duxbury as well as around the country. The Duxbury schools responded by improving the math and science curricula as well as re-emphasizing the three R's, and offering advanced programs for bright students.

By 1960, the much-needed new junior-senior high school, the present Duxbury Intermediate School building, was almost complete and the new expressway from Boston to Cape Cod was under construction. Its completion was to bring on another burst of growth in the school population, as breadwinners with young families discovered that commuting to Boston from Duxbury was now reasonable.

Duxbury was also an attractive option for families with children, partly because of the high quality of its school system. For example, long before Chapter 766 became law in 1974, Duxbury had developed programs for pupils with special needs. A program for children with reading difficulties was started in the 1950s; in 1968, a program for deaf children was begun; and in 1970, the Duxbury schools hired a speech therapist, an adjustment counselor, and teachers for the retarded and perceptually handicapped.

The high school was overflowing once more by 1965, and the intermediate and elementary schools would soon be crowded also. The solution was to build a new middle school (the present DHS building) on the former Wright estate, across St. George Street from the public library, thus preserving the campus plan of the Duxbury schools. The Eben Howes Ellison building was specifically designed for the new middle school educational program—to encourage team teaching, independent study, flexible grouping for instruction, and remedial work with individual students. However, population pressure was to eventually override these plans; the Ellison School would be used as a middle school only from 1968 to 1973.

Aerial view showing the Ellison High School, the Alden School, the Intermediate School, and the library. (*Locke Aero Photos*)

By the time Dr. Handy retired and Dr. Laurence Anderson was hired as superintendent in 1970, the high school was overcrowded again, forcing such makeshift measures as huge study hall sessions of two and three hundred in the cafeteria. A temporary solution was open campus. During the split-shift extended day, a student was not required to be on campus except when he or she actually had classes. Open campus contributed to a growing discipline problem at the high school, which exhibited itself in a range of defiant behaviors.

A more serious problem was drugs; in 1968 an intensive educational program on this topic was begun. John W. Hill, the new principal, regarded this work as "one of his most important challenges." Soon after the high school moved to the Ellison School, the extended day and open campus were dropped.

With the elementary school bursting, in 1970 the decision was made to build a second elementary school on the town-owned land on Chandler Street. But the Alden School could not wait even three years, and so from September 1971 to June 1974, the kindergarten was housed in the Sailor's Snug Harbor (since demolished) on King Caesar Road. The Chandler School, constructed on the new open space design, opened in 1973.

Beginning in the late sixties, the school system began to lose its power to pretty much run itself without having to bargain with the professional staff, the taxpayers, or the parents. The first big change was the advent of teachers' unions. "The schools brought collective bargaining on themselves in 1967," remarks Thomas Lanman, "by not paying teachers a living wage."

In the next decade, citizens would scrutinize more closely the way the schools were being run. "Parents never used to complain to the schools," says Margaret Kearney, DHS Class of 1961. "Parents never compared teachers or took it upon themselves to determine which teacher was best for their child." The state open meeting law encouraged increased accountability from the school committee and administration.

Finances in Duxbury had never been exactly loose, but 1979 brought something new—taxpayer revolt. In June 1979, just before new Superintendent Seldon Whitaker began his work, a special town meeting voted down the $6.2 million school budget, outraged at the $109,000 budget overrun. At the prospect of trimming the school budget to fit the 4 percent tax cap voted by the Massachusetts legislature, Dr. Whitaker said dryly, "It certainly will be a challenge." And it has been.

Seldon Whitaker was chosen as superintendent during a time when the Duxbury school system was under increasingly watchful surveillance by parents and taxpayers. He was personable, the better to represent the schools to the community, and he was a strong, businesslike administrator. During his five years in Duxbury, a period of financial austerity under Proposition 2½, he established a guideline for budget cuts—concentric circles widening toward lesser importance, with the teacher and the classroom at the center.

When Donald Kennedy became superintendent in 1984, growth had finally leveled off, and had even dropped slightly from the 1980 peak of 3240 children in the schools. The continuing budget squeeze has forced dropping whole programs and delaying maintenance.

In November 1985, Kennedy noted that the Duxbury school population was projected to rise slowly in the next five years, and that school costs would rise slightly faster than town income. Spiraling real estate values mean that fewer young families can now afford to move to this town, but the pressure of growth and the challenge of maintaining quality still remain the issues of education in Duxbury.

BEATRICE GORMLEY

A Student's View

When I first found out that I would be moving to Duxbury in the summer before my sophomore year in high school, I tried to find out something about what my new home town would be like. This wasn't very hard to do. I simply requested information about the town from the school. The typical characteristics covered by the town profile that I received didn't faze me—a quaint little bedroom village forty miles south of Boston; twelve thousand people, expensive houses, affluent people, high-caliber schools, gorgeous beaches, etc.

"That's nice," I yawned, "but what is there for teenagers?" I liked the idea of a good school system. Not that going to school is my favorite thing, but if I'm going, I might as well go to the best. The beaches didn't sound too bad either. But I also heard a lot about Duxbury before I ever set foot in it. It had a reputation as having one *helluva* soccer team. Duxbury also had a reputation as having one *helluva* problem with drinking and driving.

I found everything that I'd heard about Duxbury to be true. It is quaint, little, and it will always be forty miles south of Boston. The people and the houses were, for the most part, just what I expected. The school system was excellent. And the beaches—ah, the beaches. They, too, exceeded my expectations. So did the soccer team. They captured the 1984 State Championship, their fifth in eight years, as I moved in. (And in two of the three years that they didn't win, there was no State Championship.) They were a true dynasty.

The seriousness of the drinking-driving problem exceeded my expectations as well. As I grew accustomed to the school and the community, the problem worsened. I can remember sitting in homeroom in the morning and hearing the school principal's voice come over the loudspeaker, regretfully informing us that yet another of our classmates had been taken away from us. This same announcement was repeated so often that year that I got to the point where I dreaded hearing the man speak and would cringe every time I heard his voice. I lost count of the *statistics*. People became numb to what was going on. Some started looking for excuses. "There's nothing to do in Duxbury," they said.

Wrong, I say. O.K., so maybe there isn't a movie theater or a Pizza Hut in Duxbury. That doesn't mean that there is nothing to do. Young people in this town can get involved in many things. There are sports of all kinds for participants and spectators alike. Duxbury schools have consistently received the Dalton Trophy, awarded for excellence in their all-around sports program. People can also take advantage of many fine recreational facilities in town. Students can involve themselves in the performing arts as well, in both drama and music. There are school-related clubs, church organizations, scout troops, and youth groups. And of course, many young people choose to work part-time after school. By getting involved in some of these activities, teenagers make Duxbury an even better place for everyone.

About the drinking and driving? Well, it will never be completely eliminated, but the young people of Duxbury have buckled down and discouraged it as a whole. Student-led programs like *Eddie Was Here*, a play performed by students in which they spoke their own words and communicated their own feelings instead of rehearsed lines, portrayed the true story of a teenage boy's tragic death due to alcohol and drug abuse. Duxbury formed its own Students Against Driving Drunk (SADD) chapter. Ideas like "I'm Tired of the Tears," for which pink ribbons were tied around

South Shore soccer champions (1986) with their award. (*Deni Johnson*)

tree trunks throughout town, reminded us of the unfortunate accidents. These showed that abuse was stupid, that we really care, and that we don't want it to happen again. People are using their heads, for they have seen the consequences first-hand. Now they are finding better things to do.

When I first came to Duxbury, it was known as a town with a fine soccer team and a fine mess. The soccer team is still a force, and a lot of the mess has been cleaned up. Now, as I leave to go off to college, it is polishing its tarnished image, and building a greater sense of community. It is still referred to as a quaint little bedroom village forty miles south of Boston, with twelve thousand people, expensive houses, affluent people, high-caliber schools, gorgeous beaches, and so on. It still has a reputation as having one *helluva* soccer team, and it has a lot of things for young people to do.

Sean Bunn

Teaching about Duxbury

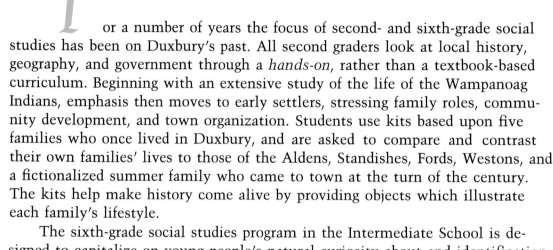

For a number of years the focus of second- and sixth-grade social studies has been on Duxbury's past. All second graders look at local history, geography, and government through a *hands-on*, rather than a textbook-based curriculum. Beginning with an extensive study of the life of the Wampanoag Indians, emphasis then moves to early settlers, stressing family roles, community development, and town organization. Students use kits based upon five families who once lived in Duxbury, and are asked to compare and contrast their own families' lives to those of the Aldens, Standishes, Fords, Westons, and a fictionalized summer family who came to town at the turn of the century. The kits help make history come alive by providing objects which illustrate each family's lifestyle.

The sixth-grade social studies program in the Intermediate School is designed to capitalize on young people's natural curiosity about and identification with their community. The year-long study begins with the Wampanoags, proceeds to explore the Pilgrims in Plymouth and Duxbury, and ends with the "Duxbury Unit," which acquaints students with Duxbury history, vital statistics, and government. Guest speakers from town departments such as police, fire, and selectmen spend a day in the Intermediate School talking to students. For this unit, each student prepares a booklet and investigates one aspect of the community. These projects are presented on Duxbury Day at DIS, the culminating activity of the year.

Duxbury is also the focus of study for *On Home Ground*, a two-year interdisciplinary course offered as an elective to high school juniors and seniors. Unlike the second- and sixth-grade studies, which are part of the social studies curriculum, *On Home Ground* is offered by the English Department. It includes

On Home Ground research at the Registry of Deeds in Plymouth. (*Carolyn B. Schindler*)

some aspects of geology, archaeology, history, art, and literature. Students are expected to use study, thinking, reading, and writing skills from each discipline. Those students who elect this course are asked to look at the geography of Duxbury through time—to see it before man arrived; when the last glaciers receded; when the earliest hunters arrived and moved across it; when tools were developed; during the development of agriculture when small bands settled down in river valleys; once tribes developed identities; and when, after thousands of years, Europeans arrived to make homes for themselves, almost obliterating the aboriginal civilization.

Once the *On Home Ground* class gets to the arrival of the Europeans, history becomes the discipline of focus. Primary and secondary sources are used; students are asked to learn the differences between them and, by reading from each, understand their strengths and weaknesses. The writings of Bradford, Winslow, and visitors to early Plymouth are contrasted to nineteenth-century romanticized versions of early Pilgrim life, such as those offered by Longfellow and the artists who painted the murals at Pilgrim Hall. Students are asked to use inference and imagination, to put themselves in the time and place of these earlier peoples. Using facts as we know them today, they develop roles for themselves in earlier times. They also realize that tomorrow's interpretations of the same data may change, or that new data may be discovered.

Following the history section, but never abandoning it, students move to the literature section of the course. They read Amasa Delano's account of his voyage off the coast of Chile, then see what Melville did with it in his short novel, *Benito Cereno*. They read Hawthorne, who introduced the concepts of religion and guilt in small town life and Arthur Miller's *The Crucible* about the Salem witch trials, and discover that a Duxbury

Duxbury students visit Plimoth Plantation. (*Carolyn B. Schindler*)

Alden was accused and imprisoned in Boston on a charge of witchcraft. Students read Thoreau, who wrote about Clark's Island and Manomet, Mary Livermore's firsthand account of her three years in Duxbury in the early 1840s, just before Partridge Academy was opened, and Mary Wilkens Freeman's *Pembroke*. Students themselves write short stories, poems, and even dramas.

Throughout the year, they meet and listen to adults in the community who are professionals in fields like art, astronomy, geology, natural history, ecology, archaeology, history, and naval construction. On field trips the classes visit the John Alden house to study colonial architecture, the Art Complex to study nineteenth-century American art, and the Drew House library and the Duxbury Room in the Duxbury Free Library, to learn research techniques. The students visit Pilgrim Hall,

Mayflower Genealogical Society, Plymouth County Registry of Deeds, Plimoth Plantation, Kennedy Library, and the new Massachusetts Archives. On their own time, individuals have attended town meetings and public lectures.

Each student undertakes a research project. Independent studies have taken many forms, all centered on Duxbury, including a science fiction novella, a trivia game, a research paper on Prohibition, and a child's illustrated history.

Time is a constant theme. The first *On Home Ground* class decided to make a time capsule for the people of Duxbury in 2085. Students brought in objects they felt represented life in Duxbury for 1985 teenagers, wrote predictions of what might happen in the intervening hundred years, and composed letters to future citizens. Along with local and national newspapers, these objects, predictions, and letters were placed in a metal container which was sealed and deposited in the vault of the Duxbury Rural and Historical Society with instructions to be opened in 2085. In addition, the entire process was videotaped, so that people in 2085 could see the town and high school as it was in 1985. Copies of the video are in the Duxbury Room of the Duxbury Free Library and the Drew House library as well as the high school library.

Our look at this place through the prism of time is not absolute and unchanging; Duxbury simply presents us with a near-at-hand subject available for our scrutiny. It is a subject we can never know completely, which is what makes it challenging and stimulating. After all, for the tiny fraction of time we are here, this is *Our Home Ground*.

CAROLYN B. SCHINDLER

Volunteers in the Schools

The Duxbury schools attract more than one thousand volunteers annually who contribute their talents and energies to a variety of endeavors that benefit students and the greater community.

Established in 1914, soon after the founding of the National Parent-Teachers Association, the PTA is Duxbury's largest volunteer organization. Each year, hundreds of members are involved in its activities which enhance the education of Duxbury's youth, and promote a positive relationship between the schools and the community. The Duxbury PTA has repeatedly won state-wide awards for leadership, creative programs, and membership growth. It has been recognized many times as a state leader for high volunteer participation.

The elementary schools and the intermediate school have their own PTA organizations. The high school has a Community Council. These groups cooperate under the coordinating umbrella of the PTA Council. In addition to providing informative public programs, a resource bank for classroom projects, and volunteer aides for classroom, library, and clerical needs, each school sponsors special activities which inspire a sense of spirit and close bonds within their school family.

The Alden PTA's annual Haunted House, eagerly anticipated by young and old alike, has for several years funded scholarships for Alden's Outdoor Education program. The Spaghetti Supper brings Alden families together for an enjoyable evening with the faculty. The children send gifts to local nursing homes through the PTA's Holiday Share-a-Gift Program, and a Toy and Game Drive provides much needed materials for indoor recess.

The Chandler PTA organizes three events which have become an integral part of that school: Surprises and Sundaes, Breakfast with Santa, and their famous Talent Show. These projects are all based on the idea of joining school and home in an atmosphere of mutual support. The Chandler PTA also funds its own scholarship for a graduating senior. In the Handicap Awareness Program for second graders, parent volunteers present the important concept of learning to understand physical and mental differences. Both Chandler and Alden have a PTA Phoning Program to ensure the safety of children by notifying the home if a child does not arrive at school on schedule.

The Intermediate School PTA focuses on increasing communications between the staff and parents, and fostering a sense of pride, enthusiasm, and unity within the school. To achieve this, they have sponsored programs such as an International Festival. As part of this project, a performance by the international dance group *Mandala* was funded, not only by a grant from New England Telephone and the New England Foundation for the Arts, but also by seventy-five individual donors from the Duxbury community. Several foreign consulates contributed books and other educational materials which the PTA placed in the intermediate school library.

The High School Community Council has initiated a joint project with the Community Garden Club and students to landscape the high school. The Community

Council also coordinates a career workshop at which community business leaders simulate realistic experiences in the job market, giving students practice interviews, résumé instruction, and helpful critiques.

The PTA Council sponsors several major activities, including the annual Kaleidoscope Fair, the funding of faculty mini-grants, a PTA scholarship, and a Fourth of July float. It provides a PTA calendar which lists the dates of all school activities, and coordinates the weekly Roster Page in the *Clipper* for school news. Since 1982, one of the PTA Council's most important commitments has been its support of Alcohol Awareness, an alliance of students, parents, and faculty dedicated to educating the community about alcohol and drug abuse.

The Creative Arts Council, funded by the PTA Council and by grants from the Institute for the Arts, the Arts Lottery, and other cultural institutions, was founded in 1976. Each year it brings more than a dozen performing and visual arts programs into the schools, supplementing the curriculum in music, theater, dance, and sculpture. It has also provided several successful artist-in-residence programs.

In addition to the PTA, the Duxbury schools have other active volunteer organizations, including the Boosters, the Gridiron Club, and the Music Promoters. Over two hundred people volunteer to raise funds for the athletic and music programs.

As the tax dollars shrink, the role of the volunteer becomes increasingly important, and with many women regularly at work, the need for volunteers becomes greater than ever. The PTA harnesses the different interests of its diverse members into a mutual objective of improving the educational experience of Duxbury's children. The PTA volunteers contribute significantly to the vitality of the Duxbury schools and directly affect the quality of life in the town, clearly reflecting the priority that the Duxbury community places on the value of a good education.

Judith Hall

Mural, *Duxbury, Massachusetts*, by Marcy Annesley Hanlon, commissioned by the 350th Anniversary Committee of the Duxbury Intermediate School. The mural hangs in the front corridor of the school. (*Fran Nichols*)

Duxbury Churches
1945 to the Present

The First Parish Chuch, Unitarian-Universalist has long shared its ample capacity and striking architectural beauty with the community, as it does today under the guidance of the Reverend Robert R. Walsh, seeming to epitomize the Unitarian-Universalist maxim, "A democratic church devoted to freedom of thought and speech in religion." Memorial Day services preceding the annual ceremony in Mayflower Cemetery are held there, as are the Choral Society's rendition of the *Messiah*, and the annual Candlelight Concert series. The Parish House is constantly busy with senior citizen events, nursery schools, and music schools, author programs, dance classes, and garden club meetings. It is in truth a community center.

The History of the First Parish Church, written by Gershom Bradford during the tenure of the Reverend Herman Lion in the late 1940s and early 1950s, describes the mark his combination of business acumen and inspiring leadership left on the church property, including the Parish House and parsonage, which was left to the church by Mrs. Sarah Peterson.

A new steeple has replaced the disintegrating predecessor, the whole gleams resplendent, a blacktop driveway has covered the former gravel. Through the enthusiastic chairmanship of the late Mrs. Abbot Peterson, base planted shrubs now soften the old severity and brilliant flowers bloom cheerfully before the doors.[1]

The First Parish Church, sitting on a slight rise above the street, is as welcoming as it is beautiful.

Volunteers fill Christmas baskets, a project sponsored by the Duxbury Council of Churches. (*Hope Pillsbury*)

The West Duxbury United Methodist Church sits on the Duxbury-Pembroke town line. Since 1867, it has served both communities as a center for neighborhood activities, as well as religious fellowship. Church suppers and fairs bring members of the two communities together in ways which are similar to much earlier rural days. Members of the congregation remember chopping wood for the church stoves and heating water on the stove to wash dishes. Today the church has *spruce-up* days on which people come to rake and plant or paint and putty. This church has always attracted people willing to take on any task.

Until recently student pastors came from the Boston University School of Theology. Dr. Roy Albert White, the present full-time minister, also serves Norwell's Church Hill Church. Outreach includes a monthly mission to Bridgewater State Prison and the support of a missionary family in Sumatra.

Hymns from a carillon dedicated in June, 1976, ring out over Snug Harbor and Washington Street environs several times daily from their location in the Pilgrim Congregational Church tower. They are just one example of this church's benefice to Duxbury. (Its early history is reported fully in an earlier chapter of this book.) During World War II, many of its activities had to be suspended; but ever since then, Pilgrim Church has enjoyed steady growth and beautification.

In 1955, an addition was made to the old building for educational purposes. In 1962, major repairs had to be made to the facade and the steeple. On a cold and rainy October day, the entire congregation was invited to watch a crane replace the spire which had rested on the ground for many months. Hot coffee was served and spirits soared as the pinnacle was deposited safely on the square tower, making the beloved old structure look once again like a true New England church.

A new parsonage was purchased in 1984, next door to the church. It is occupied by the present minister, the Reverend Stephen Hussing, who succeeded the Reverend Stephen Turrell, whose leadership (1963–1983) brought about much of the development of the modern-day Pilgrim Church.

St. John the Evangelist Episcopal Church gained full parish status in 1945. Since that time only four men have served as rectors: the Reverends John Philbrick, William Anthony, David Siegenthaler and Lewis Mills. At the time of this publication, the Reverend Paul Taylor is serving as interim rector.

Numerous young people were attracted to the church in the 1970s and 1980s, bringing a change in the

View of the First Parish Church from the Mayflower Cemetery. (*Norman Forgit*)

tone and style of worship, at a time when the Episcopal Church nationally was undergoing extensive alterations in its effort to cope with new mores and lifestyles. That St. John's Church survived these years with renewed vigor is in some measure due to the warmth of the Reverend Lewis Mills. St. John's has made an effort to expend as much of its "time, treasure and talent" on outreach programs as on its own upkeep, through work with refugees, prisoners, the Appalachian poor, and locally, the Brockton Soup Kitchen. These good works continue.

St. Paul's Church of the Nazarene has become a vital force in the growing community of Duxbury churches. It started in the 1890s with meetings in a hall over Keene's Store. These were conducted by Mrs. L. Caroline Stapes, who drove from Melrose in a horse and buggy on Saturday to be there on time Sunday morning. In the fall of 1902, money was raised through a "free-will offering" and the non-denominational Beulah Chapel was built on the Duxbury-East Pembroke border on land donated by Mr. and Mrs. Charles Hunt. In 1950, it was incorporated as the Duxbury Church of the Nazarene. In 1965, the name was changed to St. Paul's Church of the Nazarene.

A new and larger church was built on Summer Street in 1965–66, constructed in such a way that it could be converted into a ranch-style home if the mortgage was not paid. In 1986, a much larger sanctuary was added to that building to accommodate a congregation that had outgrown its quarters. The new white clapboard church was completed in early 1987, reflecting almost a century of dedication and progress.

Duxbury Christian Scientists met and studied in people's homes from 1953 until 1964, when members of the Island Creek Hall Association offered to sell their Park Street building to this informal group for the price of one dollar. That was the beginning of what is now First Church of Christ, Scientist, Duxbury. Hard work and a deep desire to share their faith with others was necessary to turn the 1870s historic hall into a habitable church. The Duxbury church, part of a world-wide denomination, also has a Christian Science Reading Room on Railroad Avenue.

Duxbury's First Baptist Church was founded by A. Wendell Drollett in his home. When the congregation grew too large for services there they moved to quarters on Washington Street. During the ministry of A. Alan Travers, the existing brick church on Tremont Street was built, as was a parsonage on Lantern Lane. The first service in the new church was Mother's Day, May 19, 1969. Additions have been made to the original structure as the congregation grew. Dr. Robert C. White is the church's leader and minister at present.

New Covenant Fellowship Church began with meetings in the homes of a few people who felt the need for a new Christian expression in Duxbury. The first Sunday morning worship was held in the Old Town Hall in September 1982. Not related to any denomination or outside group, the New Covenant Fellowship is commonly referred to as *full gospel* or *pentecostal*. David Woods, the first and present pastor, now conducts services in the Tarkiln Community Center. The congregation, which started with seven members, is growing.

The Zion Lutheran Church and Congregation Beth Jacob, both of Plymouth, the Church of Jesus Christ of Latter-Day Saints in Hingham, and the Plymouth Bay Church Assemblies of God also serve Duxbury residents.

SHIRLEY H. CARTER

The Catholic Church in Duxbury

In the early years of this century, the few Catholics gathered in Duxbury were a Mission of St. Peter's Parish, Plymouth. Until 1904, Mass was said in homes and, for a time, in Duxbury Hall. From 1904 to 1934, Duxbury Catholics attended Mass in Mattakeesett Hall, home of the Independent Order of Odd Fellows. In 1906, Father John Buckley, pastor of St. Peter's in Plymouth, had, with great foresight, purchased land from Mrs. Carrie Adams on St. George Street, where in 1934, the Catholic Church was built at a total cost of $30,000, all paid for in advance. A new church, to be completed in 1988 or 1989 on Tremont Street at the corner of Chestnut on twelve acres acquired from the Herrick family, will cost nearly $3 million.

In 1908, St. Joseph's Parish was founded in Kingston, and Duxbury became its mission from then until 1945 when Duxbury's own Holy Family Parish was established, eleven years after construction of the church building. The Reverend Andrew Haberstroh, Kingston's first pastor, was loved and admired for many years by the small mission flock in Duxbury, as was his successor, the Reverend Robert Hinchcliffe.

The 1945 establishment of Holy Family Parish delighted the fifty families who were year-round residents. At that time, about one thousand summer residents, many of them domestic help, swelled attendance during the warm months each year. Duxbury's year-round population in the early years of this century was not much over one thousand. Today it is over fifteen thousand.

The first pastor of Holy Family Parish was the Reverend John M. Manion, a Plymouth native. He served only from 1945 to 1949, but his extraordinary talents were an inspiration not only to his flock, but to many of other faiths who appreciated his charm and ecumenical spirit. He was followed by pastors whose tenures

Interior View, Holy Family Church. Christmas, 1984. (*Paul B. Spolidoro*)

were six or seven years each. An exception was the Reverend John P. Cosgrove, pastor from 1961 to his retirement in 1975. His associate pastor, the Reverend Francis Cloherty, served from 1965 to 1975.

In July 1975, the Reverend Francis X. Turke became pastor, served the traditional six years, and then became pastor of St. Agatha's in Milton. His associate pastors were the Reverend Joseph Gaudet, 1975 to 1978, and the Reverend Brian R. Kiely, who remained under the next pastor until June 1984.

The present pastor, the Reverend Monsignor William F. Glynn, came to Duxbury in his thirty-fifth year of priesthood in September 1981. Since June 1984, he has had an associate pastor, the Reverend Thomas Kopp, young, energetic, and with a fine sense of humor that combines with Father Glynn's compassion and wisdom to make the perfect team for Holy Family Parish.

Joseph K. and Grace M. Collins

The Art Complex Museum

Carl Weyerhaeuser breaking ground for the Art Complex Museum in 1969. (*The Art Complex Museum*)

he Art Complex Museum, completed in 1971, is next door to the John Alden House, built in 1653. Separated by intervening woods, two more divergent types of architecture could hardly be imagined, yet both are compatible in present-day Duxbury.

Now in its sixteenth year, the Art Complex Museum, created by the Weyerhaeuser family, provides a home for the family collections and a center for the arts in Duxbury. The idea for the museum grew from the Carl Weyerhaeuser family, with the help of Evelyn Vaughan and of Ture and Lillian Bengtz. In the family tradition, the museum would be built of wood, featuring natural light and open vistas in the sylvan setting of tall trees.

Ture Bengtz incorporated the ideas of the Weyerhaeusers and others, as well as his own, and developed a workable concept, which was formalized and refined by architect Richard Owen Abbott. In 1969, the museum began to take shape on the eleven-acre site once owned by John Alden. The free-flowing design, reminiscent of the sea, fits into the curve of a hill overlooking an excavated pond filled by natural springs, with the site beyond left untouched and wild.

After supervising the construction of the building, Ture Bengtz was named Museum Director in 1971 and continued until his death in 1973, when the larger gallery was named for him. Phoenix Hall was named in honor of Mrs. Vaughan, who, with Mrs. Weyerhaeuser, liked the symbolism of the mythological phoenix, representing a new beginning. The third major adjunct of the building is the Carl A. Weyerhaeuser Art Library.

At first, the museum was open three days a week, but as community interest grew, the schedule expanded to Wednesday through Sunday, in the afternoons. In addition to the regular Weyerhaeuser collections, always the core of the continuing exhibits, the museum regularly hosts such group shows as the Boston Printmakers, supplemented by one-man shows and traveling exhibitions. Yearly, the Duxbury Art Association has held its juried show in the Art Complex. In the realm of music, a fall and spring concert series and an outdoor summer series are presented by regional musicians.

Periodic lectures on timely art subjects are featured. Each summer, tea ceremonies are performed in the museum's Japanese tea hut by Tea Masters. The tea hut, *Wind in the Pines*, which opened in 1975, was especially designed for the museum, and is surrounded by a modified tea garden.

The Art Complex welcomes non-profit community organizations to hold various functions in its unique galleries. The South Shore Conservatory of Music launched its educational programs with a concert by the Boston Symphony Chamber Players and each year continues with a series of student and faculty recitals. The garden clubs of the community hold a number of their competitions at the museum.

With but one docent in the early years, the number has now expanded to over fifty who not only greet visitors, but also provide art education programs in the museum and in the schools, thus fulfilling a major objective of the Art Complex to work with educational institutions in the field of art. Many students from kindergarten through grade twelve have come for various workshops or class projects. In 1986, the Art Complex hosted the juried portion of *Art Works, 1986*, an exhibition by the art departments of the Duxbury schools.

Meanwhile, the exhibition schedule has steadily grown more ambitious, with such showings as the museum-organized exhibition, *The Way of Tea: Ameri-*

Alden School students Mike Drinkwater and Peter Hannon making Kachina masks. (*Art Complex Museum*)

can Art for the Japanese Tea Ceremony, and traveling shows like *The Artist and the Quilt*. Theme shows like the Barnstable County Tercentenary Exhibition of Cape Cod Artists and *Timeless Tables* (a still life exhibition) have been featured, following the policy of encouraging local and regional artists.

In 1987, the Art Complex, in cooperation with the Duxbury Rural and Historical Society, joins in celebrating the 350th Anniversary of the Incorporation of Duxbury with an exhibition entitled *Reflections*, to include paintings by Dr. Rufus Hathaway (1770–1822), a juried photographic competition of contemporary Duxbury, Sandwich cable pattern glass, and a ten- by thirty-foot photo collage created by artist Vaughan Grylls.

CHARLES WEYERHAEUSER

Duxbury Artists

Several well-know artists were painting in Duxbury in the late 1800s, including John J. Enneking, whose *Duxbury Clam Digger* is shown on page 141. Clement Drew, part-time marine artist and full-time Boston pastor, painted two views of the twin lights at Gurnet in 1866 and again in 1873. Since several members of the Drew family owned the early Peterson house on Powder Point, he probably visited there.

The Duxbury Art Association's opening exhibit was held in 1917. The association sponsored exhibits annually until 1921, then biennially. The 1923 exhibition attracted both local and well-known Boston School artists, including William Paxton, Elizabeth O. Paxton, Aldro Hibbard, Philip Hale, Lillian Westcott Hale, and Frank W. Benson. The Boston *Evening Transcript* reviewed the show:

> Among the Duxbury artists, Charles Bittinger, the President of the Association, should first be mentioned. This year his most important contribution is perhaps *On Leave in '63.* . . . Another active member of the colony is William H. Walker, for a number of years a popular cartoonist connected with the staff of *Life Magazine* who has recently swung over to the field of painting. He has a number of landscapes hung, all of considerable merit . . . The more or less radical member of the association is Miss Marjorie Conant.

Miss Conant still seemed radical to many thirty years later, when exhibiting as Marjorie Bush-Brown after her marriage. Returning to Duxbury in 1958, she was instrumental in the formation of the Bumpus Gallery. She is the best-known Duxbury painter since Rufus Hathaway.

The jury for the 1923 show, Miss Gertrude Fiske, Mr. Philip Hale, and Mr. Leslie P. Thompson, awarded first prize to Mr. Paxton for his painting entitled "Interior."

Robert C. Vose, Jr.

(top) *Sailboats on Duxbury Bay*, pencil sketch from William H. Walker's notebook. (*Robert M. Walker and William H. Walker II*); (bottom) *Gurnet Light* by Clement Drew (1866). (*Robert C. Vose, Jr.*)

200

Duxbury Music

Yankee bass viols, also called church basses, were customarily used to accompany church choirs in New England. The above instrument from the musical instrument collection of the Metropolitan Museum of Art in New York was built by William Green of Medway, Mass. in 1807. An inscription within this bass reads: "This cello was owned in Duxbury a great many years ago + was played in church. My father bought it of Seth Weston who lived near Duxbury Beach / Repaired by S.M. Briggs, South Hanson, Mass. in 1907." The church referred to was probably the third meeting house of First Parish Church. (*The Metropolitan Museum of Art, Gift of Genevieve Vaughn and Lawrence Libin, in memory of Mary Ruth McClane, 1982.*)

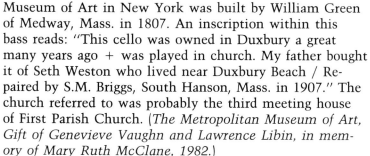

Music-making in the King Caesar House west parlor is depicted in this 1924 painting by Duxbury artist Charles Bittinger. The woman pictured is playing a square, or table, pianoforte (1790s) probably imported from London.

Title page of a piece selected from a large collection of music compiled in the 1820s by Duxbury resident Margaret C. Dickson. Many notable composers of the eighteenth and nineteenth centuries are represented in this collection, as are the great publishing houses of Europe and Great Britain.

In the fall of 1987, the Candlelight Concert Series celebrates its tenth anniversary season. This chamber music series was founded by the present artistic director, Edwin Swanborn. The performances take place in the superlative acoustics of First Parish Church, with musicians from across the United States and Canada.

In the course of its first ten years the series has become a nationally recognized presenter of fine chamber music, and is recorded by WBUR-FM (National Public Radio at Boston University). (*Edwin Swanborn*)

Edwin Swanborn

Duxbury Writers

Is Duxbury a community of those who follow the paths of literature? A casual glance at the busy social and athletic life in town might suggest not, but scratch the surface and you find that the modest man or woman you casually meet at a summer cocktail party is an author of note. Some are writers of fiction or of poetry or perhaps technical books, others of magazine and journal articles.

Richard Hughes has written books on rhetoric and literature as well as fiction. Blair McClosky, a singer and teacher, has written books on voice which have been published internationally. His co-author on one work was his wife, Barbara. James Southwood wrote a book on the Kennedy family.

Helen Philbrick and her husband, the Reverend John Philbrick, wrote several books about biodynamic gardening, one of which, *Companion Plants and How to Use Them*, has had fifteen printings.

Norman Bennett is a specialist on Africa and has edited and annotated many books and articles on that continent. Leslie Guccione, using the name Leslie Davis, writes novels which have suspense, romance, and a locale similar to Duxbury. Robert Whittier does books on boating, both maintenance and seamanship.

Harold Bush-Brown has a book on the beaux arts from an architect's perspective. Lorraine Cudmore wrote a book on the natural history of the cell. Everett Marston authored a novel, and his daughter Elsa Marston Harik has written fiction for young adults, as well as the collection, *Mysteries in American Archeology*. The Reverend Wayne Walden has written several books on Bible translations and on both the Greek and Hebrew languages.

Several very successful cookbooks were written by Duxbury residents. Ruth Wakefield, who with her husband Kenneth owned the famous Toll House restaurant in Whitman, not only invented the Toll House cookie, but also wrote a *Toll House Cookbook*. Sarah Hurlburt wrote

The Mussel Cookbook. Perhaps most prolific was Herman Smith, who not only wrote cookbooks that became collector's items, but also had a cooking column in the *Clipper*.

Duxbury selectman David Vogler has published numerous books on government. Carola Kapff Butler has written a source book on hematology. George Douglas published a book on public relations, and Helen Eaton not only wrote a book on semantic frequency, but also wrote for *Encyclopaedia Britannica*. Robert Edmunds has a published glossary of computer technology and Hugh Sloan has written books on creativity for teachers. Dr. George Starr wrote two books on decoys which are standards in the field. Ladd MacMillan wrote on Currier and Ives.

Children's book authors abound in Duxbury—Jean Poindexter Colby, Beatrice Gormley, Winona Strachan, Robert Barner, and Ruth McGibney, who with her daughter, Rica Moore, has written two books of poetry.

There are and have been poets in Duxbury—Rosemary Thomas, Terry Kennedy, Gerald Fitzgerald, and E. Huiginn among others. Sarah Wingate Taylor was dubbed the "poet of Clark's Island." Robert Lowell and his wife, Elizabeth Hardwick, lived and wrote in Duxbury for several years. John Malcolm Brinnin not only has his own books of poetry, but has written biographies and criticism of other poets. One of Brinnin's subjects, Truman Capote, summered in Duxbury, creating quite a stir when he came ashore from Clark's Island to shop at Josselyn's store in Snug Harbor. Ellen B. Simpson wrote a book on *Poets in Their Youth*.

Over the years writers for the *Clipper* have provided many historical pieces which are of great value to the researcher: Dr. Alice Bigelow, Sabina Marshall, Dr. John Adams, Henry Cragin Walker, Cecil Atwater, Mary Nye Gifford, Isabelle Freeman, Blanche White, Alison Arnold, and Priscilla Harris.

Rachel Carson got the inspiration for her famed book, *Silent Spring*, after visiting Olga and Stuart Huckins. Olga

Huckins was a well-known *Boston Herald* columnist.

There have been many genealogies written by and about Duxbury people. Gershom Bradford wrote several. Ralph Jarvis and Dr. H.C. Bumpus wrote biographies of their fathers. Elisha Mowry wrote an autobiography and Margaret Carter Metcalf compiled a book of letters written by her son, Rev. George Putnam Metcalf, while he was serving as a chaplain during World War II.

Local histories have been written by Dorothy Kelso, Laurence Bradford Wright, Sam Loring, William J. Alden, Josephine Dawes, Henry Fish, Dorothy Brownell Weston, Colonel James Truden, Captain Amaso Delano, Florence Ford, Mrs. George Green, Margie Sampson, Jane Goodwin Austin, T. C. Porter, Ethel Harper, Bern Dibner, Stephen Allen, and Frances Leach, who is an authority on Myles Standish.

Edwin Noyes' book bore the charming title, *Knee Deep in Sheep.* John Schlebecker wrote a history of American farming. Dr. Fletcher Colby wrote on urology. David Levin wrote a biography of Cotton Mather. Paul Murphy's biography, *Pascalina Popessa,* drew international attention. Writing on technical subjects are Edward Hurst, Margaret Patterson, Robert Kittridge, Peter Galassi, Fannie Hillsmith, Robert Edmunds, Peter Fossel, Leslie MacCardell, and Dr. Bernard J. Korites.

Elizabeth Whitney Post has written extensively on alcoholism, as Dr. Joseph Brenner has written on drug abuse. Dr. George Gardner combined his profession and his interest in history in a series on the psychological problems of the Pilgrims. Dr. Richard Field wrote an amusing book, *Alice in Atomland.*

Jeanne Quinzani, Sam Keith, Stephen Goodyear, and Fisher Ames, Jr., all produced books based on personal experiences, as did Lyn and Tony Chamberlain and Dawn and Robert Habgood; the Chamberlains on the best spots for cross country skiing, and the Habgoods on *Traveling with Man's Best Friend*—a dog, that is.

Cid Rickets Sumner wrote many books of fiction and non-fiction, most of which were published in several languages. Three were made into movies: *Quality,* which became the film *Pinky,* and two of her *Tammy* books. Her autobiographical books were as popular as her stories.

Although John Henry Cutler is best known locally as editor of the *Duxbury Clipper,* he is also author of many books, from adventure stories for boys, to biographies of Cardinal Cushing, Honey Fitz Fitzgerald, Caryl Chessman (that manuscript had to be smuggled out of San Quentin's death row), and James Michael Curley. He has written two books on the experiences of a small town newspaper editor, as well as a handbook, *Tips on Writing.*

This compilation of Duxbury writers is certainly not complete. No doubt there are other writers now living here, or who have lived here, but as of this writing we know not who they are.

Roberta S. Cutler

Cid Ricketts Sumner (right), with Robert D. Hale and Margaret Carter Metcalf at Westwinds Bookshop in 1957. (*Roberta S. Cutler*)

The Duxbury Clipper

The *Duxbury Clipper*, conceived over a bridge game, and for many years produced in our dining room, is still young as newspapers go. Yet, into its third decade, it has left an indelible mark on Duxbury, and perhaps because of that, has become among the most successful community weeklies in New England.

A "ma-and-pa" operation from the start, the *Clipper* was founded by my parents, John and Bobbie Cutler. Their combined knowledge of newspapers equaled that of a journalism student about to start his freshman year; now, after thirty-six years at the helm, they are walking encyclopedias of what a weekly should be.

In May 1950, when the *Clipper* was born, Duxbury had a year-round population of three thousand, the summer crowd, and a paucity of business. It did not seem a propitious time for so bold an adventure, and in launching their market surveys, the budding publishers heard many a discouraging word.

"You're out of your mind," suggested their good friend Arthur "Beanie" Beane when asked for an assessment. And the late Percy Walker, *Mr. Duxbury*, equated the idea with the old Duxbury Railroad which, as he recalled, didn't last long.

There was also the government brochure, a piece of gobbledygook from the bureaucracy, which suggested that with at least $10,000 (my parents had $400), some previous experience, and a great deal of hard work, one could achieve a "modicum" of success in publishing a weekly. Horrified by the advice, my mother stashed the document behind a bookcase, where it remained until the *Clipper* was safely afloat.

And just who were these upstarts who launched an institution? My

John H. Cutler, founder, editor, and publisher of the *Clipper*. (*Fran Nichols*)

mother, a housewife, presided over a brood of four, later five. She could sing, and act, and paint, and grow most anything. She was a whiz cook, but a newspaperwoman she wasn't. She was, however, wonderfully versatile, and could fix almost anything—two resources which proved most valuable.

My father, a Harvard Ph.D., was a skilled writer who had freelanced for several national magazines. He knew his way around Boston's newspaper row, having written for the *Globe*, the *Herald*, and the now-defunct *Boston Post*; but he was not a professional journalist. No editor ever drilled him in the rudiments of a news *lead* and he was not comfortable with the five "w's" of journalism—the who, what, where, when, and why. He had never written a *hard* news story, and he knew zero about production. He once referred to a blanket—a cylinder cover on a press—as a bedspread. Neither he nor my mother knew anything about advertising.

But they would learn, and the good merchants of Duxbury proved to be willing teachers. One, Jacob Schiff, who owned a shoestore, said he would advertise occasionally if the paper came out on Thursday, which is why Thursday became Clipper Day in Duxbury. Jack Kent, Sr., who owned the marine appliance store, later Bayside Marine, was lukewarm when my father made his pitch.

"I don't know, John," he said. "After all, most of the boys down on the waterfront know we're here."

My father pointed out the reminder factor, noting that church bells ring every Sunday to remind parishioners of the services. People needed reminding, he said. There is no record of how Jack took that, but he bought an ad, and he and his son, Jack Kent, Jr., have been aboard the *Clipper* ever since.

It was a modest beginning as the *Clipper* set sail. With six pages in the first issue, it would slowly grow to eight, and I remember the sparkle in my father's eyes when he announced, "we have to go to ten this week." In 1986, the *Clipper* averaged forty pages, often hit forty-eight, and occasionally topped fifty-two. Six pages were barely enough for the local sports.

The first issue was printed by kindly Tom Porter, who had a small press in his garage off Elm Street. It was he who gave the *Clipper* its name, my parents having toyed with such ideas as *The Alden Journal*, or *The Standish Times*, or anything, really, that didn't include the word, *Gazette*.

As the years wore on, the printers would change. Most weekly newspapers are put out by commercial printers, and that was the case with the *Clipper* until 1976, when the family took a major plunge and bought a press of its own, a Goss Community, capable of printing 18,000 copies an hour. On at least three occasions since that purchase, the publishers have enjoyed the privilege of shouting "Stop the Press," to change or add a major news story.

With the addition of the press, the *Clipper* is now a totally vertical operation at its office on South Station Street, and the offices are larger than in the early days, when the paper was produced on the dining room table at our Washington Street home. To the children, it seemed most natural to clear away the 4-H news or the high school sports report when it was time for dinner, and the dining room served the publishers well for nearly ten years, despite the fact that an occasional classified or news item would find its way into the bookcase or under the couch or behind the refrigerator. We all thought the dining room was the hub of Duxbury.

It was in that room that my parents learned the important lessons of weekly publishing. The credo evolved quickly: be provincial, keep it local; write about the schools, and town hall, and Duxbury Bay; and leave the national stories to the national press. The *Clipper* always has and always will be for and about Duxbury.

Roberta S. Cutler, co-founder of the *Clipper*. (*Fran Nichols*)

The *Clipper* survived the early days, the spaghetti days as we called them, for several reasons. There were the publishers, of course, whom I still admire greatly for their strength, their intelligence, their tenacity, and their quickness to learn. But there were other reasons as well, and atop the list was (and is) Duxbury. It is a special place that inspired loyalty and love, and my parents understood, from the beginning, I think, that the *Clipper* would succeed because of Duxbury. Duxbury is an interesting place, filled with interesting people. Someone is always off to Nepal, or home from the Orient.

From the beginning, Duxbury residents wrote for the *Clipper*. In the early days, there were "Homespun Yarns" by Grace Anthony, and "Turns of a Bookworm"

by Margaret Metcalf of Westwinds. There were wonderful contributions from Alison Arnold, Dr. Alice Bigelow, Gershom Bradford, and my grandmother, Cid Ricketts Sumner. There were (and are) "Postscripts" by Jack Post, historical pieces by Dorothy Wentworth, an occasional political column by David A. Mittell, Jr., and for too short a time, hilarious reports on the Frostbiters by Dr. Lance Bennett.

Classifieds, and letters to the editor are important in measuring the impact of a weekly, and the *Clipper* does well on both counts. Over the years, the *Clipper* has published far more letters (Sounding Off) than most papers of comparable size. That is a tribute to the readers, and to the editorial stands of the paper.

The *Clipper* prospered as Duxbury grew from a cozy, well-kept secret to a Boston bedroom. Advertising increased from meager, to modest, to healthy. After a while, the help-wanted sign went up, as my parents tired of working sixty-hour weeks. Among the editorial assistants were Jo-Ann Collins, Peggy Dunn, and Rita Luckey. Later came Sidney Arnold, Ruth Berg, and Suzanne Miller; then Judi Barrett, Maddie Merrifield, Paula Maxwell, and, of course, Priscilla Sangster, who is now managing editor.

After 36 years, Mr. and Mrs. "Clipper" are still in charge, and very much a part of what my mother calls the hectic Mondays and frantic Tuesdays. Some things, like deadlines, never change. By now, running a weekly seems a most natural enterprise, and as one who was at least present at the creation, I confess to a deep affection for "the local rag." The *Clipper* is as much a part of Duxbury as the Powder Point Bridge. For 36 years it has served as our "first rough draft" of history. It will do the same for many years to come.

DAVID S. CUTLER

The William F. Clapp Laboratories

ill Clapp (1880–1951), founder of the William F. Clapp Laboratories, Inc., was a man of many talents. Born on Halloween, he was a naturalist, a snake charmer and a people charmer, a lecturer, a well-known singer, curator of mollusks at Harvard University, and a professor at the Massachusetts Institute of Technology. He was a charismatic individual who could also be called a visionary.

A San Francisco catastrophe in 1920 was the catalyst that started Clapp Labs. In that year, numerous San Francisco Bay wharves collapsed after a marine borer attack. The United States National Research Council formed a committee to investigate that occurrence and the destructiveness of marine borers along both coasts. Bill Clapp was asked to perform studies from the Atlantic and Gulf coasts and the Caribbean Islands. Work was to be accomplished by examination of untreated wood samples submerged in the waters, removed, and replaced on a regular schedule. This method was highly successful, and with some refinements, is still in use. Data gathered provided information as to the presence of borers, their size and rate of growth, as well as species present.

Clapp isolated and described a new species from material received during that first investigation, a species that was to play an important part in research at the Laboratories many years later. As the investigation progressed, Clapp saw the need for wharf and boat owners to have pertinent, understandable information concerning marine borer attack in their particular area. He determined to have his own laboratory. While living on Boston's T Wharf, he had acquired the stone sloop *M. M. Hamilton*, which was originally used to carry Vermont granite for the Washington Monument. In the early 1930s, the Coast Guard towed the *Hamilton* from Boston to Duxbury, where it sat in a slip on the

Dr. William F. Clapp, founder of the William F. Clapp Laboratories. (*Mrs. A. P. Richards*)

south side of the Duxbury Coal and Lumber Company's wharf. Aboard the sloop, in addition to his marine work, were Clapp's pet snakes, which he used for his nature lectures.

After contacts were made with officials in railroad and steamship companies, as well as with government agencies, Clapp Laboratory was on its way. The number of test boards (now called exposure panels) increased rapidly, so the operation was moved to the barn of the Clapp's summer home on Washington Street. By 1937, there was a full-time staff of five.

With the exception of the secretary and the handyman, everyone who worked at the Lab also lived there. In the household with Bill and Nellie Clapp were Nellie Clapp's daughter and grandson, two school teachers, a widowed friend, and a cook. This melange was increased every weekend by numerous visitors. It was a busy, fun-filled household that has been described many times as the forerunner to *You Can't Take It with You.*

Pete Richards examining a sample in the laboratory which contained bathtubs set in tiers, which were supplied with water from the large cypress tank shown in the rear. (*Mrs. A. P. Richards*)

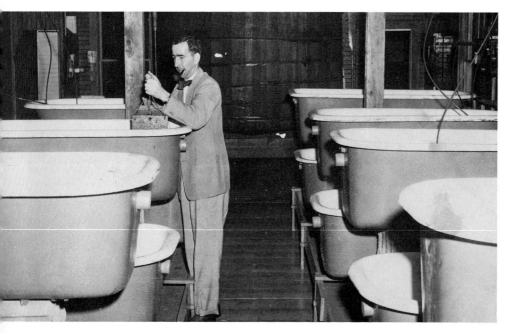

The laboratory work expanded to include wharf inspections, paint exposures, rope exposures, termite inspections, and anything pertaining to marine deterioration and its prevention. It was a hand-to-mouth existence. With the exception of the test boards, no bills were sent, and the lab was supported by contributions.

In the early 1940s, the adjacent Richardson (Winsor) property was acquired and its boathouse became the marine lab. The saltwater laboratory was equipped in a unique fashion. Tenements in South Boston were being demolished to make way for the Columbia Point housing development. The wrecking company agreed to furnish and deliver bathtubs to Duxbury for the sum of three dollars each. The tubs were thoroughly scrubbed and installed in tiers. Saltwater was pumped at high tide into a large cypress tank and gravity-fed into the bathtubs and the new laboratory was in operation—another ambition fulfilled. Nearby was a windowless building that contained a world-famous collection of examples of marine deterioration. It was at about this time that Norwich University awarded Clapp an honorary doctorate in recognition of his work in the field of marine deterioration.

The laboratories' work was known worldwide, and calls for advice came in from all over—from business magnates to individuals who had problems with "those critters." Each call was given the same attention. During World War II, the Office of Scientific Research and Development (later Office of Naval Research) requested that Bill Clapp's assistant, A. P. (Pete) Richards go to Australia and New Guinea to assess the effects marine deterioration could have on naval ships and seaplanes. It was a question as to how much information he could send home, but since the postal censor knew nothing of marine borers, all information and pertinent pictures came through unscathed.

Recognizing the need, friends from business and government got together and, on a voluntary basis, became Clapp Laboratories' first Board of Directors. These men were presidents and heads of research departments from large well-known companies, universities, and top Navy officials. In 1947, the William F. Clapp Laboratories, Inc., became a non-profit corporation.

After Dr. Clapp's death in 1951, Pete Richards (1914–1963) became President and Director of the Laboratories. Government was placing more restrictions on research performance. Gone were the days of "just pay what you think it's worth." Contract research was in. One of the publications during this period was a compilation of the results from test panel exposures maintained throughout the world. This manual, updated annually, provided those interested in building and maintaining waterfront structures with information concerning the occurrence and intensity of marine borer attack. Through the cooperative efforts of the William F. Clapp Laboratories, Inc., the Library of Congress, and the Office of Naval Research, a large volume, *Marine Borers: An Annotated Bibliography* was published in 1963. It has become one of the most important reference sources for all researchers dealing with problems of marine borers and their control.

When Richards died in 1963, the Directors of the Laboratories appointed B. R. Richards, also a marine biologist, to continue operating the laboratories in the same direction as in the past. After several years, with increasing needs for expanded types of marine biological research, and looking towards expansion, the William F. Clapp Laboratories, Inc., in 1965, became associated with Battelle Memorial Institute.

BEATRICE R. RICHARDS

Battelle Memorial Institute

Battelle Memorial Institute is the oldest and largest independent contract research organization in the world. Today, the marine research laboratory in Duxbury is a technical department of the institute's larger facility located in Columbus, Ohio. The Battelle Ocean Sciences Center, as it is now called, conducts contract research and provides technical/management services for industrial and government clients in all areas of marine science. With a staff of 165 dedicated scientists and support staff, and an annual research volume in excess of $10 million, Battelle in Duxbury is a stable, healthy organization that has become an internationally recognized leader in marine science research.

The Duxbury facility has grown in size during the past several years with the addition of a marine toxicology laboratory, a new administration building, and a chemistry laboratory. With a total of nine buildings on ten acres abutting Duxbury Bay, the laboratory has developed into a positive, viable contributor to the community by monitoring the water quality of our bay as well as providing significant educational resources to the town.

The laboratory maintains an intern program for high-school students and funds annual college science scholarships. Tours, presentations, and jobs for students, as well as training programs for teachers, are continuously provided. Battelle's annual science fairs for Duxbury students, participation in and financial support of the Art Association, an annual float entry in the Fourth of July parade, and numerous financial contributions to local charities have established Battelle as a good neighbor in the community.

Joan S. Sundstrom

Civic Associations

Jack Mowrey stands before the Kiwanis Club banner at the Mother's Day breakfast (1983). (*Fran Nichols*)

Civic groups such as the Rotary, Kiwanis, and Newcomers clubs, the American Legion, and Art Association offer members opportunities for making friends and for joining in pleasurable social and fund-raising activities. Each of those organizations furnishes scholarships for graduating high school seniors and supports other activities for young people. Several also provide services for the elderly.

The Duxbury Rotary Club was founded in 1950 as part of an international organization of business and professional men. The Duxbury club's forty-three members meet weekly for fellowship and to hear guest speakers. It sponsors a Boy Scout troop and donates to international, national, and local projects and charities. Funds have been given to high school athletic clubs and to the intermediate school PTA. Rotary's popular August auction is its primary fund-raiser.

Forty-six local businessmen, farmers, and salaried people organized the Duxbury Kiwanis Club in 1950 to serve the charitable needs of the community. Today forty, mainly white-collar activists, continue that tradition. In 1985, they completed twenty-three hands-on projects for the elderly—cleaning out gutters, cutting grass, raking leaves, trimming trees and bushes, and painting trim. In one instance, they rebuilt an entire roof; in another, they provided a television for a man in his eighties beset with Alzheimer's disease.

Each Valentine's Day, Kiwanis members deliver candy to elderly widows. The club puts up an annual Christmas tree at Hall's Corner and arranges for Santa Claus to hand out candy canes at the tree-lighting ceremony. It sponsors a youth baseball team, a Boy Scout troop, and the high school Key Club and intermediate school Builders Club for students interested in community service.

Duxbury Post 223 of the American Legion was chartered in 1927 and became most active in the years following World War II. While it no longer runs the July Fourth parade or the three-day Duxbury Days fair, it does organize the Memorial Day services and parade. On Memorial Day 1986, the Legion unveiled a marble Vietnam War memorial on the Post's grounds at Tremont and West streets. High school senior Kristen DiMascio designed the scroll-style monument.

Each year Duxbury's Legion Post donates to youth soccer, football, hockey, and the high school band, and sponsors six eleventh-grade scholars at a week-long, civic program at Bentley College. The Post also holds an annual clambake for patients at the Bay Path nursing home and a banquet to honor young people involved in Legion programs. For its 287 members, from laborers to lawyers, the Post provides comradeship.

The Duxbury Newcomers Club was founded in 1969 to promote friendship and goodwill among old and new residents. Ninety-four couples enjoyed club activities that first year. Today, 315 member couples help the town plant beach grass each spring to prevent erosion. They run the town-sponsored Easter egg hunt for tots, and hold a Lazy-Eye Clinic for nursery school children. They provide refreshments for Candidates Night at town election time, and put on a spring tea for senior citizens. Members also deliver hot lunches to the elderly and shut-ins, and aid the Council of Churches with Thanksgiving and Christmas food baskets and Christmas stockings for children.

For members, the Newcomers Club supplies a variety of emergency services. It schedules socials throughout the year, and has twenty-five special interest groups.

One of the oldest art associations in the country, the Duxbury Art Association continues as it has since its formation in 1917, a non-profit organization for

Rotary Club President Barry Williams (center), with Don Beers, Harbormaster (right) and Bob Hedd (left), honoring Duxbury teenagers who saved a girl from drowning, May 1983. (*Fran Nichols*)

promoting and supporting arts in this and surrounding communities. The association provides shows for its artist members as well as classes and a variety of activities for others, including the *Artful Adventure* trips to galleries and museums in Boston and other outlying communities. In preparing for the town's 350th anniversary, the Art Association conducted a logo contest.

The most popular of its activities is the annual festive four-day Mid-Summer Arts and Craft Show of members' works (there are 500 members, of which 350 are from Duxbury), held in the Duxbury Marine boatshed on the waterfront. The Winter Juried Art Show at the Duxbury Art Complex attracts exhibiting artists from throughout the South Shore, Boston, and beyond. Each fall, the association holds a Craft Showcase for the exhibition and sale of crafts made locally and elsewhere.

DONNA MacLEARN

Garden Clubs

Members of the Duxbury Garden Club planting the Maxwell Rose Garden by the Bluefish River (1948), Percy Walker and Abbot Peterson supervising. (*Duxbury Garden Club*)

*I*n the beautiful town of Duxbury one is immediately aware that gardens and gardening have always played an important part in its life. Early Pilgrim gardens were not only a source of food and medicine, but of enjoyment, serving as a link to gardens left behind in England and Holland.

There were no garden clubs in the early days, although many of the earliest settlers had great interest in things horticultural. Elder William Brewster (1567–1644) had beautiful lavender lilacs brought from Holland.[1] His apple orchard was one of the first established in the colonies. Other Pilgrim settlers introduced the handsome silver-leafed White Poplar, *Populus alba*, often referred to in boundary descriptions. Descendants of these early seventeenth-century plants still exist in Duxbury. The Brewster lilacs are accepted as the oldest in the New World and rootings have been sent to the National Arboretum in Washington for posterity.

In 1830, Ezra Weston's brig *Smyrna* brought home to Duxbury the charming and unknown-to-New England *Iris recticulata* from Turkey. It was planted in the Weston gardens where it grew for well over a hundred years. Jerusha Bradford Weston, wife of King Caesar II, loved to don her green riding habit[2] and ride her horse through the fields and woods of Duxbury to enjoy native wildflowers, of which the sweetly fragrant *Arbutus* (Mayflower), now our state flower, was one of her favorites.

Elizabeth Hickling Bradford, Jerusha's niece and Captain Gershom Bradford's daughter, compiled a fascinating book, *Wildflowers of Duxbury*, in 1836 from the 166 wildflower specimens she collected within the town. This book is a particularly valuable and important scientific record, especially now that so much of Duxbury has been developed for housing.

212

Both the eighteenth and nineteenth centuries were horticulturally exciting. Linnaeus had classified plant material. Gardeners of America and Europe were regularly exchanging knowledge, seeds, and plants. Great plant gathering expeditions to China, Japan, and Korea and our own far west were underway, with many new varieties of plant material added to our Arboreta. Magnificent "glass houses" were built to house exotic plant collections. Imaginations were sparked, and with more leisure time available it is no wonder that garden clubs began to be organized.

The Duxbury Garden Club, recognized as one of the oldest in the United States, was organized in the summer of 1912 by twelve summer residents "for mutual improvement in horticultural interest." All twelve were serious gardeners and most had taken a course in horticulture with Miss Helen Holmes at Simmons College. They met in each others' houses to listen to further lectures by Miss Holmes, who lived in nearby Kingston. Each of ten yearly meetings ended with coffee and crackers and a tour of the hostess' garden where problems and practical solutions were discussed and knowledge gained. Mrs. Frank Rollins Maxwell, Sr. was elected first president, a position she held through 1923. Dues were one dollar. Meetings were held every two weeks from April through September. Outside speakers were rare, since each member was required to give a well-researched paper every summer. This practice continued until 1945.

By the time of World War I, civic beautification and community service were added to club endeavors. Money was raised for the War Relief Fund and to treat the whole town to a free lecture on canning (1917).

Concurrent with Duxbury's 350th anniversary, the Duxbury Garden Club celebrates its seventy-fifth in 1987. It is a small club of forty-five members, with four

"Taking Home his Pilgrim Bride," float created by all three Duxbury garden clubs for the tercentenary parade, July 4, 1937. (*Duxbury Garden Club*)

scheduled meetings a summer, which are still held in members' homes. There has been only one male member, Mr. Arthur Train.

The Duxbury Gardeners was organized as a study group in 1931 by the daughters and friends of the Duxbury Garden Club, with Mrs. Joseph W. Lund as its first president. Its twenty-one members were active for about twelve years before they disbanded due to the war. Two years later (1945) they were invited to join the mother club, which had also grown to twenty-one members.

In 1927, when interest in horticulture was growing, several members of the Duxbury Garden Club decided a second and much larger club should be formed to accommodate all who wished to join. A large group gathered in the beautiful gardens of Dr. Nathaniel Emer-

213

son, a retired physician who devoted all his energies and talents to horticulture. They decided to form a new garden club and name it *The Community Garden Club of Duxbury* with Dr. Emerson as its first president. All future meetings were to be held in large halls or barns in order to accommodate a large membership. Soon there were over a hundred members including a number of men. For many years, it met only during the summer and a surprising number belonged to both clubs. The Community Garden Club of Duxbury has since grown to be the largest in Massachusetts with 350 members. It celebrates its sixtieth anniversary in 1987, with nine scheduled meetings a year from September to July.

Both garden clubs are members of the Garden Club Federation of Massachusetts, Inc., an organization of over 12,000 members which in turn is a member of the National Council of State Garden Clubs, Inc., with a membership of 400,000 and 215 affiliated garden clubs throughout the world. This is true flower power.

Duxbury is fortunate to have two such active garden clubs, whose interests and efforts benefit and beautify the town with such projects as: the Maxwell Rose Garden at Bluefish River, the Nash Memorial flower beds at the King Caesar House, the Memory Garden at Town Hall, plantings at Hall's Corner and Bailey's Corner, and various Arbor Day and landscaping projects from the old railroad station to the present high school. Weekly flower arrangements are made for the King Caesar House, the John Alden House, the Duxbury Library, and the Plymouth County Hospital in Hanson. Garden therapy is conducted at the Brockton Veterans Administration Hospital. The clubs have also held numerous workshops and field trips.

Garden club scrapbooks are full of National and State awards and letters of grateful appreciation, the old-est going back to World War I for a planting of fruit trees at Château-Thierry (1917) and a planting at Camp Edwards in World War II. There are many clippings about individual awards, including a Massachusetts Horticultural Society solid gold medal for a unique home garden and porch design, and blue ribbons and other awards for flower arrangements and horticultural exhibits.

Many times the garden clubs pooled resources. They waged war on ragweed and poison ivy, and won; they battled bottles and trash at the bridge, and won. They put on flower shows and created floats for the July Fourth parade. Most impressive of all were the many hampers of fresh flowers, fruits, and vegetables sent each week from 1921 through 1969 to the Benevolent Fraternity Fruit and Flower Mission in Boston, run by the Unitarian Church. Between 129 and 142 large hampers were sent each summer. Duxbury was usually "The Banner Town" for sending the most. Gasoline rationing during World War II made trip logistics to Boston incredible. During these war years *everyone* had victory gardens. Monies were raised for the "Seeds for England Fund" and another free canning lecture.

Funds for the clubs' many philanthropies and scholarships have been raised by house and garden tours, plant and greens sales, and special programs. The first scholarship was given in 1917 by the Duxbury Garden Club to a young woman for a course in "intensive training in practical farming"; the latest, given by the Community Garden Club in 1986, was two $1,000 scholarships given to two Duxbury High School graduates for study in horticulture, conservation, landscape design, and related fields.

". . . Thus out of small beginnings . . . ,"[3] Garden Club members have kept America beautiful and Duxbury as well.

PRISCILLA ALDEN CROCKER ARCHIBALD

Dateboarding

*I*n Duxbury, dateboarding is not a social activity, as it might seem. A date board is a twenty-seven- by ten-inch white wooden plaque with the name of the original owner and the date of construction printed on it. Through the Date Board Committee of the Duxbury Rural and Historical Society, the boards are issued and attached to old houses. The information usually requires considerable research to trace the title to the house and the names of former owners. It is then approved by the Date Board Committee.

In June 1968, a group of interested members of the Historical Society gathered at the home of Garvin (Mich) Bawden "to initiate a worthwhile activity for the Society, namely to find old houses which should be recognized and acknowledged by means of a suitable sign—a Date Board." The original group consisted of Bawden, an enthusiastic chairman, with members Alex Colburn, William Nash, John Cutler, George Starr, George Gardner, Donald Walker, and Dorothy Wentworth. By October of that year, only Bawden, Nash, and Wentworth were left. The number of active members has remained small, due to a fairly large turnover. The limited hours when the Registry of Deeds is open has been a definite drawback for those who work during the day.

The information for a date board is established by finding a property description in a deed, first in which the land only is sold, and the next subsequent deed in which a building or buildings are mentioned. The date board researchers know the house was built between these dates, then use some event in the owner's life, such as marriage or the sale of a former dwelling, to pinpoint the date. The architecture must be in keeping with the date also. In the Millbrook area, two properties have been traced to the original grants, but the houses standing on them are obviously not the originals.

The Josiah Kean house (c. 1680) on Keene Street, past and present.

The research can be frustrating, because of the disappointment when a deed has no further reference, because of fatigue from lifting heavy, dusty books from top shelves, and because of the nausea brought on by a combination of bifocals and microfilm. But this is so quickly compensated by the euphoria when something as simple as a missing boundary line turns up. One boundary can be the key to unlock the mystery of a whole project. The history of an old house can be compared to a jigsaw puzzle, where all the pieces fit together when it is complete.

As of April 1986, there have been 128 boards approved. Of this number, seven houses were built in the seventeenth century, forty-two in the eighteenth century, and, from 1800 to 1860, seventy-nine. When the committee was first organized, the cut-off date was 1830. As time passed, this was moved to 1850, then recently changed to 1860. Still, the waiting list is long. Research can be time consuming and sometimes tedious, so owners are encouraged to do their own. For the researcher, failure is never acknowledged, but the file is put on the back burner in hopes that some clue will be discovered later. The stack of unfinished and *stuck* material is discouraging, but not insurmountable.

Of the 128 boards, Dorothy Wentworth is responsible for 70, as well as being the inspiration and help for many others. Through her efforts, the committee struggled and survived its first eighteen years of existence and now the historical society has a good record of dated houses, an accomplishment that is a lasting contribution to the town.

VIRGINIA SEAVER

National Register District

The Old Shipbuilders District which became official June 1, 1986, extends along Washington Street and several small streets leading off it. It continues a quarter-mile from Bluefish River flag pole up Powder Point Avenue and along St. George Street.

The National Register was first established in 1935 by the Historic Sites Act, which authorized a national survey of sites significant to United States history. Under this act, only national properties that were part of the National Park System, or that had been designated as historic landmarks, were included. However, in 1966, the National Preservation Act expanded the National Register to include districts, sites, buildings and objects of significance on the local or state level.

In Massachusetts, the State Historical Commission was established in 1965 along with local commissions, such as Duxbury's, which conduct surveys and research projects for National Register nominations.

The intent of this program is not to encourage acquisitions of historic properties for museums nor to restrict private owners in the use of their buildings; rather it is to stimulate awareness of a community's historic and architectural assets, and to arouse interest in maintaining them.

Representatives from the Massachusetts Historical Commission laid down the boundaries of Duxbury's National Register District in 1982, approved its name, and determined which buildings were qualified. Specific requirements were: integrity of location, design, settings, materials, and workmanship. The area also had to be associated with events significant in the broad patterns of our history, or with the lives of persons important in our past. Lastly, the structures in it had to embody the distinctive characteristics of a type or period, or represent the work of distinguished artists or architects.

Duxbury passed all these tests. In fact, it was difficult to select any one part of town that was best qualified for this honor because the town is liberally sprinkled with fine old houses, barns, outbuildings, schools, and churches that deserve recognition. However, the Washington Street area was a small, distinct portion of Duxbury that had been created by the shipbuilding industry.

By the late eighteenth century, shipbuilding had brought new trades to town. Ropemakers, blacksmiths, barrelmakers, and sailmakers built their own capes, half-capes, and small colonial-style homes; some facing gable-end to the street, with small ells that jutted out to the rear. There are twenty or more of these modest but comfortable homes among the more substantial residences that were built later as the community grew wealthier.

Duxbury sea captains often supervised the work on their new houses. Shipwrights frequently became housewrights. They were aided in their new trade by the design books of Christopher Wren, Charles Bulfinch and Asher Benjamin, books which contained meticulous scale drawings of front and side elevations, pitched and hip roofs, front and side entrances, center and side chimneys, fenistration, cornices, dentils, and pillars, as well as interior paneling, doors, fireplaces and staircases.

Most of the larger Washington Street houses are Georgian or Federal, simple and elegant; yet every house is different. The later ones tend toward the Greek Revival display of classic design. In spite of differences in style and detail, the homes together form an authentic, homogeneous unit, a fitting monument to the sea captains and shipbuilders who were admired the world over for their high standards and business acumen.

Now the shipyards are gone but the tidy little houses and impressive mansions remain, speaking eloquently of that busy and productive time. Duxbury's Old Shipbuilders District is distinguished by the number and quality of its Colonial and Federal houses. If ever the character of a nation was reflected in the homes of its citizens, it is here.

Jean Poindexter Colby

Duxbury Rural
and Historical Society

From its very beginnings, Duxbury has evidenced an integrity that has surfaced in each generation. From Pilgrim times, its people stood four square for their beliefs, even while hewing a livelihood from the primeval forest. When their farms had become established in 1632, they "gathered" the First Church. Time then came to form a town; so in 1637 they obtained their first minister, and organized the serious business of self-government.

A century and a half later, the emphasis had shifted away from farming to the construction of vessels, the best of their kind in their day, creating a demand that made Duxbury a prime shipbuilding town. In the mid-nineteenth century, the sun was setting on the age of sail, and with it departed the golden age of the town.

But the pride remained with the knowledge that Duxbury stood for certain important values, even though the shipbuilding industry had moved on. So it was that in 1883 a group of citizens formed the Rural Society "to improve and ornament the town."

The work of the society progressed slowly, first planting trees, then installing street lights (but only, in true Yankee tradition, if the town would maintain them), then in 1887 participating in the 250th Anniversary of Duxbury's incorporation. In 1891, the society acquired its first substantial property, the land and carriage roads around Long Pond, one of the first conservation efforts on record in the Commonwealth, starting a trend in Duxbury which endures to this day.

In 1916, when the Rural Society incorporated, its activities expanded with purchasing the woodlot opposite the town buildings on Tremont Street, thus

The Federal house, now occupied by the DR&HS, was built in 1826 by Charles Drew, Jr., mariner, and remodeled by Zenas Faunce for commercial use by replacing the ground floor windows with large store windows and the single entrance with a double-width archway. In 1916, Clara May Smith Ripley, a Drew descendant, bought and presented it to the historical society. Photo taken c. 1910. (*Duxbury Garden Club*)

insuring against future deterioration near our public buildings. The Ripley family gave the Drew House that year, soon to be used as Historical Rooms.

Continually, the society worked behind the scenes, supporting worthy causes at town meeting, goading selectmen into making improvements, meanwhile attaining a membership of 200 by 1933, but not changing its name to fit its enlarging purposes until 1936, when it became the Duxbury Rural and Historical Society (DR&HS), just in time to assume a substantial role in the Tercentenary of the Town of Duxbury in 1937.

The 1960s saw major changes for both the society and the town, as the new Route 3 began to funnel newcomers into the area. In 1963, the founding of the Duxbury Conservation Commission was paralleled by various acquisitions of land by the society; but more significantly, in 1965, the DR&HS mounted a successful drive to purchase the King Caesar House, thus acquiring

a headquarters, a future museum, and a visibility which soon led to a membership of 500.

The Bradford House came to the society from the last Gershom Bradford and his brother Edward in 1968, and so did the Clark's Island property under Sarah Wingate Taylor's bequest in 1969. Concurrently, the Conservation Commission, the Massachusetts Audubon, and the society combined to form a greenbelt running almost the entire length of the town, a long step toward preserving Duxbury's rural character.

Meanwhile, to support such projects, the society started the King Caesar Mornings Lecture Series, the popular chowder suppers, an antiques auction, and later a barn sale. Subscription lectures coupled with sumptuous dinners were arranged first with the Museum of the American China Trade; and later with the Mystic Seaport Museum to net rewarding returns, both in money and in membership, which increased to 800.

Leaving her post at the Drew House only in emergencies, Sabina Crosby is rowed across Washington Street by Peter Sprosty and Phil Noyes, January 1987. (*Deni Johnson*)

The publication of Dorothy Wentworth's *Settlement and Growth of Duxbury* soon sold out the first edition and led to a series of popular pamphlets: "Tall Ships of Duxbury" and "A History of the Rural and Historical Society," together with another major work by Wentworth: *The Alden Family in the Alden House.* All were able to stand on their own financial legs.

So, too, did the Sales Department, organized and galvanized by the genius of Priscilla Mayberry, who dispensed books, cup plates, and stationery, and any merchandise that would sell to anyone who would buy— and they were legion. She was, however, far from alone.

The society was running on the efforts of nearly 200 volunteers from the president through a dozen officers, nearly fifty committee chairmen, and countless willing workers in every department, including half a hundred hostesses and a score of men available for everything from cutting brush to painting fences. Only one paid job existed in the whole organization, and that paid half-wages for perhaps eighty hours of weekly work.

For this wheel of activity there has to be a hub, and it is Sabina Crosby, Secretary of the DR&HS. In her office at the Drew House, for as long as anyone can remember, she has been cheering successes, consoling disgruntled workers, receiving and answering mail, reminding committee chairmen of responsibilities, counseling otherwise helpless presidents, and always with a pleasant "Good Morning" on the telephone, no matter who was calling.

It is to this paragon of ladylike efficiency that we dedicate this book. A pleasant "Good Morning" to you, Sabina!

JACK POST

220

Contributors

Priscilla Alden Crocker Archibald is past president of the Duxbury Garden Club.

Alison Arnold was society editor of the Boston *Herald* for many years.

Judi Barrett devotes endless hours to conservation.

Howard T. Blanchard, a firefighter himself, is the son of a former chief.

Ann Learnard Bowman is the historical society's able clerk.

Elizabeth Bradford is simultaneously a 9th and 10th generation descendant of Gov. William Bradford.

Sean Bunn is a member of the Class of 1987 at Duxbury High School.

Bradford H. Burnham is a retired Reverend Canon of the Episcopal Church.

Shirley H. Carter received her doctorate in reading and language at Boston University.

Tony Chamberlain is a distinguished reporter from the Boston *Globe*.

David E. Clapp is Director of the South Shore Sanctuaries of the Massachusetts Audubon Society.

Jean Poindexter Colby is Chairman of Duxbury's Historical Commission.

Judge Joseph K. and Grace M. Collins are early members of Holy Family Parish.

David S. Cutler runs seven newspapers, an easy job for the son of *Clipper* founders.

Roberta S. Cutler is the heart and soul of the Duxbury *Clipper*.

Alexandra B. Earle is assistant to the director of the Pilgrim Society.

Isabelle V. Freeman is descended from ten Mayflower Pilgrims.

Peter J. Gomes is Plummer Professor of Christian Morals at Harvard College.

Beatrice Gormley is author of numerous books for pre-teenage children.

Leslie Davis Guccione is a writer of romance novels.

Robert D. Hale is a lecturer, scholar, writer, and proprietor of Westwinds Bookshop.

Judith Hall is a past president of the PTA.

Priscilla Swanson Harris is the daughter of an early Scandinavian settler in West Duxbury.

Nancy M. Houghton is a member of the historical society's Research Group.

Franklin K. Hoyt is an expert on the history of the French Atlantic Cable.

Anthony Kelso is on the staff of Plimoth Plantation.

Donald Gerry Kennedy is superintendent of Duxbury Public Schools.

John Alden Keyser, Jr. is president of the Alden Kindred of America.

Cynthia H. Krusell is the town historian of Marshfield.

Ben and Peggy Lawson have been winning races in Duxbury Bay for over fifty years.

Frances D. Leach is writing a biography of Captain Myles Standish.

John P. Leonard is a thoughtful analyst and student of New England town government.

Donna MacLearn writes about Duxbury for the Quincy *Patriot Ledger*.

Margery L. MacMillan is an ardent researcher on the town's inns, restaurants and boarding houses.

Molly Matson is a librarian at the University of Massachusetts, Boston.

The Reverend Canon Robert E. Merry is an enthusiast for Duxbury history.

Stanley H. Merry, born and bred in Duxbury, has been a cranberry grower since World War II.

Robert G. Millar and Frederick T. Pratt have had much to do with preserving Duxbury's beach in its natural state.

William B. Nash was a former president of the Duxbury Rural and Historical Society.

Verna Ross Orndorff is an enthusiast for our Pilgrim heritage.

Jean Hudson Peters is the daughter and wife of physicians.

Katherine H. Pillsbury is the Duxbury Town Historian.

Jack Post, former president of DR&HS, is the guiding force behind its publishing program.

Frederick T. Potter has long maintained an active interest in the background of Duxbury.

James C. Pye, a former teacher, is a member of the historical society's Research Group.

James F. Queeny has long served as a trustee of the Duxbury Free Library.

Beatrice R. Richards is a former research scientist at Clapp Laboratory.

Priscilla Sangster was the first woman on the Duxbury Zoning Board of Appeals.

Virginia Seaver runs the Date Board Committee for the historical society.

Carolyn B. Schindler teaches the innovative *On Home Ground* course at the high school.

Joan C. Schlueter is a member of the historical society's Research Group.

The Reverend Elizabeth B. Stevens is a minister of religious education.

Joan S. Sundstrom is Assistant Director of the Battelle Marine Research Laboratories.

Edwin Swanborn is music director at the First Parish Church.

Lanci Valentine is assistant to the director of the Art Complex Museum.

Robert C. Vose, Jr. contributes his time and talent to the arts.

Dorothy Wentworth served over thirty years as Duxbury Town Historian.

Charles Weyerhaeuser is the director of the Art Complex Museum.

Marjorie Winslow is an author who has been coming to Duxbury for many years.

Benefactors

Anonymous
Abington Savings Bank
Mr. and Mrs. M. Barclay Brown
Mr. and Mrs. Charles E. Cousins
Eaton Foundation
The Ellison Foundation
Mrs. George P. Fogg, Jr.
Konrad Gesner
Grafton Memorial Fund
Mr. and Mrs. Frank S. Hyer
Mr. and Mrs. Carleton Knight, Jr.
MacDonald and Wood Real Estate
Merryland
Mrs. Verna Ross Orndorff
Mr. and Mrs. Stephen Paine
Frank F. Peard
Mr. and Mrs. James Otis Post
Rockland Trust Company
Gertrude C. Shelton
William F. Spang
Mr. and Mrs. Alexander C. Stohn, Jr.
Frances W. Sykes
Mr. and Mrs. Robert C. Vose, Jr.
Mr. and Mrs. Clarence W. Walker
Mr. and Mrs. Donald D. Walker
Mr. and Mrs. Robert M. Walker
Carl A. Weyerhaeuser Trust

Patrons

Mr. and Mrs. Ross E. Allen
Mr. and Mrs. Frederick Archibald, Jr.
Mr. and Mrs. Robert Howland Burpee
Henry W. Erving, M.D.
Mr. and Mrs. William C. Hart
Helen Delano Howe
L. Knife and Son, Inc.
Dr. and Mrs. Stanley M. Leitzes
Mr. and Mrs. George H. Lowe, III
Mr. and Mrs. Samuel W. Pillsbury
Charles T. Post, Jr., M.D.
Kenneth Shaw Safe, Jr.

Sponsors

Fanueil Adams, Jr.
Mr. and Mrs. Alvin O. Bicknell
Mr. and Mrs. Richard E. Bloodgood
G. Lincoln Dow, Jr.
DeCoursey Fales, Jr.
Mr. and Mrs. Edwin Lougee
Mr. and Mrs. Ladd MacMillan
Hollis P. Nichols
Mr. and Mrs. Kenneth R. Park
Ocean Spray Cranberries, Inc.
Norman Peterson, Jr.
The Saquish Foundation
Mr. and Mrs. David Wood Stookey
Mr. and Mrs. Arthur E. Swanson
Leo Vercollone

Friends

Margaret T. Adams
Rosamond Allen
Mr. and Mrs. Kells M. Boland
Mr. and Mrs. Thomas Burgess
Mr. and Mrs. Theodore Chadwick, Jr.
Winthrop B. Coffin
E. Raymond Corey
Mr. and Mrs. John H. Cutler
Mrs. Charles G. Davis
Dorothy M. Davison
Mr. and Mrs. Dezengotita
Patrick L. Dudensing
Robert B. Enemark
Douglas M. Gray, Jr.
Anita Haffey
Sarah Vaughan Heath
Dr. and Mrs. Hardy Hendren
Noah T. Herndon
Edward B. Hutton
Joy Mooney Jenkins
Brian Jones
Walter D. Kelleher
James G. Kelso
Mr. and Mrs. Bogert Kiplinger
Mr. and Mrs. Allen Lahey
Thomas H. Lanman, Jr.

Mr. and Mrs. Frank B. Lawson
Mr. and Mrs. T. Burke Leahey
Mr. and Mrs. Robert M. Leach
Mr. and Mrs. Robert Lindstrom
Mr. and Mrs. Malcolm MacNaught
Mrs. C. Clark Macomber
Ruth T. McGibney
Patricia Dean Metcalf
Mr. and Mrs. David Mittell
Barbara S. Mullowney
Norton Company Foundation
Dr. and Mrs. James I. Peters, Jr.
Mr. and Mrs. Paul H. Pierce
Mr. and Mrs. Harlan T. Pierpont, Jr.
Ruth C. Pratt
Mr. and Mrs. Peter A. Prescott
James Taylor Pye
Mr. and Mrs. Michael E. Reed
Rosa Lee Reynolds
William M. Riegel
Leah A. Rifkin
C. Earl Russell
John F. Spence, Jr.
Mr. and Mrs. John M. Stanton
Cid Ricketts Sumner Fund
Dr. and Mrs. Howard Ulfelder
William H. Walker, II
Mark Wenham Realty Co.
Mr. and Mrs. William H. Wheeler, Jr.

Donors

Mr. and Mrs. Frederick W. Bailey
Anne Jouett Bobseine
Mr. and Mrs. Frederick Bowes, III
Mr. and Mrs. Hamilton B. Bowman
Mr. and Mrs. Manfred Brosee
Eliot Brown
Arline M. Bunten
The Reverend and Mrs. Bradford
  Burnham
Mrs. Betsy B. Brownell
Mr. and Mrs. Allen D. Carleton
Mr. and Mrs. F. Sherburne Carter
Sabina D. Crosby

Margaret F. Currier
R.F. Danner
Mr. and Mrs. Samuel S. Dennis, III
Ann Fitzgibbons
Mrs Helen B. Fox
Mr. and Mrs. Chandler Gifford, Jr.
Lucy L. Grimm
Mr. and Mrs. John T. Hathaway, Jr.
Elizabeth W. Heath
Elizabeth Hicks
Charlotte H. Horner
Mr. and Mrs. Channing Howe
Mr. and Mrs. Delmont Irving
Mr. and Mrs. John F. Joline, III
Mr. and Mrs. Walter F. Kopke, Jr.
Dr. and Mrs. James E. Ladd
Mr. and Mrs. Robert V. Laney
Mr. and Mrs. Wilbur F. Lewis
Virginia H. Ludwig
Mrs. A.T. Lyman
Anna Karen McCarthy
Mr. and Mrs. J. Thomas Marquis
Frank D. Millet
Mr. and Mrs. Richard H. Morse
Mr. and Mrs. John B. Nash
Frances F. Nichols
Victor A. Noel, Jr.
Mr. and Mrs. George G. Palfrey
Helen L. Philbrick
Mr. and Mrs. Robert H. Pierce
Mr. and Mrs. James C. Pye
Mr. and Mrs. George L. Richards, II
Margaret W. Rogerson
Mr. and Mrs. Robert Ross
Louise Sanger
Mr. and Mrs. John J. Schlueter
Mr. and Mrs. Wilfred M. Sheehan
Nicholas J. Stasinos
The Studio of Duxbury
Mr. and Mrs. Benjamin
  A. G. Thorndike
Mr. and Mrs. Stephen W. Turrell
Robert N. Ulseth, M.D.
Mr. and Mrs. Page C. Valentine, Jr.
M.J. and K.D. Wakefield
A. A. Warlam
Mr. and Mrs. Irwin P. Zullig

Sources and Footnotes

Abbreviations Used in Notes:

BRA   William Bradford, *Of Plymouth Plantation*, Ed. Samuel Eliot Morison, New York: Alfred A. Knopf, 1979

DTR   George Etheridge, ed. *Copy of the Old Records of the Town of Duxbury, Massachusetts from 1642–1779*, Plymouth, 1893.

MAY   *Mayflower Families Through Five Generations*, Plymouth: General Society of Mayflower Descendants, 1975.

PCR   Nathaniel Shurtleff and David Pulsifer, eds. *Records of the Colony of New Plymouth in New England*. 12 vols. Boston, 1855–1861.

ALD   Dorothy Wentworth, *The Alden Family in the Alden House*, Duxbury: Duxbury Rural and Historical Society, 1980.

S&G   ———. *The Settlement and Growth of Duxbury, 1628–1870*, Duxbury: Duxbury Rural and Historical Society, 1973.

WSR   Justin Winsor, *History of the Town of Duxbury, Massachusetts, with Genealogical Registers*, Boston, 1849.

Since these sources are basic to all research on Duxbury history, they have not been listed separately in each bibliography.

Old Paths of Duxbury

1. Cynthia Hagar Krusell, *Map of Early Indian and Pilgrim Trails of Old Plymouth Colony*, 1978.

2. *Mourt's Relation: A Journal of the Pilgrims of Plymouth*, Ed. Jordan D. Fiore (Plymouth: Plymouth Rock Foundation, 1985), 53–58.

3. Harvey H. Pratt, "Three Highways of the Colonies," *Proceedings of the Scituate Historical Society* (February 22, 1918), 1–2.

4. PCR, I: 31.

5. Cynthia Hagar Krusell, "The Land Where First They Trod," *Mayflower Quarterly* 36 (1970): 117–119.

6. PCR, I: 58.

7. PCR, VI: 111.

Captain Myles Standish

1. G.V.C. Young, *Pilgrim Myles Standish: First Manx American* (Peel, Isle of Man: Mansk-Svenska Publishing Co., 1984), 10.

2. Although the house has been long gone, the homesite is maintained as a park by the town.

3. The document is dated March 23, 1649. In seventeenth-century England, the legal year began on March 25th, not on January 1st. Under the new style, adopted in the mid-eighteenth century, this would have read 1650.

4. Thomas Morton, *New English Canaan*, 1637, reprint edition (Boston, 1893), 285.

Sources

Leach, Frances D. "The Captain: Myles Standish of Plymouth Colony." Unpublished biography, 1986.

Porteus, Thomas C. "Some Recent Investigations Concerning the Ancestry of Capt. Miles Standish." *New England Historical and Genealogical Register* 68 (1914): 339–365.

———. *Captain Myles Standish: His Lost Lands and Lancashire Connections. A New Investigation.* Manchester, Eng.: Manchester University Press, 1920.

Elder Brewster

1. BRA, 253

2. Roger Williams, *Complete Writings of Roger Williams*, 7 vols. (New York: Russell and Russell, 1963), VI: 165.

3. "Elder William Brewster's Inventory and the Settlement of His Estate," *The Mayflower Descendant*, III (1901): 28.

4. *Mayflower Descendant*, III: 29.

5. Emma C. Brewster Jones, ed. *The Brewster Genealogy* (New York: Grafton, 1908), lxxvii.

6. Roger Williams, 165.

7. "Winthrop Papers," Massachusetts Historical Society *Collections*, 4th series (Boston, 1865), VII: 79.

8. WSR, 235.

9. PCR, X: 227.

10. BRA, 444.

11. BRA, 320.

12. "Love Brewster's Will and Inventory," *The Mayflower Deecendant*, II (1900): 203.

13. *Mayflower Descendant*, II: 204.

14. WSR, 235.

15. *Plymouth Church Records 1620–1859* (Baltimore: Genealogical Publishing, 1975), I: 158.

16. *Plymouth Church Records*, I: 158.

John Alden

1. Augustus Alden, *Pilgrim Alden* (Boston: James H. Earle, 1902), 81.

2. Alden, 83.

Sources

Alden Kindred of America. *Reunion Duxbury, 1926.* Holyoke, MA: Alden Press, 1926.

Alden Kindred Magazine I, 1927–28.

Robbins, Roland Wells. *Pilgrim John Alden's Progress.* Plymouth: The Pilgrim Society, 1969.

Rutheford, W. K. *Genealogical History of Our Ancestors.* N.P.: np., 1970.

George Soule

1. BRA, 444.

2. BRA, 444.

3. MAY, III, *George Soule*, Ed. Ann Borden Harding, 3, 6–7. 10; WSR, 70.

4. WSR, 89. Ed. note—[When the Plymouth Colony forces were ready to march, they received word that the Pequots had already been overwhelmed. The expedition was cancelled. (BRA, 295.)]

5. Nahum Mitchell, *History of the Early Settlement of Bridgewater* (1840; Baltimore: Gateway Press, 1970), 10–11.

6. WSR, 310.

Other First Families

1. R&H, "Abstract of Record Chain of Title and Historical Commentary to the Caliri Homestead," Unpublished abstract, 1975, iv.

2. WSR, 47; PCR, II: 50.

3. PCR, III: 5; IV: 192.

4. PCR, I: 35.

5. "Plymouth Colony," *The Mayflower Descendant* XVI (Oct 1914): 210.

6. WSR, 66; PCR, III: 177.

7. "Sketches of the Early History of Middleboro," *New England Historical and Genealogical Register* III (1814): 343.

8. WSR, 172–173.

9. PCR, XII: 16.

10. BRA, 183.

11. BRA (1898 edition), 538.

12. PCR, II: 138, 172.

13. PCR, III: 6–7.

14. PCR, II: 43, WSR, 286.

15. R&H, Herbert R. Morse, "Eagles Nest Point" ts (1943): 3.

16. DTR, 38.

Notes on the Name Duxbury

1. Many of the earliest records were destroyed in a fire prior to 1686. Early existing records consulted were: DTR; *Town of Duxbury General Records, 1781–1825; Town of Duxbury Book No. 3, 1817–1836.*

2. (Alden Bradford) "A Topographical Description of Duxborough in the County of Plymouth, Massachusetts," Massachusetts Historical Society *Collections* 1st series, II (Boston, 1793): 4.

3. James Thacher, *History of the Town of Plymouth. . . .* (1835 Yarmouthport: Parnassus Imprints, 1972), 106.

4. WSR, 11.

5. See notes listed under article on Myles Standish: Porteus, *Recent Investigations*, 339; Young, 10; Lawrence Hill, "Gentlemen of Courage—Forward: The Line of Myles Standish within a History of England," ts (1986): 175.

Sea and Shore

1. BRA (1898 edition), 192.

2. Thomas Lechford, "Lechford's Manuscript Notebook," *Archaeologia Americana*, 12 vols. (Worcester, 1885), VII: 418–419.

3. Massachusetts Archives Collection, "Registers of Vessels," *Commercial*, VII: 231.

4. ——, *Valuations*, 161: 455; 162: 292.

5. DTR, 17

6. DTR, 272.

The Bradfords

1. Gershom Bradford, *In With the Sea Wind* (Barre, MA: Barre Publishers, 1962), 42.

2. Bradford, *Sea Wind*, 42.

3. Bradford, *Sea Wind*, 84.

4. Bradford, *Sea Wind*, 40.

5. Gershom Bradford, *Yonder is the Sea* (Barre, MA: Barre Publishers, 1959), 13.

6. Bradford, *Yonder Sea*, 17.

7. Bradford, *Yonder Sea*, 39.

8. Bradford, *Yonder Sea*, 213.

The Westons

1. Samuel Eliot Morison in *Maritime History of Massachusetts* notes that *canoe* was a word used for a small rowboat (Boston: Houghton Mifflin, 1924), 148; Ezra Weston, 3rd, "Weston Family of Duxbury, Mass," manuscript notebook, 146, New England Historic Genealogical Society. Note: In Duxbury, Ezra Weston, 3rd is known as the 4th.

2. Ezra Weston, 3rd, 150.

3. R&H, "Tribute to Gershom Bradford Weston" (N.A.: n.p., 1852), 6.

4. "Tribute," 13.

Joshua Winsor

1. Nina Fletcher Little, "Doctor Rufus Hathaway, Physician and Painter of Duxbury, Massachusetts 1770–1822," *Art in America* (Summer 1953): 115.

2. Little, 97.

3. Dorothy Wentworth, "The Solomon Washburn House," *Duxbury Clipper*, 18 March, 1982: 25.

4. WSR, n162.

5. Little, 98.

Sources

"Dateboard Notebooks." R&H.

Potter, Frederick T. *Tall Ships of Duxbury, 1815–1850.* Duxbury: Duxbury Rural and Historical Society, 1982.

Rufus Hathaway

Little, Nina Fletcher, "Doctor Rufus Hathaway, Physician and Painter of Duxbury, Massachusetts 1770–1822." *Art in America* 31.3 (Summer, 1953): 96–115.

Richards, Lysander Salmon. *History of the Town of Marshfield.* Vol II Plymouth: Memorial Press, 1901. 2 vols.

Versailles, Elizabeth Starr, compiler. *Hathaways of America.* Northampton, MA: Gazette Printing, 1970.

Sylvanus Sampson

1. The name was variously spelled, even by Captain Sampson himself.

2. This is the date that has been passed down through the Sampson-Winslow family. No documents have been found to authenticate it.

3. WSR, 17.

Author's note—The items herein quoted, reprinted, or synopsized are from the papers left in the store by Captain Sampson.

Shipping Era Houses

1. Gertrude Hall, "The Charm of Old Duxbury," *Indoors and Out* (July, 1906): 165.

2. R&H, Pauline Winsor Wilkinson, "Life in Duxbury–1840," ts (1921).

3. John Everett Chandler, "The Colonial House," quoted in newspaper article by Willard de Lue, n.d. Duxbury Free Library.

4. R&H, Frances K. Fogg, "The Wallpapers of the King Caesar House Parlors," ts (1967): 1–2.

5. R&H, Welthea Little Sprague, Interview, Oct. 31, 1888, ts "Dateboard Notebook 2".

Sources

Connally, Ernest Allen. "The Cape Cod House: An Introductory Study." *Journal of the Society of Architectural Historians* XIX:2 (May, 1960)

Cummings, Abbott Lowell. *Architecture in Early New England.* Sturbridge: Old Sturbridge Village, 1958.

Doane, Doris. *A Book of Cape Cod Houses.* Old Greenwich, CT: Chatham Press, 1970.

McAlester, Virginia and Lee McAlester. *A Field Guide to American Houses.* New York: Alfred A. Knopf, 1985.

Cordwainers

1. Elizabeth C. Bolton, letter addressed to: "My dear and very busy Doctor," [Probably Reuben Peterson] 9 Feb. 1937, Duxbury Free Library.

Schooling in Duxbury

1. WSR, 72.

2. WSR, 74.

3. *The Partridge* 27.1 (Nov., 1940): 1.

4. Mary A. Livermore, *The Story Of My Life,* Women in America (1899, New York: Arno Press, 1974), 373. **Ed. Note**—Mary Ashton Rice Livermore (1820–1905), teacher, author, lecturer, and reformer. Her autobiography chronicles recollections of her three-and-a-half years in Duxbury.

5. Livermore, 369.

6. Livermore, 370.

7. Livermore, 372.

8. Waldo E. Long, *The Story of Duxbury, 1637–1937* (Duxbury: Duxbury Tercentenary Committee, 1937), 19–20.

Author's note—Specific citations from school committee records are drawn from the "Minute Book of the Duxbury School Committee, 1858–84" and the *Annual Reports of the Town of Duxbury, 1937–1945.*

Road and Rail

1. *Badger and Porter's Stage Register*, #3 (Boston, 1825), 2.
2. *Old Colony Memorial* 7 May, 1842.
3. R&H, Pauline Winsor Wilkinson, "Memoir".
4. Mildred Glass, personal interview, 1986.
5. "Helen Eaton Remembers," *Duxbury Clipper* 8 May, 1975, C 11.
6. Steven Currier, personal interview, 1986.

Sources

Annual Reports of the Town of Duxbury, 1840–1900.
Earle, Alice Morse, *Stage Coach and Tavern Days*. Williamstown, MA: Corner House, 1977.
Hager, Louis and Albert Handy, eds. *A Complete History of the Old Colony Railroad*. Boston, 1893.
Report of the Board of Railroad Commissioners on an Investigation into the Affairs of the Duxbury and Cohasset Railroad Company. Boston, 1877.

Benjamin Smith

Massachusetts. Society of the Commonwealth. *Massachusetts Soldiers and Sailors of the Revolutionary War*. Boston: Wright and Potter Printing, 1896–1908.
United States Census Office. *1st Census, 1790; 2nd Census, 1800; 3rd Census, 1810; 4th Census, 1820*.
Vital Records of Duxbury, Massachusetts, to the year 1850. Boston: New England Historic Genealogical Society, 1911.
(For the guardianship case) Probate record dated 2 July, 1765 Plymouth County Massachusetts, Probate Records Office.
(For Court suits against Smith) Konig, David Thomas, ed. *Plymouth County Records 1686–1859*. IX, Common Pleas, April, 1784, entry 336 (1784 suit); XIV, Common Pleas, November, 1830, entry 59 (1830 suit). Wilmington, DE: M. Glazier, 1978.
(For property deeds) Plymouth County Massachusetts, Registry of Deeds. Book 110: 257–8 (1809 deed); Book 169: 148 (1830 deed).

Sailing and Racing

1. George A. Green, letter quoted in foreward, *Handbook of Racing Rules and General Information* by Ralph Lawson (Duxbury: Duxbury Yacht Club, 1927).

The Wright Estate

1. Edmund Brownell Weston, *In Memoriam* (Providence: privately printed, 1916), 57.
2. Pauline Pyle, "Last Days for Opulent Mansion," *Patriot Ledger* [Quincy] 11 Nov. 1966: 9.
3. "William Wright," obituary, *Old Colony Memorial*, 12 Dec. 1912.
4. *Annual Report of the Town of Duxbury* (1919), 55.
5. Pyle, 9.

Sources

Annual Reports of the Town of Duxbury, 1888–1920. "Wentworth Papers," R&H.

Physicians

1. BRA, 260.
2. WSR, 154.
3. Pauline Winsor Wilkinson, "Life in Duxbury, 1840," *Duxbury Clipper* 8 May, 1975: 6.

Sources

Dwyer, Gladys R.; Hathaway Ethel; Hayes, Sally and Charles; Leighton, Katheryn; MacMillan, Marjorie; Noyes, Priscilla; Wadsworth, Elden; Walker, Virginia and Donald. Personal interviews. Apr. and May, 1986.
Peterson, Elizabeth S. "History of Duxbury Nurse Association," ts. [c. 1956].
Wadsworth, Horace Andrew, ed. *Wadsworth Family in America*. Lawrence, MA, 1883.
Willison, George F. *Saints and Strangers*. New York: Reynal and Hitchcock, 1945.

The Theatre

Crocker, Harriet; Cutler, Roberta S.; McClosky, D. Blair; Thompson, Roz. Personal interviews. Sept. 1986.

The Bridge

1. "Gurnet beach," *Boston Sunday Herald* 8 Oct. 1892: 22.
2. Gershom Bradford, "As Bridge Neared Completion," *Duxbury Clipper* 8 May 1975: 13.

Clams

1. BRA, 116.

Duxbury's Mayflower Heritage

1. BRA, 60.
2. Waldo E. Long, *The Story of Duxbury, 1637–1937* (Duxbury: Duxbury Tercentenary Commission, 1937), 19.

3. BRA, 236.

World War II in Duxbury

Adams, Dunkin; Arnold, Alison; Hoyt, Alice and Franklin; Loring, Atherton, Jr.; Personal interviews. 1986.
The Log of Duxbury Flotilla #600. Privately published, n.d.

Preserving Duxbury

1. S&G, 2.
2. *Annual Report of the Town of Duxbury* (1926), 107.

Education Since 1946

Annual Reports of the Town of Duxbury. 1946–1983.
Beeby, Shelly; Christo, Nancy; DeWolf, Helen; Handy, Everett; Kearney, Margaret; Lanman, Thomas, Jr,; Solberg, Marcia. Personal interviews. Spring, 1986.

Teaching About Duxbury

Author's Note—This article was written with the assistance of Kathleen Dunn and Judith Fosdick.

Volunteers in the Duxbury Schools

Author's Note—This article was prepared with the assistance of Rebecca Chin.

Today's Churches

1. Gershom Bradford, *History of the First Parish Church* (Duxbury: Women's Alliance, 1953), 22.

Garden Clubs

1. Tercentary marker located on Marshall St., near the site of Elder Brewster's homestead.
2. Copy of Rufus Hathaway's portrait of Jerusha Bradford Weston at the King Caesar House.
3. BRA, 236.

Dateboarding

Author's Note—There are many sources available for tracing the history of an old house. The Plymouth County Registry of Deeds holds copies of recorded deeds. The Probate Court has copies of wills. Town records of vital statistics are invaluable, especially the consolidated vital records through 1850. Real estate listings and assessments in town reports are helpful, as are family genealogies when available. The 1833 Ford map, and some later maps, show the owners of existing houses.

Credits

Credits not accompanying each illustration or shown below are from the collection of the publisher.

Frontispiece: Nathaniel Winsor, Jr. house entrance.

Part Titles: page 1, Duxbury Beach, birds in flight. (David C. Twichell); page 47, The bark Smyrniote, built in 1859 at William Paulding's Duxbury shipyard; page 111, Tennis party c. 1890. The first young lady on the left is Anna Coffin (Mrs. Edward Elms, III) and the third from the left is her sister Laura. (Barbara B. Gifford and Anna B. Millar); page 167, The Duxbury Art Complex Museum. (Fran Nichols)

Timeline photo credits (pages 104–109) listed by year of corresponding text reference: 1605, Houghton Library, Harvard University; 1637, 1675, Massachusetts Historical Society; 1765, 1773, Library of Congress; 1794, Massachusetts State Archives; 1849, 1973, Fran Nichols; 1892, 1927, Jean Stasinos; 1954, Carleton Knight, Jr.